Genders and Sexualities in History

Series Editors
Joanna Bourke, Birkbeck College, University of London, London, UK
Sean Brady, Birkbeck College, University of London, London, UK
Matthew Champion, University of Melbourne, Melbourne, Australia

Palgrave Macmillan's series, Genders and Sexualities in History, accommodates and fosters new approaches to historical research in the fields of genders and sexualities. The series promotes world-class scholarship, which concentrates upon the interconnected themes of genders, sexualities, religions/religiosity, civil society, politics and war.

Historical studies of gender and sexuality have, until recently, been more or less disconnected fields. In recent years, historical analyses of genders and sexualities have synthesised, creating new departures in historiography. The additional connectedness of genders and sexualities with questions of religion, religiosity, development of civil societies, politics and the contexts of war and conflict is reflective of the movements in scholarship away from narrow history of science and scientific thought, and history of legal processes approaches, that have dominated these paradigms until recently. The series brings together scholarship from Contemporary, Modern, Early Modern, Medieval, Classical and Non-Western History. The series provides a diachronic forum for scholarship that incorporates new approaches to genders and sexualities in history.

Neil Penlington

Men Getting Married in England, 1918–60

Consent, Celebration, Consummation

palgrave
macmillan

Neil Penlington
Independent Scholar
London, UK

ISSN 2730-9479　　　　　　　ISSN 2730-9487　(electronic)
Genders and Sexualities in History
ISBN 978-3-031-27404-6　　　　ISBN 978-3-031-27405-3　(eBook)
https://doi.org/10.1007/978-3-031-27405-3

© The Editor(s) (if applicable) and The Author(s), under exclusive license to Springer
Nature Switzerland AG 2023
This work is subject to copyright. All rights are solely and exclusively licensed by the
Publisher, whether the whole or part of the material is concerned, specifically the rights
of translation, reprinting, reuse of illustrations, recitation, broadcasting, reproduction on
microfilms or in any other physical way, and transmission or information storage and
retrieval, electronic adaptation, computer software, or by similar or dissimilar methodology
now known or hereafter developed.
The use of general descriptive names, registered names, trademarks, service marks, etc.
in this publication does not imply, even in the absence of a specific statement, that such
names are exempt from the relevant protective laws and regulations and therefore free for
general use.
The publisher, the authors, and the editors are safe to assume that the advice and information in this book are believed to be true and accurate at the date of publication. Neither
the publisher nor the authors or the editors give a warranty, expressed or implied, with
respect to the material contained herein or for any errors or omissions that may have been
made. The publisher remains neutral with regard to jurisdictional claims in published maps
and institutional affiliations.

Cover credit: Stockbyte/Getty Images

This Palgrave Macmillan imprint is published by the registered company Springer Nature
Switzerland AG
The registered company address is: Gewerbestrasse 11, 6330 Cham, Switzerland

To James

Series Editors' Preface

In *Men Getting Married in England, 1918–60: Consent, Celebration, Consummation*, Neil Penlington explores the complex yet riveting history of marriage and masculinity in modern Britain from the end of the First World War to the 'golden age of marriage' in the 1950s. He focuses on questions of consent and capacity (including the meaning bestowed on non-consumption), love and romance, courtships and engagement, wedding rites and etiquette, and honeymoons. It is a sensitive, nuanced and carefully argued book that explores the social, economic and religious forces that influenced mid-twentieth-century masculinities. As such, it contributes not only to knowledge of the past but also to understanding current questions about manhood and marriage. In common with all the volumes in the 'Gender and Sexualities in History' series, *Men Getting Married in England* is a multifaceted and meticulously researched scholarly study. It is an innovative contribution to our understanding of gender and sexuality in the past.

London, UK   Joanna Bourke
London, UK   Sean Brady
Melbourne, VIC, Australia   Matthew Champion

Acknowledgements

Thank you to my brilliant doctoral supervisor Prof. Joanna Bourke, and to Prof. Matt Cook for helping me over the finishing line. Thanks also to my examiners: Prof. Claire Langhamer and Prof. John Tosh. This project was possible because of a scholarship from the Department of History, Classics and Archaeology at Birkbeck, University of London.

CONTENTS

1	**Introduction**	1
	References	23
2	**Consent and Capacity**	29
	Affinity	33
	Polygamy	39
	Age	45
	Mental Capacity	56
	Conclusion	64
	References	66
3	**Engagement**	69
	Words	74
	Intimacy	81
	Things	83
	Pressures	91
	Conclusion	101
	References	104
4	**The Wedding**	107
	Wedding Etiquette Manuals	111
	Newspapers	120
	First-Person Wedding Narratives	128
	Conclusion	143
	References	145

xii CONTENTS

5 **Non-consummation** 149
Non-consummation, the 1912 Royal Commission
and the 1937 Act 157
'Wilful Refusal' and the Purpose of Marriage 162
Re-consummation: 'Sex' as Condonation 175
Proof of (Non)Consummation 180
Conclusion 184
References 186

6 **Honeymoon** 189
Planning 194
Location 200
Experience 210
Conclusion 220
References 222

7 **Conclusion** 225

Index 231

Abbreviations

BLSA	British Library Sound Archive
Church Commission	*The Church and the Law of Nullity of Marriage: The Report of a Commission appointed by the Archbishops of Canterbury and York in 1949 at the request of the Convocations*
NLSC	National Life Stories Collection
Royal Commission Minutes 1956	*Minutes of Evidence taken before the Royal Commission on Marriage and Divorce, 1952–1956*
Royal Commission Report 1956	*Royal Commission on Marriage and Divorce, Report 1951–1955*

LIST OF FIGURES

Fig. 5.1 Divorce and nullity decrees granted in England and Wales, 1918–1954 (1918, $n = 100$)   152

Fig. 5.2 Divorce and nullity petitions filed in England and Wales, 1918–1954 (1918, $n = 100$)   153

Fig. 5.3 Approximate success rate (%) in divorce and nullity cases   154

Fig. 5.4 Nullity decrees granted in England and Wales by type, 1918–1954   155

Fig. 5.5 Divorce and nullity petitions filed in England and Wales by husband or wife, 1918–1954 (Source: Royal Commission on Marriage and Divorce, Royal Commission on Marriage and Divorce: Report, 1951–1955 [London, 1956], 357–61)   156

CHAPTER 1

Introduction

In the 1950s, weddings were everywhere, an almost unavoidable facet of English popular culture and daily life. As historian Claire Langhamer points out, the 'marriage day itself became increasingly commercialised, and overtly romanticised in the mid-century, setting the stage for the large-scale spectacles so characteristic of modern wedding celebrations'.[1] Even though the number and proportion of religious ceremonies declined slightly during the first half of the century, newspapers increasingly presented weddings as 'white weddings'. These weddings were formal, elaborate ceremonies taking place before a large number of guests and followed by a reception and increasingly by a honeymoon holiday. This book addresses what the big wedding meant for men and masculinity, by taking the 1950s 'golden age of marriage' as an endpoint and showing the changes in the process of getting married between 1918 and 1960.

Weddings pervaded popular culture. Newspaper reporting of weddings went from coverage of royal and 'society' weddings in the 1920s to the 'white weddings' of all social classes in the 1950s. This period also saw the arrival of mass cinema attendance and, as sociologist Chrys Ingraham has shown, a large proportion of cinema films featured a white wedding

---

[1] Claire Langhamer, 'Afterword' in Alana Harris and Timothy Willem Jones (ed.), *Love and romance in Britain, 1918–1970* (Basingstoke: Palgrave, 2015), 246.

© The Author(s), under exclusive license to Springer Nature Switzerland AG 2023
N. Penlington, *Men Getting Married in England, 1918–60*, Genders and Sexualities in History, https://doi.org/10.1007/978-3-031-27405-3_1

1

either as incidental to the plot or more often as the 'happy ending'.[2] The number of weddings increased during this period and it would appear that the scale of the average wedding—the number of guests—also increased. This meant that people in the 1950s were far more likely than those in the 1920s to be invited to a wedding, or to notice a wedding in the high street or village church on a Saturday afternoon. The increased likelihood of being invited to weddings meant that it was not just those who were arranging a wedding who had preparations to make, as wedding guests had to reply to invitations, buy presents, dress appropriately and possibly arrange transport and accommodation. Through a close reading of first-person testimonies, newspapers and etiquette manuals, the complexities and contradictions of masculinity will be shown by revealing power relations between men and women, between men, and between generations. The marrying man is considered in relation to his fiancée/wife and other family, especially his parents and his new in-laws. The iterative reconstruction of masculinity is shown by assessing the tension and complicity between the groom man and father, and father-in-law.

The English marriage laws changed during this period. Legal changes in the definition of a valid marriage and related discussions of the age of marriage consent, affinity, mental capacity and polygamy reveal English marriages and masculinities in relation to the European and Colonial Other, as well as movements in legal and cultural definitions of childhood, and shifts in medical and psychological definitions of mental capacity. The redefinition of consummation of marriage shows the gendered purpose of marriage and the requirements of 'normal' male sexuality. These facets of masculinity are explored through examination of 'official' discourses of marriage including parliamentary, legal, ecclesiastical and medical/psychological sources. Newspapers are used to suggest how knowledge of marriage law circulated. Evaluation of these 'official' discourses of marriage will demonstrate that constructions of married masculinity were based on assumptions of class, race and Englishness. Further, there was tension between Church and State, and between Christian and secular perceptions of the purpose of marriage, and therefore of 'sex' and masculinity.

The mid-twentieth century, and especially the 1950s, has been called variously the 'golden era of romance', the 'golden era of courtship' and

---

[2] Chrys Ingraham, *White weddings: Romancing heterosexuality in popular culture* (London: Routledge, 1999).

the 'golden age' of marriage.[3] There was an expectation that a man would get married. The average age of first marriage decreased steadily throughout the century with the youngest age in the 1960s. At the same time, the rate of marriage per capita increased throughout the period, especially after the Second World War (see Table 1.1). The average man married at 26.5 in 1919, and 24 in 1962. The highest peacetime male marriage rate was in 1957. The proportion of religious wedding ceremonies remained steady during this period as 'Christian Britain survived into the 1950s'.[4] The Church of England however experienced a decline in the number of weddings solemnised by its clergy. In 1919, 60% of marriages were solemnised by Church of England—the highest number ever recorded—but by the end of the period, fewer than half of weddings were in Anglican churches. In contrast, there was an increase in the proportion of register office weddings and the number of weddings of other Christian denominations. Jewish marriages held steady, while the number of Roman Catholic marriages more than doubled.

Our journey through consent, celebration and consummation will examine marriage and masculinity in England throughout the process of getting married. Although primarily a history of masculinity, other approaches such as performativity, ritual theory and the tourist gaze will show some of the gendered meanings of the 'invented traditions' of marriage during this period. This will show some of the changes, complexities and contradictions of masculinity by considering marrying men within a nexus of class, race and religion.

* * *

This book builds on the studies on marriage emerging since the expansion of social history in the 1960s, and includes the recent turn towards studies of marriage in relation to singleness, love and romance. Historians have assessed the gendered power relations between husbands and wives,

---

[3] Timothy Willem Jones and Alana Harris 'Introduction: Historicizing "modern" love and romance' in *Love and romance in Britain, 1918–1970* ed. Alana Harris and Timothy Willem Jones (Basingstoke: Palgrave, 2015), 14; Phil Hubbard, *Cities and sexualities* (Abingdon: Routledge, 2012), 137; Alana Harris, *Faith in the family: A lived religious history of English Catholicism, 1945–82* (Manchester: Manchester University Press, 2013), 131.

[4] See Callum Brown, *The death of Christian Britain: Understanding secularisation 1800–2000* (London: Routledge, 2009. First published 2001), 169.

Table 1.1 Marriages in England and Wales, 1919–1962

Selected Years[1]	All marriages	Civil ceremonies (%)	Religious ceremonies[2]				Median age at marriage (single men only)	Males marrying per 1,000 unmarried males
			All (%)	Church of England and Church in Wales (%)	Roman Catholic (%)	Other (%)		
1919	369,411	23	77	60	5	12	26.5	69.6
1924	296,416	24	76	58	6	13	26.0	53.6
1929	313,316	26	74	56	6	12	26.0	55.2
1934	342,307	28	72	54	7	12	26.4	59.3
1939	439,694	—	—	—	—	—	26.2	74.4
1944	302,714	—	—	—	—	—	24.9	54.5
1947	401,210	—	—	—	—	—	25.8	73.0
1952	349,308	31	69	50	10	10	25.1	67.6
1957	346,903	28	72	50	12	11	24.4	70.0
1962	347,732	30	70	47	12	11	24.0	65.6

[1] Limited types of ceremony data are available before 1962

[2] Percentages may not add to 100 due to rounding

Source ONS—Number of marriages, marriage rates and period of occurrence (Table 3, Historic marriage numbers and rates), Marriage Statistics Historical Series (Table 4, Marriages: Median age at marriage by sex and previous marital status, 1846–2007), Marriage Statistics Historical Series (Table 1, Marriages: Type of ceremony and denomination, selected years 1837–2007 [numbers])

1 INTRODUCTION 5

and more recently marriage in an era of rising individualism. Feminist historians have looked at the institution of marriage by focusing on the home and work lives of wives and mothers, and have concluded that the companionate marriage was more an ideal than a reality. Shared sexual pleasure was often a dream and although improvements in contraception led to smaller families, women bore the 'double burden' of paid work and unpaid domestic labour.[5] Gender historians—taking masculinity and femininity as relational—have explored the tensions and negotiations within marriage. Joanna Bourke's *Working-class Cultures* looks at power relations between husbands and wives by studying paid labour, 'housework' and sexual relations.[6] Earlier work on the companionate marriage has been joined by historical research on the tension between marriage and individualism. Marcus Collins coined the term 'mutuality'—which he defines as 'the notion that an intimate equality should be established between men and women through mixing, companionate marriage and shared sexual pleasure'—to argue that the twentieth century saw a rise and eventual decline in male and female expectations of marriage largely because of the rise of 'individualism'. Collins modifies the earlier findings of feminist historians by showing that the institution of marriage was not only oppressive to women but that men increasingly found it difficult to live up to the 'mutual' ideal.[7] The commonest reason given for divorce in the mid-twentieth century was adultery. Langhamer focuses on 'extra-marital sex' in post-war England to show a 'discursive construction of marriage' that was suffused with 'newly emergent tensions between mutuality and individualism and love and sex'. It was in this context that '[m]arital infidelity attained a new prominence within public discussions of sexual and emotional life' in post-war England.[8] This book will build on these historians' notions of power relations inside and outside

---

[5] For example, Finch, Janet and Penny Summerfield, 'Social reconstruction and the emergence of companionate marriage, 1945–59' in *Marriage, domestic life and social change: Writings for Jacqueline Burgoyne (1944–88)* ed. David Clark (London: Routledge, 1991).

[6] Joanna Bourke, *Working-class Cultures: Gender, class and ethnicity* (London: Routledge, 1994), chapters 3, 4.

[7] Marcus Collins, *Modern love: An intimate history of men and women in twentieth-century Britain* (London: Atlantic Books, 2003), 4, 7, 213–4.

[8] Claire Langhamer, 'Adultery in post-war England', *History Workshop Journal* 62 (Autumn 2006), 88, 94, 110.

the home, the relational categories of masculinity and femininity, and the rise of individualism to show the tensions and expectations of masculinity during the process of getting married.

The sex lives of the married have also been the object of historical scrutiny. Many historians have perhaps rightly seen changes in contraception and abortion as being important issues in determining the sex life of married couples. Hera Cook uses a combination of marriage/sex manuals, demographic statistics and developments in contraception to try to understand the extent of married couples' sexual repertoires and the meanings they attach to them. Cook argues that there was a 'long sexual revolution' culminating in the 1960s, during which men and especially women were able to enjoy sex without 'fear of pregnancy'.[9] Oral historian Steve Humphries showed in the 1980s that sex during the period 1918 to 1960 was largely confined to the marital bed. In most cases, if sex took place before marriage it was between a couple who would eventually get married.[10] More recently, Kate Fisher and Simon Szreter, also using oral history interviews, collapse the binary of duty/pleasure to argue that in the period under research married people (especially women) combined both. Fisher and Szreter are right to argue that historians have found it 'easier to find interesting sources for the study of the sexuality of marginalised groups'. They cite the work of Jeffrey Weeks, Frank Mort and Matt Houlbrook for making use of 'medical, judicial, religious and related primary sources'.[11] In this book, scrutiny of both personal testimonies and 'official' sources shows changing definitions and purposes of married sex to examine the complexities of masculinity and male sexuality. In a sense, this draws influence from Matt Houlbrook's *Queer London*, which takes a Queer look at the sexual geography of London between 1918 and 1957, by analysing sex that definitely did not happen in the marital bed. Houlbrook demonstrates that a variety of 'male sexual practices and identities coexisted, intersected, and overlapped'. Heterosexuality and 'normality' were not always coterminous: men, in certain situations, would choose same-sex sexual partners without

---

[9] Hera Cook, *The long sexual revolution: English women, sex, and contraception 1800–1975* (Oxford: Oxford University Press, 2005), 338.

[10] Steve Humphries, *A secret world of sex: Forbidden fruit: The British experience, 1900–1950* (London: Sidgwick & Jackson, 1988), 26.

[11] Kate Fisher and Simon Szreter, *Sex before the sexual revolution: Intimate life in England, 1918–1963* (Cambridge: Cambridge University Press, 2010), 46, 326.

feeling a loss of masculinity or seeing themselves as anything other than 'normal'.[12] Houlbrook's questioning of 'normal' sexuality is instructive when looking at marriage. As Robyn Wiegman and Elizabeth A. Wilson have argued, a norm is not a 'singularity' but is 'wide-ranging' and 'ever moving'.[13]

The act of getting married centres on the wedding. Historians and others have analysed the marriage ceremony to place it within a nexus of economic, social and cultural factors. Historian John Gillis's important study of British marriages from 1600 to the 1970s shows differences in marriage customs according to class and region. Gillis's *longue durée* approach allows him to conclude that recent changes in marriage and cohabitation are a return to an earlier norm. Following a 'history from below' approach pioneered by E. P. Thompson's *Making of the English Working Class*, social historian Gillis, charts the rise, demise and rise again of the big 'plebeian' wedding over four centuries. Gillis argues that, rather than a triumph for romantic love, the re-emergence of the big working-class wedding in the mid-twentieth century demonstrates that the working-class married couple could only exist within a larger support network. The wedding was a way of bringing these people together at the start of the marriage. Further, Gillis argues that the 'reritualisation' of the wedding was because of the lack of control working-class people had in other aspects of their lives.[14] More recent scholarship has taken a theoretically informed approach to analysing wedding rites. Sociologist Chrys Ingraham deploys Marxian critical theory to show that the rise of the 'white wedding' in the United States makes both heterosexuality and its concomitant gender stereotypes appear natural, reinforces the racial hierarchy, and bolsters consumer capitalism. Borrowing from Jacques Lacan and Louis Althusser, Ingraham coins the term 'heterosexual imaginary' to show that heterosexuality appears as timeless and unchanging, and its role in structuring gender, class and race is left 'unexamined'. Her analysis of the 'wedding-industrial complex' reveals the ways in which films, magazine publishers, clothing retailers, travel agents and others

---

[12] Matt Houlbrook, *Queer London: Perils and pleasures in the sexual metropolis, 1918–1957* (London: University of Chicago Press, 2006), 7, 171.

[13] Robyn Wiegman and Elizabeth A. Wilson, 'Introduction: Antinormativity's queer conventions', *differences* 26, No. 1 (2015), 16.

[14] John Gillis, *For better, for worse: British marriages, 1600 to the present* (Oxford: Oxford University Press, 1985), 5, 260–1.

create an illusion that romantic heterosexuality, and therefore gender, is changeless.[15] Literature scholar Elizabeth Freeman takes a different approach in her study of weddings and forms of belonging in American culture. Freeman builds on the notions of performativity developed by Eve Sedgwick to show that 'marriage seems to be destabilised rather than reinforced by the semiotic performance of the wedding',[16] meaning that the cross-gender coupling, and gender itself, is shown by the wedding ceremony to be fictive and unstable by demonstrating the other forms of relationship (belonging) that are present: for example, parents, siblings, friends and a whole array of weddings guests. By building on these scholars' work, this book shows that marriage rituals—engagement, wedding and honeymoon—change over time, that the white wedding normalises normative gender and sexuality within wider social, cultural and economic discourses, and that the wedding fails to create a stable, unified couple that is separate from other relationships.

Historians have also uncovered the variety of marriage-like relationships that were not perhaps sanctified by Church or State in a wedding ceremony. Katherine Holden's study of singleness in England from 1914 to 1960 combines oral history interviews with the deconstruction of opposites. To provide a more sophisticated way of understanding the emotional and sexual lives of 'single' people, Holden collapses the binary of single/married and demonstrates that the meaning of each are in dialogue and not antithesis. Holden gives a 'voice' to those who are on the 'periphery of marriage' to show the complexity and emotionality of 'singleness' during an era when 'the popularly held belief' was that 'marriage was the normal adult condition'.[17] Historians have also considered the historically variable shapes, definitions and meanings of family. Historian Matt Cook's work on Queer families in the first half of the twentieth century shows that 'family—as an actual network of people and as a conceptual and ideological framework—was and remains key to queer men, albeit in different and shifting ways'.[18] The 'other'

---

[15] Ingraham, *White weddings*, 16, 26.

[16] Elizabeth Freeman, *The wedding complex: Forms of belonging in modern American culture* (London: Duke University Press, 2002), 34.

[17] Katherine Holden, *The shadow of marriage: Singleness in England, 1914–60* (Manchester: Manchester University Press, 2007), 6, 10, 216.

[18] Matt Cook, 'Families of choice? George Ives, queer lives and the family in early twentieth-century Britain', *Gender & History* No. 1 (April, 2010), 15.

models of relationship or family, and the figures of bachelor and spinster, helped to define marriage, and the married, as 'normal'. These historians demonstrate that working outside of binary thinking can provide original and convincing historical analysis of marriage and kinship in this period. This book, though focusing on men marrying women, questions binary constructions of sex, gender and sexuality.

Another relevant strand of historical work is the analysis of love and romance in the twentieth century. Langhamer uses a range of different sources in her 'social history of heterosexual love and commitment'. By supplementing Mass Observation material with social studies, feature films and teenage comics, Langhamer shows that the 'well-worn view of post-war Britain as stable, conservative, and emotionally controlled' is inaccurate and that instead 'new understandings of love and partnership' created 'tensions and contradictions'. The rise of romantic love brought closer 'scrutiny' of relationships, with many people increasingly unwilling to live 'loveless' lives.[19] In the Palgrave edited volume entitled *Love and Romance in Britain, 1918–1970*, historians have employed a variety of sources to problematise 'the 1950s as a golden era of romance'. This collection of essays draws on a wide range of sources to show that 'tensions surrounding competing expectations, gendered interpretations and unequal power relations were present throughout modern love's "golden era"'.[20] In her contribution, Langhamer concludes that the 'mapping of romantic love onto heterosexual marriage was, for example, a key characteristic of the age'.[21] Stephen Brooke also demonstrates this in his analyses of the interrelation between popular culture and subjective experience of 'love'. Brooke shows that 'for ordinary people, heterosexual "love" and "romance" were increasingly found in and refracted through stories encountered in popular culture', but that this did not 'displace emotional realism and material pragmatism'.[22] Throughout this book, 'love' and

---

[19] Claire Langhamer, *The English in love: The intimate history of an emotional revolution* (Oxford: Oxford University Press, 2013), xvi, 1, 4, 207–8.

[20] Alana Harris and Timothy Willem Jones, 'Introduction' in *Love and romance in Britain, 1918–1970* ed. Alana Harris and Timothy Willem Jones (Basingstoke: Palgrave, 2015), 14, 15.

[21] Langhamer, 'Afterword', 245.

[22] Stephen Brooke, '"A certain amount of mush": Love, romance, celluloid and wax in the mid-twentieth century' in *Love and romance in Britain, 1918–1970* ed. Alana Harris and Timothy Willem Jones (Basingstoke: Palgrave, 2015), 81, 94.

'romance' appear in a range of sources as ideals that the marrying man was increasingly expected to provide or participate in: for example, the romantic marriage proposal, white wedding and honeymoon. Although this rich historiography of sex, love and romance provides context and inspiration for approaching source material, this book lies principally within the history of masculinity. The ideas behind this book stem from the conference at Birkbeck College in 2008 that resulted in the volume *What is Masculinity? Historical Dynamics from Antiquity to the Contemporary World* edited by John Arnold and Sean Brady. In their introduction, Brady and Arnold draw attention to four areas of importance for historians of masculinity.[23] First, they highlight the need for source criticism, since different source bases could lead to very different research outcomes when historicising masculinity in different periods and for different men. Secondly, they point out that male–male relationships are just as important as male–female when considering masculinity. Thirdly, historians should consider masculinity 'with regards to status, age, profession, religion, ethnicity and national identity'. This is especially important when considering masculinity in mid-twentieth-century England since 'in modern times it is likely that "national identity" would be a key and recurrent accompaniment to ideas of masculinity, both within a European context of competing nation states, and (with added racial aspects) in a colonial context'. Finally, acknowledging that many scholars had focused on 'representation' or 'codes' of masculinity, Brady and Arnold called for historians to explore 'the experience of cultural mediated reality'.[24] Following a colloquium five years earlier at the University of Sussex, Karen Harvey and Alexandra Shepard asked 'What Have Historians Done with Masculinity?', in response to John Tosh's important 1994 essay 'What Should Historians Do with Masculinity?' Harvey and Shepard questioned the temporal boundaries of historians' research and stated the importance of exploring the 'ways in which the history of masculinity is in tension with existing periodisation'. They

---

[23] Similar themes are found in Karen Harvey and Alexandra Shepard, 'What have historians done with masculinity? Reflection on five centuries of British history, circa 1500–1950', *Journal of British Studies* 44, No. 2 (April 2005), 274–80; Heather Ellis and Jessica Meyer 'Introduction' in *Masculinity and the other: Historical perspectives* ed. Heather Ellis and Jessica Meyer (Newcastle: CambridgeScholars, 2009), 1–18.

[24] John Arnold and Sean Brady, 'Introduction' in *What is masculinity? Historical dynamics from antiquity to the contemporary world* ed. John Arnold and Sean Brady (Basingstoke: Palgrave, 2011), 3, 4, 5.

suggested that researchers were finding that the 'emerging long-term picture is one of tidal change and deep continuity, rather than linear transformation'. They found that historians of masculinity had 'concentrated on culturally and commercially dominant groups of men' and that analysis was needed that assessed both 'cultural codes' and 'subjective experience', and that the latter may yield 'evidence of the subtleties of change'.[25] Although there has since been a range of excellent studies of masculinity in this period,[26] none has assessed married masculinity in a cross-class study using a diverse range of sources.

This book explores some of the continuities of modern masculinity—domesticity, paid labour and male–male interactions while subordinating women—to show the shifts and contradictions in mid-twentieth-century masculinity in England. Placing the locus of change, not with the two world wars, but with socioeconomic drivers in the 1930s and 1950s, the research shows some of the linkages and dissonances between 'representation' and 'experience' of masculinity. Male–male relations are considered in tension with the male–female, and English masculinity is placed within the context of colonial tensions and a desire among some to compare well with 'civilised' nations. The masculinity of marrying men is considered within a nexus of overlapping identities such as class, race and religion.

* * *

[25] Harvey and Shepard, 'What have historians done with masculinity?', 274, 277, 279–80; See John Tosh, 'What should historians do with masculinity?—Reflections on nineteenth-century Britain', *History Workshop Journal* 38 (1994).

[26] For example, Lucy Delap, '"Be strong and play the man": Anglican masculinities in the twentieth century' in *Men, masculinities and religious change in twentieth-century Britain* ed. Lucy Delap and Sue Morgan (Basingstoke: Palgrave, 2013), 119–45; Laura King, *Family men: Fatherhood and masculinity In Britain, 1914–1960* (Oxford: Oxford University Press, 2015); Stella Moss, 'Manly drinkers: Masculinity and material culture in the interwar public house' in *Gender and material culture in Britain since 1600* ed. Hannah Greig, Jane Hamlett, Leonie Hannan (Basingstoke: Palgrave, 2015), 138–52; Helen Smith, *Masculinity, class and same-sex desire in industrial England, 1895–1957* (Basingstoke: Palgrave, 2015); Juliette Pattinson, '"Shirkers", "scrimjacks" and "scrimshanks"?: British civilian masculinity and reserved occupations, 1914–45', *Gender & History* 28, No. 3 (2016), 709–27.

This book falls within the history of masculinity, perhaps best typified by the work of historian John Tosh.[27] The history of masculinity has from its inception sought to historicise masculinity from an anti-sexist perspective.[28] The model of masculinity initially suggested by Tosh is a historicised version of the 'hegemonic masculinity' model developed by sociologist R. W. Connell.[29] Connell's sociological model simultaneously explains the hierarchies of different masculinities and the continuing domination of women by men, by keeping 'power relations of gender always in view'.[30] Based on Antonio Gramsci's concept of hegemony, the hegemonic masculinity is always insecure and unstable and can be resisted and challenged. Hegemonic masculinity is a sociological model that is useful to historians since, as Connell argues, masculinities are 'created in specific historical circumstances'[31] and as the hegemonic masculinity gathers men with values that appeal to men with 'very different interests',[32] it is therefore a model that can be applied across social classes. Gramsci stated, in his critique of Italian fascism, that '"spontaneous" consent' is 'given by the great masses of the population to the general direction imposed on social life by the dominant fundamental group'.[33] When applying Gramsci's concept of hegemony to masculinity, Connell argues that men yield the 'patriarchal dividend' by being complicit in exclusive heterosexuality, the sexual double standard and male 'right'

[27] For example, John Tosh, *A man's place: Masculinity and the middle-class home in Victorian England* (London: Yale University Press, 1999).

[28] Michael Roper and John Tosh, 'Introduction: Historians and the politics of masculinity' in *Manful assertions: Masculinities in Britain since 1800* ed. Michael Roper and John Tosh (London: Routledge, 1991), 7.

[29] Tosh, 'What should historians do with masculinity?', 192; R. W. Connell, *Masculinities* (Cambridge: Polity, 1995), 76–81.

[30] John Tosh, 'Hegemonic masculinity and the history of gender' in *Masculinities in politics and war: Gendering modern history* ed. Stefan Dudink, Karen Hagemann and John Tosh (Manchester: Manchester University Press, 2004), 55.

[31] Connell, *Masculinities*, 77; R. W. Connell, *The men and the boys* (Cambridge: Polity, 2000), 13.

[32] Tosh, 'What should historians do with masculinity?', 192.

[33] Antonio Gramsci, *Selections from the prison notebooks*, ed. and trans. Quintin Hoare and Geoffrey Nowell Smith (London: Lawrence & Wishart, 1998. First published 1971), 12.

1 INTRODUCTION   13

to paid work.[34] This 'complicity' is historically specific since it varies according to time and place. During the late nineteenth and early-twentieth centuries, the requirements of hegemonic masculinity were marriage with paternity, to be head of household, to have 'breadwinner' status with dignified employment, and to have access to male social networks. These were the aspirations of men from the middle class and working class; indeed, such values were a vital part of the labour movement.[35]

Social class was important during the period 1918 to 1960 and is therefore an important category of analysis in this book. As Tosh points out 'gender status cannot be reduced to class status', and it is important to determine how social class inflected masculinity and *vice versa*. Class is difficult to define and historicise. In her gender history of *Working-Class Cultures*, Bourke is wary of analysis of social class that assumes '"trickle down" theories and "embourgeoisement"' of the working class and instead considers working-class people as individuals rather than simply researching their institutions such as 'trade unions, workingmen's clubs, community pressure groups, and policy parties'.[36] Tosh in his groundbreaking work on middle-class masculinity in Victorian England accepts that the term 'middle class' is difficult to define. He argues that it 'is misleading to think of a unified bourgeoisie' and that it is 'in some ways more realistic to accept the residual implications of the term "middle" class'. Tosh therefore defines the middle classes by what they were not rather than what they were, and contends that 'the middle classes were distinguished from the aristocracy and gentry because they worked regularly for living, and from the working class because they did not stoop to manual labour'.[37] Tosh therefore implies the triadic, occupation-based class structure of the upper, middle and working class.

It is important to understand some of the movements and undercurrents of the English social-class structure during this period, and this

[34] Connell, *Masculinities*, 76–81; Tosh, 'What should historians do with masculinity?', 192.

[35] Sean Brady, *Masculinity and male homosexuality in Britain, 1861–1913* (Basingstoke: Palgrave, 2005), 32–6, 47; Lynne Segal, *Slow motion: Changing masculinities, changing men* (Basingstoke: Palgrave, 2007. First published 1990), 248–9.

[36] Tosh, 'What should historians do with masculinity?', 190; Bourke, *Working-class cultures*, 1.

[37] Tosh, *Man's place*, 13.

also demonstrates the difficultly the historian has in defining social class. Historian Ross McKibbin has tried to measure the power and population of the social classes during this period. McKibbin argues that although difficult to define, 'there was undoubtedly an upper class' during this period and he tentatively estimates their number at 40,000. Although declining in number, and possibly in wealth and influence, the upper class could variously comprise 'the old aristocracy', the 'gentry', those who were the political elites attached to the peerage by birth, marriage, or social affiliation, or simply those 'people who could be categorised in no other way'. Also hard to define are the middle classes. McKibbin shows that some contemporary commentators adopted an 'income criterion' of £250 a year. This would have allowed a middle-class 'style of life' and would have 'excluded the great mass of the manual working class'. McKibbin argues that this figure of £250 a year 'has little value' to the historian and perhaps what 'mattered was occupation and the social aspirations and manners which occupation demanded'. On this basis, and because of 'their very strong sense of not being working-class', the office clerk 'must be regarded as middle-class'. At the other end of the 'middle' class, in the 'higher professionals', there were 'spectacular' changes as the number of lawyers and clergy decreased to be overtaken by those in 'engineering and scientific professions'. Across the period, there was a fall in the number of employers and a rise in the number of 'salaried employees' especially those in 'lower professions' such as 'managers and administrators'. McKibbin argues that in this period the English middle class had 'become predominantly a technical-scientific-commercial-managerial class' and 'surprisingly quickly'. Based on *occupation*, McKibbin estimates that twenty-two per cent of the English population were middle class in 1921 and twenty-eight per cent in 1951. Although in numerical decline across the period, the working class was by far the largest group. McKibbin estimates that seventy-eight per cent of the English population were working class in 1921 and seventy-two per cent in 1951. Within the decline in overall numbers, it is important to note that the number of skilled workers declined more rapidly than the semi-skilled or unskilled, partly because of the rapid decline of '"staple" industries' such as coal, textiles, shipbuilding and heavy engineering.[38] Although less than perfect,

---

[38] Ross McKibbin, *Classes and cultures, England 1918–1951* (Oxford: Oxford University Press, 1998), 2, 44–7, 49, 106–7.

McKibbin's occupational definition allows the historian to show change over time across and within social classes.

The definition of social class used in this book is based on occupation and follows the triad of upper, middle and working class. This pragmatic approach is similar to that of social historian John Gillis who compares marriage by social class without defining class.[39] Working class is taken as those who work in manual jobs, and lower-middle class as clerk-level office jobs or, for example, a steelworks junior manager. Upper-middle class is defined as professional (for example, medical, scientific, senior financial), with middle class falling in between these two, such as a steelworks manager. Upper class is taken to mean those from aristocratic or ennobled families. This definition is not unproblematic since, for example, steelworkers may have their differences and antagonisms within their own group, and further that a steelworker could be wealthier than a clerk. As Bourke shows, across this period, the '"class" structure has persisted' despite changes in relative wealth. Class by itself is perhaps not an ideal descriptor. Since, as historian David Cannadine argues, social class 'has a geography as well as a history',[40] where possible men, and women, are introduced into the narrative of this book with some basic *individual* details such occupation and region or city. This should allow transparency such that the reader can see how the individual has been categorised. Categorising men into occupational groups is however expedient to show some of the varied masculinities during this period.

The sources used suggest both an overarching masculinity, and differences between class-based masculinities. A range of sources reveals definitions of marriage and married sexuality, as well as men's subjectivities. At the heart of this is power: power between men and women, power between men, power between generations and power to define sex and marriage. Power is inextricably linked to discourse, the variety and scope of knowledge bases within which a subject can articulate her or his own self.[41] Tosh initially suggested that the ways in which men continuously

---

[39] Gillis, *For better, for worse*, 4.

[40] Bourke, *Working-class cultures*, 5; David Cannadine, *The rise and fall of class in Britain* (New York: Columbia University Press, 1999), 19.

[41] John Storey, *Cultural theory and popular culture: An introduction* (Harlow: Pearson, 2001. First published 1997), 78.

affirm and demonstrate their masculinity could be evaluated in the interrelated sites of home, work and all-male association.[42] In this book however a series of overlapping sites are considered (for example, legal cases, marriage proposals, honeymoon planning) to assess the relative power of men and women, and therefore constructions of masculinity. The first category of sources is those that could be called 'official', including parliamentary debates, legal cases, liturgy books and medical journals. Historian Frank Mort uses a Foucauldian approach, the analysis of power through discursive eruption, in his work on sex and 'official knowledge' because '[d]iscourse analysis works best wherever intellectuals have staked out distinctive monopolies on truth'.[43] Mort later explained that his 1980s 'attempt to integrate Foucault with a feminist emphasis on the gendered power relations that a history of modern sexuality is imbedded in' was targeted, along with other researchers at the time, at 'the classic terrain of the "the social" which shaped modern strategies of government'.[44] In this book, the gendered 'truths' of 'official' definitions of marriage show masculinity in relation to social class, race and religion, but are part of a larger picture including the popular press and subjective experience.

Subjective experience is intertwined with the performance of sex, gender and social class. Early performativity theory was not concerned with sex, gender and sexuality. Work on performativity started with philosopher J. L. Austin and his 1955 Harvard lecture series published subsequently as *How to Do Things with Words*. Austin was interested in the ways in which certain statements, called 'performatives' (for example, 'I do' at a wedding ceremony) appear to perform the action rather than merely describe it. Austin was not interested in the veracity or falsity of utterances but in the level of infelicity. For example, there is no essential untruth in a bigamist uttering 'I do' at a wedding ceremony, but it would be inappropriate. Implicit in this model is the importance of context and circumstance. For Austin 'constative' statements, for example 'the cat is on the mat', may appear to describe something, but are actually performative because such utterances are in themselves performing and affirming. Following from this, all utterances, or speech acts, are

[42] Tosh, 'What should historians do with masculinity?', 192.

[43] Frank Mort, *Dangerous sexualities: Medico-moral politics in England since 1830* (London: Routledge, 1987), 4, 6–7.

[44] Frank Mort, 'Victorian afterlives: Sexuality and identity in the 1960s and 1970s', *History Workshop Journal* 82 (Autumn, 2016), 206.

therefore performative.[45] Post-structuralist Jacques Derrida reconfigured Austin's performativity to take account of the repeated ways in which language is used rather than as just one-off speech acts. For Derrida, elements of language, or discourse, become signs detached from their original context that are cited and repeated. Signs themselves have a 'repetitive and citational structure'. For example, the 'I do' at a wedding ceremony works only because it is part of an 'iterable model'.[46] Language therefore performs acts through the citation and repetition of existing discursive practices. Philosopher Judith Butler builds on Derrida and Austin to provide a model that explains how sex, gender and sexuality are constructed simultaneously through cited and repeated performative acts. In the same way that 'I do' relies on a recognised and implicit series of performatives, so '[g]ender is the repeated stylisation of the body, a set of repeated acts within a highly rigid regulatory frame that congeal over time to produce the appearance of substance, of a natural sort of being'.[47] For Butler, a subject cannot exist without being gendered.[48] This book explores the connection between constructions of valid capacity and consent, the performance of the wedding ceremony, the linguistic definitions and corporal acts of consummation, and notions of married masculinity and 'normal' male sexuality.

Newspapers are an important source for historians of modern gender and sexuality, and they are included here to show the ways in which notions of marriage, masculinity and male sexuality were popularly circulated, including reports of court cases and parliamentary debates that affected marriage law. The newspaper articles are from the leading broadsheet, *The Times*, and from the *Daily Mirror* and the *Daily Express*, because during this period they 'led the field in circulation terms'.[49] As Tosh points out, the mass media play an important role in 'reinforcing

---

[45] J. L. Austin, *How to do things with words* (Oxford: Oxford University Press, 1962), 4–6, 14–15, 17, 145–7.

[46] Jacques Derrida, 'Signature event context' in Jacques Derrida, *Margins of Philosophy* trans. Alan Bass (Chicago: University of Chicago Press, 1984. First published 1982), 326.

[47] Judith Butler, *Gender trouble: Feminism and the subversion of identity* (Abingdon: Routledge, 2008. First published 1990), 45.

[48] Judith Butler, *Bodies that matter: On the discursive limits of "sex"* (London: Routledge, 1993), 8.

[49] King, *Family men*, 9–10.

the dominant expressions of masculinity'.[50] Newspaper historian Adrian Bingham assesses the way the popular press reported sex in the mid-twentieth century. Bingham shows that newspapers continued to present marriage as the only acceptable place for sexual intimacy, but that increasingly 'sexual compatibility' was more important. By the 1950s, popular newspapers continued to support the institution of marriage but held that marriages were 'not unbreakable' and also stated the 'importance of a mutually enjoyable physical relationship for a healthy marriage'. Bingham's sophisticated use of newspaper archives and analysis of readership allows him to argue that divorce reporting 'offered readers a convenient opportunity to satisfy some of their curiosity about sexual indulgence and moral transgression while maintaining their attachment to conventional values'.[51] Newspapers in this book show the changing meanings attached to marriage, masculinity and male sexuality specifically in relation to the process of getting married.

Newspapers show change, but it is tradition that plays a crucial role in any ritual. Through scrutiny of ceremony, historians can reveal some of the complex forces that were at play in culture, society and personal lives in the past. Historian Eric Hobsbawm's concept of 'invented tradition' is instructive here. Hobsbawm defined an invented tradition as

> a set of practices, normally governed by overtly and tacitly accepted rules and of a ritual or symbolic nature, which seek to inculcate certain values and norms of behaviour by repetition, which automatically implies continuity with the past.[52]

This is crucial, as ritualist Catherine Bell argued, since a 'ritual that evokes no connection with the past is apt to be found anomalous, inauthentic, or unsatisfying by most people'. For every ritual, including weddings, 'there is a thick context of social customs, historical practices, and day-to-day activities'. Rituals change over time and are 'never

---

[50] Tosh, 'Hegemonic masculinity', 44.

[51] Adrian Bingham, *Family newspapers? Sex, private life, and the British popular press 1918–1978* (Oxford: Oxford University Press, 2009), 46, 79, 143–4.

[52] Eric Hobsbawm, 'Introduction: Inventing traditions' in *The invention of tradition* ed. Eric Hobsbawm and Terrance Ranger (Cambridge: Cambridge University Press, 1983), 1.

1 INTRODUCTION   19

simply or solely a matter of routine, habit, or the "dead weight of tradition".[53] The understanding that rituals combined elements of old and new, and existed and changed within competing social contexts informs the gendered reading of marriage proposals, asking the father for his daughter's hand in marriage and, of course, the wedding day itself.

Traditions and rituals suffuse etiquette manuals, a source in which historians can find gendered meanings of the idealised marriage process. The period 1918 to 1960 saw a flurry in the publication of etiquette manuals aimed at helping wealthier couples to arrange their weddings. Although the wedding etiquette manual dates back to the mid-nineteenth century,[54] the interwar years saw an increase in the publication of the number of titles that detailed how to organise a 'traditional' wedding including who should make decisions, how to dress, the choice of venue and choreography of the ceremony. Etiquette manuals also told men how to propose and how to arrange a honeymoon. The readership of etiquette manuals was narrow, consisting of wealthier readers, and etiquette manuals are not a good source for showing change over time since their *raison d'etre* was to present the 'traditional' wedding as unchanging. However, as sociologist Cas Wouters explains, etiquette manuals 'may reveal a mixture of actual and ideal behaviour, but these ideals are *real*'.[55] These idealised weddings and honeymoons are also found to an extent in newspapers and personal testimonies.

These sources do not just demonstrate discursive patterns and eruptions, but also suggest some of the marriage discourses available to men as they narrated their lives and constructed their sense of self. Personal testimonies—chiefly autobiographies and archived oral histories—show

[53] Catherine Bell, *Ritual: Perspectives and dimensions* (Oxford: Oxford University Press, 1997), 145, 171; Catherine Bell, *Ritual theory, ritual practice* (Oxford: Oxford University Press, 2009. First published 1992), 92.

[54] For example, *The etiquette of courtship and matrimony: With a complete guide to the forms of a wedding* (London, 1852) [and Second Edition in 1865]; *A manual of the etiquette of love, courtship and marriage. By a lady* (London, 1853); *The etiquette of love, courtship and marriage. To which is added, the etiquette of politeness* (Halifax, 1859); *Etiquette, politeness, and good breeding: Embracing all forms and ceremonies in the etiquette of marriage, etc.* (London, 1870); *How to woo; or, the etiquette of courtship and marriage* (London, 1879); *The etiquette of marriage* (London, 1902); G. R. M. Devereux, *The etiquette of engagement and marriage, etc.* (London, 1903).

[55] Cas Wouters, *Sex and manners: Female emancipation in the West, 1890–2000* (London: Sage, 2004), 10.

the agency men had in constructing their subjectivities, their own sense of themselves. As historian Penny Summerfield has shown, first-person narratives can help us understand the ways in which subjects construct their own sense of themselves from available intersecting and differentiated discourses to which they had access.[56] These sources need to be treated critically: both oral histories and autobiographies are typically constructed long after the event. The subject of an autobiography or oral history seeks to construct a narrative of her or his life that is meaningful[57] and these meanings are distorted or created.[58] However, as Kate Fisher argues, the subjective nature of oral history allows 'subjectivities [to] form the analytical focus'.[59] The link between subjectivity and experience is also important. Joan Scott's contribution on this issue is important: it is 'not individuals who have experience, but subjects who are constituted through experience' she observes.[60] This is useful to consider in the study of men's experiences and masculinity as a subjective identity; I am interested in the meanings men attached to their experiences of getting married. The oral history sample is from the collections in the British Library Sound Archive (BLSA) and has been compiled by using search terms such as 'proposal', 'engagement', 'wedding', 'honeymoon' and then sifting to remove irrelevant interviews on the basis of content (e.g. 'business proposal'), time period or geography. The sample includes interviews from a range of collections including general content such as the BBC Millennium Memories and more specific interviews, for example Alan Dein's 'Lives in Steel'. The sample covers weddings that took place

[56] For such an approach see Penny Summerfield, *Reconstructing women's wartime lives: Discourses and subjectivity in oral histories of the Second World War* (Manchester: Manchester University Press, 1998), 9–14.

[57] Megan Doolittle, 'Missing fathers: Assembling a history of fatherhood in mid-nineteenth-century England', University of Essex: Unpublished Ph.D. thesis (1996), 173; Alessandro Portelli, 'The peculiarities of oral history', *History Workshop Journal* 12 (1981), 103–4.

[58] John Burnett suggests that autobiographers 'record the most significant events and the sharpest emotions' in John Burnett, *Idle hands: The experience of unemployment, 1790–1990* (London: Routledge, 1994), 1; Joanna Bourke argues that authors could 'lie' in Bourke, *Working-class cultures*, 29.

[59] Kate Fisher, *Birth control, sex and marriage in Britain, 1918–1960* (Oxford: Oxford University Press, 2006), 14.

[60] Joan W. Scott, 'The evidence of experience', *Critical Inquiry* 17, No. 4 (Summer, 1991), 779.

1 INTRODUCTION 21

in the years 1918 to 1961, the interviewees' dates of birth range from 1891 to 1939. All social classes are covered and there is a geographical spread from Newcastle to the West Country. The overall number of oral histories is thirty-nine women and fifty-six men.

Readers will notice that much of this book involves people telling stories about themselves and this can provoke an emotional response. Historians are also telling a story: partly personal, partly gleaned from the chosen historical sources. Although historians cannot omit or distort evidence,[61] they interpret sources and present historical research subjectively. The process of choosing and editing the material included in this research can leave readers, who are also shaped by personal circumstances and cultural context, wanting more. What happened to the couple who separated after thirty-three years of unconsummated marriage? What did the older man do when his grown-up children objected to him marrying a younger woman? Did the English woman return to India with her polygamous husband? The footnotes may lead intrigued readers to more detail, but often not. The desire to know more about individual human joy and suffering is therefore shared by me: often, I too long to know *what happened next*.

* * *

This book follows the process of getting married through three important stages: consent, celebration and consummation.

Not all marriages were valid since not any couple could legally marry and this restriction changed during the period 1918 to 1960. Chapter 2 'Consent and Capacity' considers these legal changes regarding who could marry, and what they reveal about masculinity in respect to class, race and religion. A close reading of 'official' discourses—parliamentary debates and nullity test cases in English Civil Law—shows the gendered silences during debates about capacity and consent, the power relations between husbands and wives, and the discursive construction of English marriage. Masculinity is explored through dissection of legally acceptable marriage and in particular the law regarding affinity, polygamy, age and mental capacity. Although sexual agency was complicated, marriage was premised on the man as the breadwinning head of household and the woman as housewife and child carer, and further that men often married

---

[61] Richard J. Evans, *In defence of history* (London: Granta, 1997), 121.

for reasons of pragmatism. English masculinity was in part defined against the colonial Other as protective of women and children.

Chapter 3 assesses 'Engagement' during a period, 1918 to 1960, in which engagement to marry was effectively a legally binding contract and a man who reneged on a promise of marriage could find himself in court for 'breach of promise'. By assessing codes of engagement to reveal the tensions and expectations of masculinity, this chapter asks what pressures were on the marrying man, especially in relation to his (potential) kinship network. A gendered reading of breach of promise cases, newspaper reports, oral histories and etiquette manuals shows the power relations between fiancé and fiancée, and between generations. Men were to propose but had to ask permission from the woman's father, or even an employer or superior officer, but there was a shift from codes of honour to love and romance. A woman was caught in a triangle between two men—her father and her future husband. Men, supposedly independent (especially from their mothers), were often constrained by others.

Chapter 4 'The Wedding' shows the increased ritualisation of the wedding and the normalisation of the now *traditional* 'white wedding', during the period 1918 to 1960, and asks what the rise of the big wedding tells us about masculinity and male sexuality. Etiquette manuals, newspapers and oral histories show some of the different ways of narrating the wedding, and some of the social-class-inflected gender power relations. The 'white wedding' became increasingly popular and newspapers represented it as being available to all, and many men wanted a 'proper' church wedding with as many of the tropes of the idealised 'white wedding' as possible. The combination of old and new and the gendered wedding preparations and choreography created a timeless masculinity based on the breadwinning head of household. Although posited as the bride's 'big day' with the couple at the centre, the wedding and reception were sites in which a man could display his masculinity by engaging in fraternisation with his best man and other male wedding guests.

The wedding did not *complete* the marriage and it had to be consummated by a single act of penile-vaginal intercourse. Chapter 5 'Non-Consummation' asks what a shift from religious to increasingly secular definitions of consummation meant for masculinity and male sexuality by examining medical, legal, ecclesiastical and parliamentary sources. Debates about consummation of marriage in newspapers reported a crisis of relations between Church and State, as the Church lost ground to more secular definitions of sex and marriage. The new, secular purpose of marital sex, and a shift from biological to psychological definitions of impotence, reinforced the 'normal' man as the active, regularly, penetrating partner in a heterosexual marriage and gave primacy to male sexual pleasure contrary to the notion of companionate marriage.

Chapter 6 looks closely at the 'Honeymoon', the final stage of getting married during which consummation would ideally take place. Masculinities of newly married men, especially in relation to social class, revealed through a close reading of first-person testimonies, etiquette manuals, newspaper reports and railway posters. This chapter follows the structure of a honeymoon: planning, location and experience. The planning of a honeymoon allowed men to demonstrate their connections and knowledge outside the home, and many men were increasingly able to provide a 'romantic' honeymoon. Men transformed into the subject position of 'husband' surrounded on holiday by their own social class, and masculine independence was in tension with dependence on others in order make the honeymoon happen.

This book reveals the complexities of masculinity over a four-decade period from the end of the Great War to the start of the 1960s, by using a wide range of sources to look at the seemingly narrow, straightforward process of getting married. Most men married in this period but not all men could legally marry. The laws of consent and capacity defined who could, and could not, marry. These laws changed with the passing of parliamentary legislation, and judgements in nullity test cases. It is with these changes, and their gendered formation and application, that we start our exploration of masculinity and marriage through the journey of consent, celebration and consummation.

REFERENCES

Anon. 1852 [and Second Edition in 1865]. *The etiquette of courtship and matrimony: With a complete guide to the forms of a wedding.* London.

Anon. 1853. *A manual of the etiquette of love, courtship and marriage. By a lady.* London.

Anon. 1859. *The etiquette of love, courtship and marriage. To which is added, the etiquette of politeness.* Halifax.

Anon. 1870. *Etiquette, politeness, and good breeding: Embracing all forms and ceremonies in the etiquette of marriage, etc.* London

Anon. 1879. *How to woo; or, the etiquette of courtship and marriage.* London.

24   N. PENLINGTON

Arnold, John and Sean Brady. 2011. Introduction. In *What is masculinity? Historical dynamics from antiquity to the contemporary world*, ed. John Arnold and Sean Brady, 1–14. Basingstoke: Palgrave.

Austin, J.L. 1962. *How to do things with words*. Oxford: Oxford University Press.

Bell, Catherine. 1997. *Ritual: Perspectives and dimensions*. Oxford: Oxford University Press.

Bell, Catherine. 2009. First published 1992. *Ritual theory, ritual practice*. Oxford: Oxford University Press.

Bingham, Adrian. 2009. *Family newspapers? Sex, private life, and the British popular press 1918–1978*. Oxford: Oxford University Press.

Bourke, Joanna. 1994. *Working-class cultures: Gender, class and ethnicity*. London: Routledge.

Brady, Sean. 2005. *Masculinity and male homosexuality in Britain, 1861–1913*. Basingstoke: Palgrave.

Brooke, Stephen. 2015. "A certain amount of mush": Love, romance, celluloid and wax in the mid-twentieth century. In *Love and romance in Britain, 1918–1970* ed. Alana Harris and Timothy Willem Jones, 81–99. Basingstoke: Palgrave.

Brown, Callum. 2009. First published 2001. *The death of Christian Britain: Understanding secularisation 1800–2000*. London: Routledge.

Burnett, John. 1994. *Idle hands: The experience of unemployment, 1790–1990*. London: Routledge.

Butler, Judith. 1993. *Bodies that matter: On the discursive limits of "sex."* London: Routledge.

Butler, Judith. 2008. First published 1990. *Gender trouble: Feminism and the subversion of identity*. Abingdon: Routledge.

Cannadine, David. 1999. *The rise and fall of class in Britain*. New York: Columbia University Press.

Collins, Marcus. 2003. *Modern love: An intimate history of men and women in twentieth-century Britain*. London: Atlantic Books.

Connell, R.W. 2000. *The men and the boys*. Cambridge: Polity.

Cook, Hera. 2005. *The long sexual revolution: English women, sex, and contraception 1800–1975*. Oxford: Oxford University Press.

Cook, Matt. 2010. Families of choice? George Ives, Queer lives and the family in early twentieth-century Britain. *Gender & History* 22 (1): 1–20.

Delap, Lucy. 2013. "Be strong and play the man": Anglican masculinities in the twentieth century. In *Men, masculinities and religious change in twentieth-century Britain*, ed. Lucy Delap and Sue Morgan, 119–45. Basingstoke: Palgrave.

Derrida, Jacques. 1984. First published 1982. Signature event context. In *Margins of philosophy*, ed. Jacques Derrida. Trans. Alan Bass, 309–30. Chicago: University of Chicago Press.

1 INTRODUCTION   25

Devereux, G. R. M. 1903. *The etiquette of engagement and marriage, etc.* London.

Doolittle, Megan. 1996. Missing fathers: Assembling a history of fatherhood in mid-nineteenth-century England. Unpublished Ph.D. thesis: University of Essex.

Ellis, Heather and Jessica Meyer. 2009. Introduction. In *Masculinity and the other: Historical perspectives*, ed. Heather Ellis and Jessica Meyer, 1–18. Newcastle: Cambridge Scholars

Evans, Richard J. 1997. *In defence of history*. London: Granta.

Finch, Janet, and Penny Summerfield. 1991. Social reconstruction and the emergence of companionate marriage, 1945–59. In *Marriage, domestic life and social change: Writings for Jacqueline Burgoyne (1944–88)*, ed. David Clark, 7–32. London: Routledge.

Fisher, Kate and Simon Szreter. 2010. *Sex before the sexual revolution: Intimate life in England, 1918–1963.*Cambridge: Cambridge University Press.

Fisher, Kate. 2006. *Birth control, sex and marriage in Britain, 1918–1960.* Oxford: Oxford University Press.

Freeman, Elizabeth. 2002. *The wedding complex: Forms of belonging in modern American culture*. London: Duke University Press.

Gillis, John. 1985. *For better, for worse: British marriages, 1600 to the present*. Oxford: Oxford University Press.

Gramsci, Antonio. 1998. First published 1971. *Selections from the prison notebooks*. Trans. Quintin Hoare and Geoffrey Nowell Smith. London: Lawrence & Wishart.

Harris, Alana and Timothy Willem Jones. 2015. Introduction. In *Love and romance in Britain, 1918–1970*, ed. Alana Harris and Timothy Willem Jones, 81–99. Basingstoke: Palgrave.

Harris, Alana. 2013. *Faith in the family: A lived religious history of English Catholicism, 1945–82*. Manchester: Manchester University Press.

Harvey, Karen, and Alexandra Shepard. 2005. What have historians done with masculinity? Reflection on five centuries of British history, circa 1500–1950. *Journal of British Studies* 44 (2): 274–280.

Hobsbawm, Eric. 1983. Introduction: Inventing traditions. In *The invention of tradition*, ed. Eric Hobsbawm and Terrance Ranger, 1–14. Cambridge: Cambridge University Press.

Holden, Katherine. 2007. *The shadow of marriage: Singleness in England, 1914–60*. Manchester: Manchester University Press.

Houlbrook, Matt. 2006. *Queer London: Perils and pleasures in the sexual metropolis, 1918–1957*. London: University of Chicago Press.

Hubbard, Phil. 2012. *Cities and sexualities*. Abingdon: Routledge.

Humphries, Steve. 1988. *A secret world of sex: Forbidden fruit: The British experience, 1900–1950*. London: Sidgwick & Jackson.

Ingraham, Chrys. 1999. *White weddings: Romancing heterosexuality in popular culture*. London: Routledge.

Jones, Timothy Willem and Alana Harris. 2015. Introduction: Historicizing "modern" love and romance. In *love and romance in Britain, 1918–1970*, ed. Alana Harris and Timothy Willem Jones, 1–19. Basingstoke: Palgrave.

King, Laura. 2015. *Family men: Fatherhood and masculinity In Britain, 1914–1960*. Oxford: Oxford University Press.

Langhamer, Claire. 2006. Adultery in post-war England. *History Workshop Journal* 62: 86–115.

Langhamer, Claire. 2013. *The English in love: The intimate history of an emotional revolution*. Oxford: Oxford University Press.

Langhamer, Claire. 2015. Afterword. In *love and romance in Britain, 1918–1970*, ed. Alana Harris and Timothy Willem Jones, 245–253. Basingstoke: Palgrave.

McKibbin, Ross. 1998. *Classes and cultures, England 1918–1951*. Oxford: Oxford University Press.

Mort, Frank. 1987. *Dangerous sexualities: Medico-moral politics in England since 1830*. London: Routledge.

Mort, Frank. 2016. Victorian afterlives: Sexuality and identity in the 1960s and 1970s. *History Workshop Journal* 82 (Autumn): 199–212.

Moss, Stella. 2015. Manly drinkers: Masculinity and material culture in the interwar public house. In *Gender and material culture in Britain since 1600*, ed. Hannah Greig, Jane Hamlett, and Leonie Hannan, 138–52. Basingstoke: Palgrave.

Pattinson, Juliette. 2016. "Shirkers", "scrimjacks" and "scrimshanks"?: British civilian masculinity and reserved occupations, 1914–45. *Gender & History* 28 (3): 709–727.

Portelli, Alessandro. 1981. The peculiarities of oral history. *History Workshop Journal* 12: 96–107.

Roper, Michael, and John Tosh. 1991. Introduction: Historians and the politics of masculinity. In *Manful assertions: Masculinities in Britain since 1800*, ed. Michael Roper and John Tosh, 1–24. London: Routledge.

Scott, Joan W. 1991. The evidence of experience. *Critical Inquiry* 17 (4): 773–797.

Segal, Lynne. 2007. First published 1990. *Slow motion: Changing masculinities, changing men*. Basingstoke: Palgrave.

Smith, Helen. 2015. *Masculinity, class and same-sex desire in industrial England, 1895–1957*. Basingstoke: Palgrave.

Storey, John. 2001. First published 1997. *Cultural theory and popular culture: An introduction*. Harlow: Pearson.

Summerfield, Penny. 1998. *Reconstructing women's wartime lives: Discourses and subjectivity in oral histories of the Second World War*. Manchester: Manchester University Press.

Tosh, John. 1994. What should historians do with masculinity?—Reflections on nineteenth-century Britain. *History Workshop Journal* 38: 179–202.

Tosh, John. 1999. *A man's place: Masculinity and the middle-class home in Victorian England*. London: Yale University Press.

Tosh, John. 2004. Hegemonic masculinity and the history of gender. In *Masculinities in politics and war: Gendering modern history*, ed. Stefan Dudink, Karen Hagemann, and John Tosh, 41–58. Manchester: Manchester University Press.

Wiegman, Robyn and Elizabeth A. Wilson. 2015. Introduction: Antinormativity's queer conventions. *Differences* 26(1):1–25.

Wouters, Cas. 2004. *Sex and manners: Female emancipation in the West, 1890–2000*. London: Sage.

CHAPTER 2

Consent and Capacity

If any of you know cause, or just impediment, why these two persons should not be joined together in holy Matrimony, ye are to declare it – Banns from the *Book of Common Prayer*[1]

Under English law, the legally essential component of marriage is freely given 'consent'.[2] Derived from the laws of ancient Rome, English marriage could be contracted only between two parties—a man and a woman—who have *consensus*[3] and therefore have the capacity to consent to marriage. During the period 1918 and 1960, English marriage consent law changed in two ways. First, new legislation moved the boundaries of marriage by restricting or relaxing access to marriage: the Age of Marriage Act (1929) raised the marriage age; the Marriage (Prohibited Degrees of Relationship) Act (1931) and the Marriage (Enabling) Act (1960) relaxed some prohibitions of affinity; and the Matrimonial Causes Act (1937) introduced restrictions for 'mental deficients', those of 'unsound

---

[1] *The Book of Common Prayer* (London: Ebury, 1992), 307.

[2] Consent must be given without 'duress' and the 'duress need not be confined to fear of bodily harm', since '[t]error of the mind will be sufficient to make the contract void'. See *Scott (falsely called Sebright) v Sebright* (1886).

[3] William Van Ommeren, 'Mental illness affecting matrimonial consent', *Canon Law Studies* 415 (1961), whole vol.

© The Author(s), under exclusive license to Springer Nature Switzerland AG 2023
N. Penlington, *Men Getting Married in England, 1918–60*, Genders and Sexualities in History, https://doi.org/10.1007/978-3-031-27405-3_2

29

mind', those with venereal disease[4] or those pregnant by another man[5] at the time of the wedding ceremony. Secondly, a number of legal test cases, including polygamy, set precedents that altered the definition of marriage consent, and therefore changed the boundaries of marriage. This chapter will unpick the straightforward notion of agreeing to marry to reveal the gendered meanings and implications of seemingly gender-neutral marriage consent laws—of who could or could not marry. By moving beyond the categories of active/passive, we will see some of the complexities and contradictions of masculinity and male sexuality, and the tension between desire and pragmatic decision-making.

This chapter shows changing notions of marriage consent through a close reading of strands of legal sources and related debate and commentary: parliamentary legislation, and legal test cases in which precedents were set. New parliamentary legislation regarding marriage consent introduced in this period was gender neutral but a gendered reading of the parliamentary debates illustrates the implicit and explicit motivations for passing the new laws regarding age of marriage, affinity and mental capacity were often highly gendered. The second strand of marriage consent law considered here is marriage annulment, or nullity. A court could annul a marriage if it was found to be 'defective', and lacking in consent, at the time of the wedding ceremony. It was possible for a marriage to be contracted between, for example, underage people or a couple who were too closely related, but such marriages could be retrospectively annulled regardless of whether the parties were cognisant of the impediment at the time of marriage, or whether there was deception or ignorance of the law. The legal cases in this chapter do not therefore reveal the prevalence of 'illegal' marriage. It is impossible to say, for example, how many bigamous or consanguineous marriages there were because many would not have come before the courts and the process for stopping illegal marriages was itself very flimsy. Although, as historian Matt Cook states, '[t]here is no straightforward correlation between the

---

[4] This was not discussed in parliament during the passage of the 1937 Act, and the only nullity test case was *C v C* [1946] 1 All ER 562, which compelled physicians to provide evidence in such a case.

[5] This was not discussed in parliament during the passage of the 1937 Act, and the only nullity test case was *Smith v Smith* [1947] 2 All ER 741, which was concerned with 'marital intercourse' as condonation of the marital offence of pregnancy by another man. Sex as 'condonation' is discussed in Chapter 5 'Non-Consummation'.

morality and norms of the law and the morality and norms of society',[6] nullity test cases that set legal precedents can reveal changing notions of marriage and are suggestive of the range of marriages and sexual intimacies that existed at the time. These unusual cases demonstrate some of the taboos and boundaries men and women transgressed, consciously or otherwise, and further the ways in which legal interpretation of that transgression often depended on gender. Moreover, when giving judgement, judges often gave examples of what might happen if they did or did not grant a nullity and set a legal precedent. This can lead to a variety of imagined marriage possibilities that may or may not have actually existed already.

The relatively small number of legal cases reviewed is both rich in detail and highly influential legally since each case marked a change in marriage consent law. These test cases changed the law because the resulting judgement set a legal precedent, rather than a law change enacted by parliament. Changes in marriage consent law and the often gendered reasons for such legal change allow the historian a glimpse at the wider discourses of masculinity that were circulating at the time. The approach taken examines all of the cases listed in the appropriate categories in the *Blackstone's Index*, a leading index of historical precedent-setting law cases.[7] The cases examined here—because of their legal significance—have been kept in detail and each has a detailed judgement.[8] The result is not an exhaustive explication of affinity, polygamy, age and mental capacity in relation to marriage. Instead, the method used narrowly looks at how the law of marriage consent changed who could have access to the institution of marriage during this period and the gendered meanings that were implicitly or explicitly stated during the process of changing the law. Although this does not show directly the everyday experience of married masculinity, the seemingly straightforward process of law changes

---

[6] Matt Cook, 'Law' in *Palgrave advances in the modern history of sexuality* ed. Matt Houlbrook and H. G. Cocks (Basingstoke: Palgrave, 2006), 70.

[7] Maxwell Barrett (ed.), *Blackstone's Marriage Breakdown Law Index: Case precedents, 1900–1997* (London: Blackstone, 1998); Maxwell Barrett (ed.), *Blackstone's Family Law Index: Case precedents, 1900–1997* (London: Blackstone, 1998). An alternative approach would be to examine a random sample of cases. This would possibly reveal some different cases with different characteristics, but would be difficult to achieve since very few post-1858 nullity case files exist and there are none after 1937.

[8] The details can be found, for example, on the *Lexis* database.

throws up elements of masculinity in relation to class, race and religion. By taking a narrow approach, it is possible to focus on some rich and important sources that reveal the conflicting ways in which masculinity was constructed and reiterated, as laws restricted or relaxed access to marriage and therefore had a real impact on the lives of men and women by determining which relationships were legitimate in the eyes of the State.

This gendered assessment of marriage consent and capacity during the period 1918 to 1960 is set within the context of shifting social, political and cultural attitudes of the time. Examination of marriage consent shows some of the connections between marriage, sex, race, religion and class.[9] Fear of rising divorce—though more a fear than a fact for most of the period—created anxiety about the institution of marriage.[10] This led to a desire by some to relax the marriage consent laws to make it easier for some people to marry: for example, removing restrictions on marriage within certain degrees of affinity. There was concern too that the *wrong* people were marrying and procreating, and eugenicists argued that endemic levels of unemployment in the interwar period were more about genetics than economics.[11] For example, it will be shown that 'mental defectives' were among those deemed unfit to procreate and were barred from marrying. The interwar period also saw rising anxiety about England's place in the world. Now, no longer the dominant superpower, Britain was increasingly dependent on its Empire for trade and status; especially after 1931, when Home Rule and eventually independence for India, the 'Jewel in the Crown' of the empire, looked increasingly inevitable in the 1940s.[12] Polygamy test cases brought English judgement of Indian and Egyptian, Hindu and Muslim marriage at a time when Britain was about to lose those colonies. Age of marriage consent

---

[9] This follows Pamela Haag's historical study of consent in the US. Pamela Haag, *Consent: Sexual rights and the transformation of American liberalism* (Ithaca: Cornell University Press, 1999), xviii.

[10] The divorce rate was two and a half times higher after the Second World War compared to before it. The big increase in divorce, however, started in the 1970s. Lawrence Stone, *Road to Divorce: England 1530–1987* (Oxford: Oxford University Press, 1990), 402.

[11] Martin Pugh, '*We danced all night': A social history of Britain between the wars* (London: Vintage, 2008), 161–4, 197.

[12] Bernard Porter, *The Lion's Share: A short history of British Imperialism, 1850–1995* (Harlow: Longman, 1996), 306, 322–5.

debates were framed within wider unease about how Britain compared with 'civilised' nations, and how the English could set an example to the Other.

This examination of marriage consent demonstrates that the boundaries and expectations of marriage changed during the period 1918 to 1960, and, further, reveals some of the ways in which marriage, masculinity and male sexuality intersected with notions of class, race and religion. Each section of this chapter—affinity, polygamy, age and mental capacity—will show some of the different and overlapping concerns and anxieties about marriage. The affinity section explores masculinity in the tension between protecting younger women from predatory men, and preventing perceived jealously between sisters over desirable men. Polygamy test cases reveal how the Anglican-inflected English legal system judged Hindu and Muslim marriage towards the end of the British Empire. The debates about age of marriage demonstrate the concerns politicians and campaigners had about England's standing in the world and their determination to portray English marriage as modern. The mental capacity section shows the willingness of lawmakers to exclude those deemed unfit to procreate. In each of these areas, the definitions of marriage assumed and reinforced the gender positions of the female homemaker and child carer, and male provider and protector. Marriage consent law created men as sexually active, but the sexual agency of women was recognised. Changes in the laws of marriage consent provide a glimpse into English marriage and the idealised Englishman at a time of declining religious observance and at the end of Empire.

AFFINITY

Delphine Monica Peal married Captain Daryl Robert Peal in 1921 in India, and the couple made English legal history a decade later. In 1930, the *Daily Mirror*, under the headline 'Married His Aunt', reported that the Peals were 'admittedly nephew and aunt',[13] and therefore tacitly transgressed a taboo. *Peal v Peal*, the only nullity test case[14] during this period regarding prohibited degrees of marriage, concerned a couple who

---

[13] 'Married His Aunt', *Daily Mirror*, 8 July 1930, 6.

[14] 'Christian Indian marriage invalid as fell within prohibited degrees of consanguinity (not withstanding dispensation from Catholic church); on retention of domicile be different generations of Britons living abroad'. *Blackstone's Marriage Breakdown*, 294.

'were at the time of the ceremony of marriage British subjects of the Roman Catholic faith resident in India'. The petitioner was the 'daughter of the paternal grandfather of the respondent' and therefore within the prohibited degrees of affinity and consanguinity in English law, but had had dispensation from the Roman Catholic Church locally. After deciding that a previous case, *Lopez v Lopez* (1885), involving 'Goanese' (sic) Christians was not relevant because the Peals were British subjects, albeit living in India for four generations, the judge found that this case was subject to English law and the marriage was declared invalid. Giving judgement Lord Merrivale explained that in British India there were 'various classes of persons governed by different systems or codes of personal law' and that it was 'inevitable that laws... operating in the complex political, social and racial conditions which exist in India, should produce doubtful cases for decision in the Indian Courts'. This case set a precedent under English marriage law and one that further defined British subjects in India as essentially White. Merrivale continued: 'What is really in question here is whether British subjects in India who happen to be or may become Roman Catholics are, as regards competency to marry, persons in a distinct and legally different class from their British fellow subjects'.[15] This judgement defined English marriage as ideally Anglican *and* White, since Roman Catholic marriage was subject to Anglican restrictions if the spouses were White.

The *Peal* case involved an aunt and nephew, and that degree of affinal relationship—along with uncle and niece—was the subject of parliamentary debates about affinity, and therefore familial desire, leading the eventually to legislative change in 1931. Throughout the debates about prohibited degrees of marriage, there were two competing strands of argument. First, those in favour of relaxing the laws of affinity claimed that it would help provide a 'natural' second mother for children in the event of the death of their biological one. Secondly, opponents of the relaxation were concerned that it would create rivalry between sisters for male affection. These two stands of argument complicate the notion of active-male and passive-female sexuality, but not gender roles. In both arguments, the woman was the child carer and homemaker and the man the breadwinner and provider.

---

[15] *Peal v Peal* (1931) 100 LJP 69. Also 'Peal vs. Peal', *The Times*, 8 July 1930, 5.

2 CONSENT AND CAPACITY 35

The parliamentary debates considered here form part of a sequence starting with the Deceased Wife's Sister's Marriage Act, 1907; the Deceased Wife's Sister's Marriage Act (1907) Amendment, 1921[16]; the Marriage (Prohibited Degrees of Relationship) Act, 1931; the Marriage Act, 1949; and the Marriage (Enabling) Act, 1960. The 1931 Act extended the possibility of marriage 'of persons with their nephew or niece' and can be seen as an evitable response to the unintended consequences produced by the Acts of 1907 and 1921. Sir Arthur Shirley Benn, who moved the second reading of the Bill in 1927, pointed out that it was important 'to get rid of an anomaly' because it 'was possible for a man to marry his deceased wife's sister or for a woman to marry her deceased husband's brother, but it was not possible to for them to marry the children of either'.[17]

Although the language of the Marriage (Prohibited Degrees of Relationship) Act (1931) was gender equal, comments made in parliament during the passage of the Act were highly gendered. For example, barrister and Labour M. P., Sir H. Slesser opposed the Bill. Described by the *Daily Express* as 'Solicitor-General in the Socialist Government [and] a pillar of Anglo-Catholicism',[18] Slesser assumed that women were passive in sexual and marriage consent by stating that it would

> be a very bad thing that when a man was mixing on normal terms of intimacy with his wife's relations there should be any possibility of his marriage with young girls who might be regarded as practically on the footing of his daughters.[19]

This assumes that young women needed to be protected from potentially predatory men, a concern during this era.[20] Secondly, Slesser reminded the House that '[t]he whole argument upon which the Deceased Wife's Sister Bill was based was simply that the deceased wife's

---

[16] The Act allowed a man to marry his deceased brother's widow thus making the law gender equal, albeit written from a male point of view. From the female perspective this Act allows a woman to marry her deceased husband's brother.

[17] 'Parliament', *The Times*, 5 March 1927, 7.

[18] 'Marriage to a Niece', *Daily Express*, 5 March 1927, 2.

[19] 'Parliament', *The Times*, 5 March 1927, 7.

[20] Matthew Waites, 'The age of consent and sexual consent' in *Making Sense of Sexual Consent* ed. Mark Cowling and Paul Reynolds (Aldershot: Routledge, 2004), 76–7.

sister would normally make a good guardian to look after the children'.[21] In this strand of argument, active/passive sexuality links with male/female gender roles in which the women should 'look after children' and, implicitly, that the man should be the provider. This gendered line of argument continued two decades later. The final law change regarding affinity in this period, the Marriage (Enabling) Act of 1960, was first rejected by parliament in 1949, but the debates took a more sexual tone and posited the man as sexually active and acquisitive. Conservative peer Lord Mancroft introduced his Bill to 'permit a person to marry the sister or brother of a divorced spouse', but found opposition from the Church of England and 'no encouragement from the [majority Labour] Government'. Mancroft's chief motivation appeared to be a case involving an NCO, 'Sergeant Smith' from his regiment who fell in love with a sister-in-law who had been 'mothering' his small child.[22] This was a similar motivation to the passing of earlier legislation: the gendered notion that a family should comprise a male breadwinner and female child carer.

The 1960 Act relaxed the rules of affinity further by replacing the word 'deceased' in these Acts with the word 'divorced'. The discussion about the marriage of divorcees reflected the new social realities that divorce had become more widespread and more politically and socially acceptable. In 1960, Lord Beveridge supported the Bill and expressed concern for the 'innocent victims—the children'. He stated that if 'a man [was] driven to divorce his wife after she had borne him children he should be free to provide for them, as completely as possible' including giving them 'a second mother by marriage if that seemed to him to be desirable'.[23] Here the architect of the Welfare State (itself based on a model of family with a male 'breadwinner'),[24] William Beverage, reinforced a view of marriage and family in which the man is the 'provider'. The woman is the child carer but the man knows what is 'desirable' in the upbringing of *his* children. Historian Katherine Holden argues that the 'maiden aunt was a common character in children's and adult fiction throughout the

---

[21] 'Parliament', *The Times*, 5 March 1927, 7.

[22] Hansard, Parliamentary Debates, House of Lords, *vol. 161 (24 March 1949), cols. 693–730.*

[23] 'Extended Right To Remarry', 27 January 1960, 6; 'Let Them Wed Sisters-In-Law', *Daily Mirror*, 21 January 1960, 9.

[24] See, for example, Noel Whiteside, *Bad Times: Unemployment in British Social and Political History* (London: Faber and Faber, 1991), 12–3.

nineteenth and twentieth centuries' and further that 'older unmarried aunts attached to families remained ubiquitous throughout the early and mid-twentieth century'. This was especially the case among the class of 'colonial families who sent them home from abroad to be educated'.[25] Beveridge clearly delineated the roles of male and female relatives in family life by explaining the role of the 'Auntie':

> Every one of us knows how dear 'Auntie' is to many families of children. When we in my family had not enough, my sisters adopted an aunt and she was a very dear 'Auntie' to us all. If children have not an aunt, they will often invent one.[26]

The Archbishop of Canterbury made the opposite claim about the presence of an 'Auntie', that there were 'cases in which the disturbance caused by the disappearance of the real mother and the transformation of the aunt into a second mother will be very real'.[27] Here, the presence of 'Auntie' is a disturbance, but the example is gendered in the same direction. It is based on the same gendered assumption that a female relative could be a replacement for a wife and mother, and the man would continue being the breadwinner, albeit with a different sexual and marriage partner. This strand of debate also shows that on eve of the so-called Sexual Revolution of the 1960s, marriage was seen by many as pragmatic as much as romantic. A (second) marriage could be more about childcare than love.

There was, however, a different strand of argument in this debate and one that further complicated the notions of masculinity and femininity, especially in respect of sexuality. Dating back to the early affinity debates in the mid-nineteenth century, women were depicted as being seductive in capturing a man, and ruthlessly competitive with other women to secure a husband. This line of argument did not appear in the interwar debates when the focus was more about the care of children, but increased after the Second World War, at a time when the debates became more sexual

---

[25] Katherine Holden, *The Shadow of Marriage: Singleness in England, 1914–60* (Manchester: Manchester University Press, 2007), 167.

[26] Hansard, Parliamentary Debates, House of Lords, *vol. 220 (26 January 1960)*, cols. *652–95.*

[27] Ibid.

in content. Lord Mancroft in summarising, and perhaps parodying, the argument against his own Bill stated that his opponents thought

> that the wife will feel less secure as the sister-in-law can enter the family circle; that the sister-in-law may eventually be in a position, should affairs so dictate, to marry the husband; that since she must obviously be a frequent visitor to the house her position there is a disturbing one; and that she will be reluctant to come to the house knowing that she may eventually be in a position to marry her brother-in-law. But, my Lords, she comes in now, and she is in a position, putting it crudely, to commit adultery with the husband.

Mancroft's argument against this was taken from a male point of view and created the male as sexually active: 'I should have thought that if a man were blackguard enough to seduce his sister-in-law he would do it whether marriage was ultimately possible or not'. The Archbishop however looked at it from the woman's point of view:

> At present she is entirely free of any suspicions and fears of her sister; she has a firmly-based security. But once that has gone, the door is open, and there is room for suspicions and jealousies unknown before. The sister may become a supposed or a real rival to her sister.'[28]

In making this argument, the archbishop was echoing comments made by William Gladstone a century earlier. In 1849, Gladstone argued against a Bill to allow a man to marry his deceased wife's sister by claiming that 'the purity of sisterly love itself... was threatened to be tainted by the invasion of possible jealousies'.[29] This creates femininity as potentially scheming and riven with jealousies, to such an extent that both men and women need the law as protection. The man here is desirable—economically and sexually—and the women are competing for him. These two strands of argument—that the wife's sister would make a good mother for the children, and that relaxing the laws of affinity would create

---

[28] Hansard, Parliamentary Debates, House of Lords, *vol. 161 (24 March 1949), cols. 693–730.*

[29] Quoted in Adam Kuper, 'Incest, cousin marriage, and the origin of the human sciences in nineteenth-century England', *Past and Present* 174 (February, 2002), 164.

rivalry between sisters—complicate the notion of active-male, passive-female sexuality, but both enforce the binary of male breadwinner and female child carer.

Legislators who sought to constrain familial desire were primarily concerned that children should have a 'mother', but assumed that women were prone to jealousy and envy of each other in pursuit of a desirable man. The parliamentary debates framed women as seducers of men, but portrayed men themselves as more likely to act upon their sexual desires, even within the family. These desires were however shaped by pragmatic decisions. Although sexual agency in these debates is contradictory, gender roles are constructed as male breadwinner and female housewife. Case law regarding affinity defined marriage as primarily White and Anglican, something that is also shown in polygamy cases.

POLYGAMY

When Kathleen Lawson married Nawal Baindail on 5 May 1939 in a civil marriage ceremony at Holborn register office, she did not know that her new husband had already been married at a Hindu ceremony in Muttra in the United Provinces, on the plains of India. Her subsequent desire to annul the marriage would result in one of only four test cases involving bigamy[30] or polygamy during the period 1918 to 1960.[31] Three cases appeared before the courts in 1945 and each involved an 'English' woman and an 'Indian' man. These test cases created new precedents for polygamy and also brought the English courts into judgement of 'Hindoo' marriage both in England and in British India. This provides the historian with an opportunity to reveal a view of marriage taken by the English judiciary with regard to race and religion just before Indian independence from the British Empire. Although there was no legislative change regarding polygamy, these law-changing test cases show that English marriage law was forced to confront alternative systems of

---

[30] This chapter focuses narrowly on nullity test cases that resulted in a marriage law change in order to show changes in who could or could not validly marry. Langhamer discusses bigamy criminal cases and shows that there was a 'century high of 986 cases in 1943', tailing off to 240 for the period 1950–1954, Claire Langhamer, *The English in Love: The intimate history of an emotional revolution* (Oxford: Oxford University Press, 2013), 203.

[31] In a sixth case, the judgement in *Sowa v Sowa* [1960] 3 WLR 733 was overturned in 1961.

marriage and kinship at a time of imperial divorce between Britain and India. In doing so, English marriage was contrasted with the perceived Otherness of the Indian race and of Hinduism. Unlike many of the examples cited in parliamentary debates regarding affinity, these polygamy cases involve a woman who did not know about the marriage impediment and a man who did. The fourth case involved an Egyptian Islamic marriage at precisely the time when tension was growing in British-ruled Egypt, the early 1950s. This case had a different outcome, since the English woman was deemed to be fully cognisant of what she was doing at the time of the ceremony. These cases were also heard at a time of the ideal of companionate marriage: polygamy did not fit into the modern English model of married 'mutuality'.[32]

The view of the British in India and in the imperial metropole was that Indian men could be categorised into 'manly' or 'effeminate'. As historian of masculinity Mrinalini Sinha points out, there was 'the colonialist stereotype of "effeminacy"' based on the 'the elaborate colonialist ethnography of "martial" and "non-martial" races in India'. The British perception of Indian masculinity was based on a combination of religion and region. Contrasts were drawn 'between the so-called "manly" peoples of the Punjab and the North-West Frontier and the "effeminate" peoples of Bengal and the more "settled" regions of British India, or between virile Muslims and effeminate Hindus'.[33] The measure of manliness was applied with prejudice. Marriage, though seen as an important element of British masculinity,[34] was not enough for an Indian man to be considered 'manly'. In the 1930s, war historian and Knight Lieutenant General, Sir George Fletcher MacMunn found that 'early marriage' was one of the factors that led to 'the lack of martial aptitude among people of the plains'.[35] Indian officers were also prone to drawing a distinction between

---

[32] For example, Adrian Bingham, *Gender, Modernity, and the Popular Press in Inter-War Britain* (Oxford: Oxford University Press, 2004), 236; Alison Light, *Forever England: Femininity, Literature and Conservatism between the Wars* (London: Routledge, 1991), 8; Marcus Collins, *Modern Love: An intimate history of men and women in twentieth-century Britain* (London: Atlantic, 2003), passim.

[33] Mrinalini Sinha, 'Giving Masculinity a History: Some contribution from the historiography of Colonial India', *Gender and History* 11, No. 3 (November 1999), 447.

[34] Sean Brady, *Masculinity and Male Homosexuality in Britain, 1861–1913* (Basingstoke: Palgrave, 2005), 23.

[35] Lionel Caplan, 'Bravest of the Brave', *Modern Asian Studies* 25, No. 3 (1991), 582.

martial and non-martial races. Hordit Singh Malik, Deputy Commissioner of Lahore 'expressed the belief that with character and training boys of non-martial races should make good officers'. English officers however felt that '[e]arly marriage prevented Indian officers from getting the training at Mess which was important'.[36] It would appear that in the all-male army environment a married Indian man was not always considered one of the 'men'. Srini also argues that 'British masculinity, no less than native masculinity' was 'shaped by the contingent practices of colonial rule'.[37] The nullity test cases and parliamentary debates demonstrate the extent to which the establishment's relationship with India shaped its perceptions of gender, sexuality and marriage. In the three cases that involved a Hindu man, the man was from the 'plains' and could have been seen as 'effeminate' in the colonial context. The nullity test cases are a useful way of seeing English masculinity as defined against the colonial Other.

In *Baindail (otherwise Lawson) v Baindail* (1945), the husband's appeal was rejected and a nullity granted to Kathleen Lawson, thus annulling their six-year marriage. In judgement, the judge stated that it would

> be wrong to say that for all purposes the law of domicile was conclusive and there were some things that the Courts would not allow a man to do whatever status the law of his domicile gave him. Slavery provided an obvious example.

This drawing of moral equivalence between polygamy and slavery created contemporary English marriage as modern and morally superior to the Otherness of Hindu marriage. The judgement continued:

> If this English ceremony were held valid, disastrous consequences might flow from the fact that the respondent would then be entitled to the consortium of her husband. For, if he decided to return to India, it would be her duty to follow him there, and she might find herself, under Hindu law, obliged to share her husband with his Indian wife.... The Courts were bound to regard an Indian marriage as an effective bar to ceremony of marriage over here.

---

[36] '"Indian Sandhurst" Committee', *The Times*, 23 December 1925, 11.

[37] Sinha, 'Giving masculinity a history', 454.

The judge implicitly recognised polygamous Indian marriage and concluded that his judgement had been 'decided with due regard to common sense'. The judge in this case created male sexuality as aggressive and acquisitive in order to protect the passive woman from it. Race inflected this case, as an innocent (she did not know he was already married) White woman is potentially at risk from the perceived Otherness of non-White male sexuality. The gender roles of husband and wife are clearly demarked: the man is the decision-maker and it is the woman's 'duty to follow him'. Further, this judgement depicts Indian marriage and home life as Other, exotic and backward in that the English woman would be 'obliged to share her husband with his Indian wife'. In this law-changing case,[38] English gender, marriage, sexuality, domesticity, religion and culture are held to be superior to that of the Indian Other.[39]

Also in 1945, *Mehta (otherwise Kohn) v Mehta*,[40] a woman domiciled in Britain married an Indian man, but she thought she was going through a ceremony in Bombay to convert to the Arya Samaj (described in court as a Hindu 'sect') in 1940. This ceremony was required because his parents did not want him to marry her or anyone who was 'a Christian or a white woman', thus showing that the English were an inferior Other to others. She had no intention to marry on that day and realised that the ceremony was a wedding only when she was presented with an English marriage certificate after repeating 'Hindustani' words that she did not understand. This nullity case hinged on whether it was 'a marriage in the Christian, sense of the term "marriage"' and therefore equated English marriage with the Christian ideal of monogamy. The petitioner's counsel argued that potentially the husband could convert to 'orthodox Hinduism' and marry additional wives, and could therefore turn a monogamous marriage into polygamy. This case therefore reinforced notions of passive femininity and female sexuality, and active, acquisitive male sexuality. It also equated English marriage with Christian marriage. The judge cited the earlier case *Hyde v Hyde* (1866), a case involving Mormon polygamy and adultery,

---

[38] 'Potentially polygamous Hindu marriage recognised so second marriage bigamous', *Blackstone's Marriage Breakdown*, 185.

[39] All citations taken from *Baindail (otherwise Lawson) v Baindail* [1945] 2 All ER 374 as reported in *The Times*, 31 January, 1946, 6.

[40] 'Monogamous marriage entered into by person whose religion allowed to marry polygamously was a valid marriage; no intent to marry meant marriage null', *Blackstone's Marriage Breakdown*, 280.

and stated 'I conceived that marriage, as understood in Christendom, may for this purpose be defined as the voluntary union for life of one man and one woman, to the exclusion of all others'. This firmly places English marriage within the realms of 'Christendom', presumably alongside those countries that were White and Western. The Mehta marriage was judged to have been monogamous at its inception, therefore this Hindu marriage was 'Christian within the sense of the term "marriage"' and the court had jurisdiction to grant an annulment.[41]

In the same year, the judgement in another case, *Srini Vasan (otherwise Clayton) v Srini Vasan* (1945),[42] found that a previous potentially polygamous Hindu marriage was valid, but only as a pragmatic means to allow nullity or divorce. The wedding of Dr. Narayana Srini Vasan, a Hindu man from Madras, and Grace Clayton, an Englishwoman, took place in Blackburn register office. He had already married 'a Hindu girl' in a ceremony that 'took place according to Hindu rites' in Trivandrum. Miss Clayton was unaware of any impediment to marriage and 'believed that at that time the respondent was a bachelor'. Justice Barnard, in judgement, declared that 'the Hindu marriage in 1933 would be recognised as valid by the Courts of British India, though potentially polygamous' and further that

> it would be strange if English law were to afford no recognition of polygamous marriages when England was the centre of a great Empire whose Mohamedan and Hindu subjects numbered many millions.... [and to] deny recognition of a Hindu marriage for the purpose in hand would, in my opinion, be to fly in the face of common sense, good manners and the ordered system of tolerance on which the Empire is based.

This judgement was in keeping with the policy of allowing different religions an element of religious freedom in British India, but it also clearly stated that to do otherwise 'English law would be encouraging polygamy'. That is to say, that polygamy was acceptable in India among Indians, but it was contrary to English marriage. Justice Barnard stated that the 'Divorce Court, for obvious reasons, would not entertain a matrimonial cause for the purpose of granting relief or enforcing rights in

---

[41] All citations taken from *Mehta (otherwise Kohn) v Mehta* [1945] 2 All ER 690.

[42] 'Second marriage of man already party to polygamous marriage in India a nullity', *Blackstone's Marriage Breakdown*, 328.

respect of a marriage lacking the characteristic of monogamy'. This tacit acceptance of polygamy in certain marriages defined gender and sexuality along racial and religious grounds.[43]

The final polygamy case in the sequence of test cases in this period involved an Islamic marriage in Egypt. The 1938 marriage between Marjorie Elizabeth Risk (née Yerburgh) and Abdul Hamid Mustafa Risk was not annulled when it appeared before the courts in 1950. *Risk (otherwise Yerburgh) v Risk*[44] was essentially a test of court jurisdiction following the Law Reform (Miscellaneous Provisions) Act (1949), which stated that a wife may petition for nullity or divorce if she 'is resident in England... for a period of three years immediately before the commencement of proceedings'.[45] The Risk wedding took place in Egypt at the Muslim 'Karmuz religious court' in Alexandria in a ceremony that 'stipulated that the husband might take two, three or four wives at one and the same time'. Marjorie Risk described herself to the court as a 'Christian' but the judge did not grant her a nullity since English law 'stressed the monogamous character of marriage and ... recognised no other'. Since she had shown agency and had actively entered into the potential polygamous marriage willingly, there was nothing the English courts could do.[46]

These polygamy test cases show how English Law—in these examples the judiciary, not parliament—confronted Otherness, and interracial marriage, at a time of Imperial tensions. While we cannot be sure of the timing,[47] these cases provide a glimpse at the 'official' English view of marriage and masculinity in India and Egypt at a time of unrest and

---

[43] All citations taken from *Srini Vasan (otherwise Clayton) v Srini Vasan* [1945] 2 All ER 21 as reported in *The Times*, 18 May 1945, 8.

[44] 'Court cannot make nullity adjudication in respect of polygamous marriage', *Blackstone's Marriage Breakdown*, 310.

[45] 'High Courts of Justice', *The Times*, 28 October 1950, 4.

[46] *Risk (otherwise Yerburgh) v Risk* [1950] 2 All 973.

[47] The precise timing of a nullity case is difficult to determine. As it was instigated by a plaintiff, an annulment is a case that can be initiated at any time after a marital impediment has been found. There would also be a time lag before the case was heard in court, especially a precedent-setting case that could make its way up to the High Court. It is interesting that the Indian polygamy cases here were all heard in 1945. This could be a coincidence (three couples independently wanted their marriage annulled at roughly the same time) or it could be that these cases are simply part of the post-war 'spike' in nullity and divorce cases. See Figs. 6.1 and 6.2.

agitation for independence in each country.[48] The notion of monogamy in English marriage was held to be a Christian virtue and these law-changing cases recognised Hindu and Muslim polygamy and accepted, even expected, it among Indians, and Egyptians. Whether Egyptian, English or Indian, the roles of husband and wife were firmly fixed with the man as the decision-making head of household. The judgements defined gender and sexuality in racial and religious terms: the male Colonial Other was inherently sexually aggressive and acquisitive, and Hindu and Muslim marriage as backward compared to Christian marriage in modern England. English masculinity is, in contrast, protective of innocent English women, but only up to a point. The Egyptian case shows that the law would not protect a woman who was complicit in entering an illegal marriage. The problem of women actively entering illegal marriages was also found in age of marriage consent cases.

AGE

The marriage between Margery Graimes Fowler and Hubert Alfred Carr started in a church in Chingford, Essex in September 1930 and ended in court in January 1936 with a decree of nullity. Although the *Daily Express* reported the case under the headline 'Bride of 15 is Freed',[49] it was uncontested. This would suggest that both parties wanted the marriage to end.[50] *Carr (otherwise Fowler) v Carr* was the first precedent-setting[51] nullity case since the passing of the Age of Marriage Act (1929), which raised the age of marriage consent from twelve for females and fourteen for males to sixteen for both. At the time of the wedding ceremony, Miss Fowler had been aged fifteen years and eleven months. The *Carr* case shows that it was possible for one of the parties to lie about her or his

---

[48] Negotiations for Indian independence began in 1945. See for example 'Chronology' in *The Oxford History of the British Empire: Volume IV – The Twentieth Century* ed. Judith M. Brown and Wm. Roger Louis (Oxford: Oxford University Press, 1999), 727; After 1947, the British presence in the Middle East became increasingly unstable, and eventually there were 'violent demonstrations and riots in Egypt against the British garrisons' in the early 1950s, leading to British withdrawal in 1954, Porter, *The Lion's Share*, 333.

[49] 'Bride of 15 is Freed', *Daily Express*, 14 January 1936, 5.

[50] It is impossible to say how many 'happy' underage marriages there were in this period.

[51] 'Marriage void as one of the parties thereto had only been fifteen when marriage celebrated', *Blackstone's Marriage Breakdown*, 203.

age—in this case the bride actively told the vicar and her husband that she was seventeen—and become married.[52] There were two conflicting arguments regarding age of marriage consent in parliamentary debates. First, some in favour of raising the age of consent wanted to protect underage girls from predatory men. Secondly, some of those who were arguing against raising the marriage age wanted to protect men from mendacious young women—perhaps like Miss Fowler—who lied about their age. These two conceptions of gender—which also depended on class-based notions of childhood—are contradictory and allocated agency in different ways.

At the start of the period, the age of marriage consent was different from the age of consent. The age of consent—the age at which a subject could consent to penile-vaginal intercourse—was sixteen for males and females. After the Hardwick Act (1753) the age of marriage consent was twenty-one or with parental permission fourteen for males and twelve for females.[53] In practice, by the period under discussion, a marriage involving a minor without parental permission was not declared void,[54] therefore the effective age of marriage was twelve and fourteen. As historian Joanna Bourke argues the age of consent marks the point at which a person becomes a full legal subject.[55] However, there was discrepancy between age of consent and age of marriage consent during the period in between the Criminal Law Amendment Act, 1885 and the Age of Marriage, 1929. The latter set the marriage at sixteen, with parental permission. This difference in age laws allowed sex with a twelve-year-old female or fourteen-year-old male under the 'veil' of marriage. The difference between the age of consent and age of marriage also shows that 'sex' and 'marriage' are interrelated but with different expectations. Although age of consent created a *legal* subject, perhaps age of marriage in this period created an *adult* subject. Further, as will be shown, some politicians pointed out that under contemporary definitions of consent,

---

[52] *Carr (otherwise Fowler) v Carr* (1936) 80 SJ 57 HC PDAD; also *The Times*, 14 January 1936, 5.

[53] See also *Arnold v Earle* (1758) 2 Lee 529, 161 ER 428, William Latey and D. Rees, *Latey in Divorce* (London, 1945), 166.

[54] *Phillimore's Ecclesiastical Law* (abridged by Philip Jones) (2nd edn 1895) (Cardiff: Greenfach, 2004), 69.

[55] Joanna Bourke, *Rape: A history from 1860 to the present day* (London: Virago, 2007), 83.

sexual consent could be one act of coitus; marriage consent amounted to perpetual sexual consent on the part of the woman.

The perceived boundary between childhood and adulthood varied according to social class, and this led to class prejudice regarding the transition to adulthood. It is important to understand that the mostly middle-class and upper-class participants in the age of marriage debate would have held age norms that were typical of their social class. Although working-class and middle-class average marriage ages started to converge during the mid-twentieth century, it was still the case that those who went on to pursue higher education postponed marriage for longer. Working-class people were more likely to leave school earlier and start work sooner. They were also more likely to start 'dating' at a younger age and consequently married at a younger age than their middle-class and upper-class counterparts. Indeed, an element of middle-class respectability was the belief that working-class parents sent their children out into the world too early.[56] Dating back to the mid-nineteenth century, juvenile 'delinquency' was seen as a problem that existed among working-class young men (and boys) especially in large towns.[57] This concern about 'male youth' grew during the Depression of the 1930s.[58] These class-biased assumptions of childhood, youth and manhood were circulating during the time of debates about age of marriage.

Many of those in favour of raising the age of marriage were motivated by the desire to protect young women from older men. The Age of Marriage Act (1929) made direct reference to the Criminal Law Amendment Act (1885) and further sealed the legal definition of sexual consent as being between an active male and passive female since the earlier Act 'was premised upon the view of sexual activity between man and women in which the female is passive, while the male takes the sexual initiative and must obtain her consent'.[59] But, in an amendment added at a late stage regarding 'indecent assault' against an underage spouse, the Act is

[56] John Gillis, *Youth and history: Tradition and change in European Age Relations, 1770-present* (London: Academic Press, 1981), 181, 188, 193.

[57] Eileen Yeo, '"The boy is the father of the man": Moral panic over working-class youth, 1850 to the present', *Labour History Review* 69, No. 2 (August 2004), 187.

[58] Matt Houlbrook, *Queer London: Perils and pleasure in the sexual metropolis, 1918–1957* (London: University of Chicago Press, 2005), 234.

[59] Matthew Waites, *The age of consent: Young people, sexuality and citizenship* (Basingstoke: Palgrave, 2005), 69.

48 N. PENLINGTON

clearly gendered: 'it shall be sufficient defence to prove that at the time of the offence he [the husband] had reasonable cause to believe that the girl in respect of whom it is alleged to have committed was his wife'.[60] This also shows that rape within marriage was not illegal. The 'girl' therefore was not only giving marriage consent but perpetual sexual consent. It also suggests that a woman could actively lie about her age in order to marry a man.

The protecting of young girls and its concomitant gendered notion of consent is present in the debate leading to the final passage of the 1929 Act. Government figures, given by Lord Salisbury, demonstrated 'the magnitude of the evil...[of] marriage of girls under sixteen'.[61] Those in favour, especially the Bill's sponsor Lord Buckmaster, stated that the Act would protect girls from older men. This reinforced the notion of active-male and passive-female sexuality, but also a masculinity in which a man was to be responsible for protecting vulnerable (young) women from male sexual predators. Across the period, as historian Matt Houlbrook argues, the sexual abuse of children was to 'transgress a fundamental boundary in modern British culture and the man who would do so was a threatening, depraved figure increasingly set apart from the society he inhabited'.[62] Buckmaster gave an example of a case 'three or four years' earlier, i.e. the mid-1920s, in which

> a child of 12 or 13—her exact age is not quite clear—was raped by a man of 29, and the man was charged with rape before the magistrate. It was then suggested that, if he married the girl, she would be unable to give evidence against him, and he might be acquitted of the charge, and that was done, and this man, who ought to have been sent to gaol for the longest possible period that the law permits, was allowed to enter into a union blessed by the law with the little creature against whom he had perpetrated this unforgivable wrong.[63]

In this example, passive females needed protection from predatory males, but there was no discussion about rape within marriage. Consent

---

[60] Age of Marriage Act. 1929, Section 1.1.

[61] 'Bar on Marriage under 16', *Daily Express*, 20 February 1929, 2.

[62] Houlbrook, *Queer London*, 234.

[63] Hansard, Parliamentary Debates, House of Lords, *vol. 72 (19 February 1929), cols. 961–70.*

was something that was, or should have been, sought by a man and given by the woman. The act of giving marriage consent was, for the woman, to give perpetual sexual consent. This was spelt out explicitly by Buckmaster himself:

> At this moment it was a criminal offence for a man to have relations with a girl under the age of 16. She was incapable of consenting. Was it not a remarkable thing that what the girl was not capable of consent to once she could consent to in perpetuity, and that by the law she was enabled to protect the man from his criminal action by the mere process of going through the ceremony of marriage?[64]

This reiterates the same notion of consent as the 1885 Criminal Law Amendment Act: a man is sexually active, sexually acquisitive and sexually attracted to young women. Buckmaster was not questioning the idea that marriage consent for a women should be anything other than sexual consent 'in perpetuity'. At the Select Committee stage, Buckmaster repeated the importance of protecting young women from older men: '[r]elations between a man and a girl under the age of sixteen constitute a grave criminal offence, and the reason is that the man has taken advantage of the girl's inexperience and immaturity'.[65]

On the issue of illegitimate children, Buckmaster continued his line of reasoning: that consent is requested by the man and given by the woman. He argued however against the proposition that a girl under sixteen should marry because she was pregnant:

> I am bound to say I find it difficult to hear with patience such an argument as that.... What is going to happen to her—this child, who is going to be made the wife of a man who has taken advantage of her in such a manner as that?[66]

In the way this example is framed, the man has the sexual agency since he 'has taken advantage' of a passive female. Opponents of the Bill continued to argue that illegitimacy should be a central concern in regard

[64] 'Parliament', *The Times*, 20 February 1929, 7.

[65] Hansard, Parliamentary Debates, House of Lords, *vol. 72 (28 February 1929), cols. 1203–19.*

[66] Hansard, Parliamentary Debates, House of Lords, *vol. 72 (19 February 1929), cols. 961–70.*

to age of marriage consent. In arguing that the 'Bill ought to receive a little more consideration', Earl Desart and gave an example of a case

> in 1926, of a man of eighteen and a girl of fifteen. He had got her into trouble. She was pregnant. The man wanted to marry her, and the girl wanted to marry him. Both sets of parents consented. The National Society for the Prevention of Cruelty to Children were interested, and they wrote both to the boy and the girl, holding the view that criminal proceedings seemed to be a tragedy. They were married, and no proceedings were taken... [otherwise] Her character would be smirched. Her child would be illegitimate.[67]

In this case, Desart is arguing the opposite of Buckmaster: that the 'girl' should marry the older man and that he should not be prosecuted for getting 'her into trouble'. However, the lines of consent are the same in both arguments: the man asks for consent and the woman consents, or not. For the government, the Marquis of Salisbury added that in '64 per cent of the cases the girl [marrying under the age of sixteen] is pregnant before the marriage'.[68] Further, that marriage 'gives a particular status to the man and particularly to the woman'.[69] This genders the institution of marriage by claiming that it is an institution that protects women and gives them 'status'. This forecloses discussion about what marriage means for men and the ways in which the institution of marriage could be harmful to women. Salisbury did however recognise the agency of women by reminding Peers that the 'feelings of the girl' should not be 'ignored'.[70] Politicians were concerned with protecting girls, but they also thought this was the duty of husbands. Before arriving at an age of sixteen for both sexes, the government reported that because of 'the protective duties assumed by husbands, it might be desirable to raise the

---

[67] Hansard, Parliamentary Debates, House of Lords, *vol. 72 (28 February 1929), cols. 1203–19.*

[68] Ibid.; The Bishop of Southwark also pointed out that sixty-five per-cent of 'marriages of girls at 15' were because 'a child was expected', 'Age of marriage' *The Times*, 26 March, 1929, 9.

[69] Hansard, Parliamentary Debates, House of Lords, *vol. 73 (12 March 1929), cols. 397–425.*

[70] Hansard, Parliamentary Debates, House of Lords, *vol. 72 (19 February 1929), cols. 961–70; 'Bar on Marriage under 16', Daily Express, 20 February 1929, 2.*

minimum age for marriage in the case of males to seventeen or eighteen'. This was rejected because the Select Committee concluded that it would create unintended consequences which would have left young women unprotected because an unequal marriage age would 'conduce to increased immorality because it would enable a young man to promise marriage to a girl of sixteen which he could repudiate on reaching his own legal age'.[71]

While the sponsors of the Bill were motivated by protecting girls from men, some in the debate were concerned about protecting men from being seduced by young women who lied about their age in order to get married. This led to an amendment being added to the Bill before it was passed into law. This line of argument placed agency with the female subject as she actively ensnared a seemingly passive male. Mr Harris—Assistant Secretary at the Home Office—wanted confirmation that a man of 'say 24' would not be prosecuted for 'carnal knowledge' if the 'girl' had lied about her age and turned out to be under sixteen.[72] This use of the term 'carnal knowledge' complicates sociologist Matthew Waites' argument that it connotes active-male sexuality and passive-female sexuality in age of consent law,[73] since the woman is actively claiming to be older than her age in order to engage in marriage and sexual intimacy. The Director of Public Prosecutions, Sir Archibald Bodkin, giving evidence to the Select Committee added a racial element and drew attention to the '[c]ases [that] frequently arose in which young girls, many of them Jewesses from Poland, advance their ages in order to get married, and were not above forging consents'.[74] Bodkin was more concerned with 'protecting the men' from this and the threat of prosecution under 'criminal law' resulting from accidentally marrying an underage female. He further went on to explain that he thought that the age of marriage was the wrong issue. On the subject of those marrying at twelve and fourteen, Bodkin stated that he had 'never heard of any persons in this country having been married on reaching those ages' but that '[t]here was, undoubtedly, a very considerable amount of immorality among young people between the ages of 13 and 16. The majority of the cases which

---

[71] '16 the Minimum Age of Marriage', *Daily Mirror*, 26 April 1929, 26.

[72] 'Age of marriage' *The Times*, 26 March, 1929, 9.

[73] Waites, 'The age of consent and sexual consent', 76.

[74] Bodkin did not give any evidence for this claim, nor can any be found.

had been reported to him were cases of incest, which was rife in the country'.[75] Bodkin, here, is moving beyond the binary of active/passive used by others in the debate by arguing that 'young people' of both sexes had sexual agency. Buckmaster himself conceded that men needed protection from the law and from women who lie about their age:

> If a man is charged with having had unlawful connection with a girl under the age of sixteen, it is to be a defence if it can be shown that he married her reasonably believing that she was sixteen when he married her. If the marriage were declared void under this Bill he might have been defenceless.[76]

An amendment was therefore made to the Bill protecting a man who had 'reasonable cause to believe that the girl … was his wife', that is to say that he genuinely thought she was old enough at the time of the wedding ceremony.

This amendment contained both male and female sexual agency, but it was the protection of young women that was at the heart of an important tranche of debate: comparison with other countries. One country was mentioned more than any other in the debate about age of marriage, and used as a counterpoint to acceptable English marriage: India. When leading a delegation in 1927 to the Home Secretary to argue for an increase in the marriage age, Eleanor Rathbone of the National Union of Societies for Equal Citizenship (NUSEC) stated that '[e]ven in China and Egypt the age is higher' and that by having a low age of marriage the 'bad example set by Britain had its repercussion in places like India'. She further claimed that average age of marriage was 26, but 'the law was misunderstood in tropical countries, where the impression was held that marriages in Britain at the earliest stages were very frequent'. The Home Secretary, Sir William Joynson-Hicks, agreed but added a different comparison by stating that 'it is very undesirable for the marriage age in England to be lower than the age in most other civilised countries'.[77] This comparison stemmed from a report in 1927 in which the League

---

[75] 'Age of Marriage', *The Times*, 22 March, 1929, 13.

[76] Hansard, Parliamentary Debates, House of Lords, *vol. 74 (30 April 1929), cols. 258–63.*

[77] 'The marriage age', *The Times*, 9 November 1927, 11.

of Nations Advisory Commission for the Protection and Welfare of Children and Young People compared Great Britain unfavourably to other countries in the League of Nations for two reasons. First, Britain had a low age of marriage, and, secondly, Britain had 'a minimum age of marriage... lower than the age of consent'.[78] Bringing gender explicitly into the debate, Joynson-Hicks replied that the League of Nations report was concerned with the 'traffic' of women and children in some countries, but added that there were 'no grounds for thinking that such abuses occurred in this country'.[79] This line of debate about age of marriage consent concerned the protection of women from men and was set firmly in an international context but with 'England' compared with both 'civilised' countries and also those racially inferior tropical countries. This was in spite of some evidence to the contrary provided by a 'woman doctor formerly connected with the Women's Medical Service in India' who examined over 1,100 cases in Bombay and found that average age of the mother at first birth was twenty-and-a-half, and only twelve babies were born to mothers who were sixteen or under. She, however, conceded that similar studies needed to be conducted in other parts of India.[80]

During the passage of the 1929 Act, politicians created an opposition between English marriage and the foreign Other. Lord Buckmaster, the Act's sponsor, made a comparison with the Indian Other by claiming that 'this country was profoundly stirred by the ... revelations with regard to child marriages in India' and more generally the 'child marriages [that] were permitted in non-Christian lands, yet none the less, married or no, it is a criminal offence for a man to have relations with a girl under the age of 13 years'. This was a year older than in Britain. Buckmaster concluded that 'we ought ... to put our own house in order before we start to arrange other people's'. There was concern also for England's standing in the world. The Archbishop of Canterbury was concerned that '[a]bove all, England should be freed from the taunt that her age of marriage was so low'. He was making comparisons with Japan, Siam, Cuba and countries in Europe. The Assistant Secretary to the Home Office stated that the low age of marriage consent in Britain 'compares unfavourably with

---

[78] Advisory Commission for the Protection and Welfare of Children and Young People (League of Nations), *The age of marriage and the age of consent* (Geneva: League of Nations, 1927), 3, 5, 22.

[79] 'House of Commons' *The Times*, 31 March 1927, 8.

[80] 'Age of marriage in India' *The Times*, 25 October 1928, 15.

54   N. PENLINGTON

that in many other countries, and surprise has been expressed that Great Britain and her Dominions have been content with it.... It [gave] a bad impression of our moral standards to other countries'.[81] It is clear, therefore, that the Age of Marriage Act (1929), which raised the marriage age to sixteen in England was passed with comparison with other countries in mind. English lawmakers wanted England to compare favourably with other nations by protecting women from men.

The second of only two age of marriage consent nullity test cases in this period, the first being *Carr*, involved Roman Catholics who had been married in Austria. This test case, *Pugh v Pugh* (1951), was ostensibly a test of English Law jurisdiction.[82] The marriage received press attention in October 1946 as the *Daily Express* reported the forthcoming wedding of the 'Captain and the Countess'.[83] The case was brought by a Hungarian-born woman, a Countess, who was married at the age of fifteen years and six months in a Roman Catholic ceremony to 'an Englishman domiciled here [in England]'. The judge held that the Age of Marriage Act (1929) could 'extend beyond the sea' and the marriage was declared void. The judge found a 'distinction' between Lord Lyndhurst's Act (1836)—'founded on Christian doctrine'—and the Age of Marriage Act—'founded on social and moral grounds'. He explained that the 'common law before the Age of Marriage Act, 1929, was this: By canon law which continued and in spite of the Reformation a boy of fourteen years could marry a girl of twelve'. This creates an opposition between English Civil Law and Roman Catholic Canon Law. The judge continued:

> According to modern thought it is considered socially and morally wrong that persons of that age, at which we now believe them to be immature

---

[81] 'Parliament', *The Times*, 20 February 1929, 7; 'Bar on Marriage under 16', *Daily Express*, 20 February 1929, 2; 'Parliament', *The Times*, 13 March 1929, 8; 'No Marriages under 16', *Daily Express*, 26 March 1929, 3.

[82] *Pugh v Pugh* [1951] 2 All ER 680; reported as *Pugh (otherwise Eperjesy) v Pugh* 1951 in *The Times*, 13 July, 1951. 'Marriage validity tested by reference to husband's domicile (here English) so marriage with under-sixteen year old invalid; Age of Marriage Act 1929, s. 1(1) has extra-territorial effect; applies to Britons wherever married', *Blackstone's Marriage Breakdown*, 300.

[83] 'And now, because she was then 15, their marriage ends in London', *Daily Express*, 13 July 1951, 5.

and provide for their education, should not have the stresses, responsibilities and sexual freedom of marriage and the physical strain of childbirth.... Child marriages are by common consent believed to be bad for the participants and bad for the institution of marriage.[84]

This states the purpose of marriage as coitus leading to procreation and places English Law as morally superior to Roman Canon Law, and English marriage as superior to the European Other. By stressing that 'Acts making carnal knowledge of young girls an offence are an indication of modern views on this subject', the judge was reiterating the binary of active-male sexuality and passive-female sexuality, and that an important facet of English masculinity was to protect women.

The law change resulting from *Pugh* confirmed the jurisdiction of English marriage law overseas, but did so in a gendered way, and reinforced gendered citizenship. The judgement in *Pugh* applied only because the *man* was a British subject. This reinforced the gendered definition of British citizenship in the British Nationality and Status of Aliens Act (1914), which stated that 'the wife of a British subject shall be deemed to be a British subject, and the wife of an alien shall be deemed to be an alien'.[85] This law, reinforced in *Pugh*, placed the man as head of household: the British man always kept his citizenship, but a woman lost hers if she married a foreigner. Citizenship was a masculine privilege.

In the passing of legislation regarding age of marriage consent and the related legal test cases, marriage consent implied perpetual sexual consent on the part of the female. There was no attempt to change this. Social class influenced notions of childhood and sexual agency were defined by the opposing arguments of those who wanted to protect girls/women from predatory men, and those who wanted to protect men from deceitful girls/women. English age of marriage law was defined with comparison with other countries. English men, through marriage, were to set an example to the Indians and hold their own among the 'civilised' men of the world. Case law, meanwhile, confirmed an Anglican view of marriage and that British citizenship was a masculine privilege.

[84] *Pugh v Pugh*.
[85] British Nationality and Status of Aliens Act. 1914, s. 10 (1).

Mental Capacity

'Plan to Prevent Marriage of the Mentally Unfit' blazed the main front-page headline in the *Daily Express* on 21 February 1929. The newspaper reported on a 'memorandum signed by fifty leading representatives of the Church, the law, medicine and philanthropy' who wanted to 'prevent the marriage of defectives'. In a typical example of the eugenics discourses circulating widely at the time, the article stated that it was 'recognised that mental deficients are incurable, that they are more fertile than normal people, and that their children are nearly always mentally unsound'. The newspaper indignantly pointed out that it was 'hardly credible, but the authorities sometimes allow the marriage of mental deficients'.[86] Less than a decade later the Matrimonial Causes Act (1937) restricted marriage so that mental deficients, as defined by the Mental Deficiency Act, 1913, could not legally marry. The spread of concern about mental deficiency far outweighed the numbers. At the time of 1937 Act, one contemporary calculation gave the number of 'persons suffering from mental disease' at 154,000, of whom 62,000 were married. There were a further 79,000 'mentally defective population under care'[87] and presumably were not in a position to marry.

Categorisation of mental deficiency in this period was social-class based. Historian John Welshman shows that 'mental deficiency' was linked to class, especially by those who worked in social policy. In the interwar period, the 'feeble-minded' were deemed to cause most social problems, but after the Second World War the blame lay with a new category: the 'problem family'.[88] A Foucauldian approach allows literature scholar Clare Hanson to show how eugenics discourses exaggerated the concern about 'mental deficiency', even though those classed as mentally deficient (including 'minor sub-normality') were approximately two per cent of the population in the immediate post-war period. Hanson argues that 'professionals' in psychiatric medicine, social medicine and education reinforced the 'assumption that "mental deficiency" was a working-class

---

[86] 'Plan to prevent marriage of the mentally unfit', *Daily Express*, 21 February 1929, 1.

[87] David Perk, 'Insanity and divorce: Some medical considerations', *British Medical Journal* 2, No. 4003 (September 25, 1937), 198.

[88] John Welshman, *Underclass: A history of the excluded since 1880* (London: Bloomsbury, 2013. First published 2006), 57–8, 77.

phenomenon'. Although the link between social class and mental deficiency went back to the nineteenth century, Hanson argues that it gained 'new currency' after the Second World War because of a link between post-war reconstruction and eugenic thought. The 'problem families' were seen to be 'over-active' and there was a fear of 'miscegenation... that of cross-breeding between a defective and a "normal" individual'.[89]

Mental capacity was also gendered with explicit roles for husbands and wives. This was partly because of the male dominated psychiatric profession. Legal scholar Ezra Hasson found that increasingly during the nineteenth century 'medical men' appearing as expert witnesses had greater 'influence' through 'their testimony on judicial decision making'.[90] At the end of that century, there were 'eight women working as medical officers' in British psychiatry hospitals, and only forty more by the interwar period. Between 1925 and 1935, there was 'intense debate within the psychological movement on the question of femininity, female sexuality, and the psychology of women'.[91] As sociologist Joan Busfield shows, the 'idea of a link between pregnancy or childbirth and changes in mood or emotion is an old one' and women in the twentieth century were 'assumed, by virtue of a distinctive biology, to be more psychologically vulnerable than men'.[92] Hasson argues in his study of nineteenth-century insanity nullity cases that 'English law has not constructed insanity as intrinsic to the individual, but rather as something that is determined by his or her abilities within the context of a particular situation': a concept known as 'compartmentalisation'. In relation to marriage consent, a person had to show 'an appreciation of the nature of the marriage contract... centred on the responsibilities and obligations of the married state'. Hasson found in his analysis of nine nullity cases that insanity and 'unsound mind' could be gendered through the 'identification of inappropriate behaviour' such as 'behaviour that deviates from the social and cultural norm'. For example, to be classified sane women had to demonstrate that they understood

---

[89] Clare Hanson, *Eugenics, literature and culture in Post-War Britain* (Abingdon: Routledge, 2013), 3, 40, 46, 49.

[90] Ezra Hasson, 'Capacity to marry: Law, medicine and conceptions of insanity', *Social History of Medicine* 23, No. 1 (2010), 16.

[91] Elaine Showalter, *The female malady: Women, madness, and english culture, 1830–1980* (London: Virago, 1987), 127, 199–201.

[92] Joan Busfield, *Men, women and madness: Understanding gender and mental disorder* (Basingstoke: Palgrave, 1996), 155, 158.

their marriage role as 'caring for her husband and raising children'.[93] Men were therefore expected to be something other, to be the psychologically strong and stoical breadwinner.

The law regarding 'unsound mind' and marriage consent changed twice in the interwar period, first with a test case in 1923 and again in the Matrimonial Causes Act (1937). In a precedent-setting case, *Forster (otherwise Street) v Forster* (1923), the law changed to exclude those suffering from delusions at the time of the wedding from the institution of marriage. Despite the presumed psychological vulnerability of women, Ethel Margaret Forster (née Street) filed for nullity against former army captain Arthur Addison Forster in an uncontested case. The petitioner's case was that the husband 'for some time before the ceremony had been, of unsound mind and incapable of contracting marriage'. To 'laughter' the judge asked, 'Did you ever know anybody who was in a condition to understand all the consequences of matrimony?' On the evidence of an expert witness, an 'examiner in mental diseases for the University of London', it was stated that the husband was a 'chronically weak-minded young man with a tendency to insanity in his nature which would be brought about by alcohol'.[94] The judge cited *Durham v Durham* (1885) that 'a mere comprehension of the words of the promises exchanged is not sufficient' and the question before him was 'whether the respondent was mentally capable of understanding the nature of the marriage contract and the duties and responsibilities which it creates'. In granting a nullity, the judge stated that the husband had a history of suffering from delusions and 'the evidence of his family' was that 'he was not normal'. He did not have the 'capacity to perform any of the obligations' of a married man, since his notion 'that he was an officer holding responsible and trusted command' was nothing more than a 'deluded belief'.[95] This 'weak' man was unable to act as responsible protector and provider for his wife.

Forster more firmly placed 'unsound mind' alongside incurable 'insanity' as a bar to marriage, and this was added to legislation in 1937 combined with the definition of 'mental deficiency' as set out in the 1913 Act. The Matrimonial Causes Act (1937) implemented the findings of

---

[93] Hasson, 'Capacity to marry', 1, 7, 10–11.

[94] 'High Court of Justice', *The Times*, 14 June 1923, 5.

[95] 'High Court of Justice', *The Times*, 17 July 1923, 5.

the 1912 Royal Commission on Divorce and Matrimonial Causes. Those who gave evidence on nullity were chiefly concerned about implementing a ground for insanity and another for venereal disease. Representing the Eugenics Education Society, Dr F. W. Mott, a physician, and Mr J. E. Lane, a surgeon, thought that such grounds were vital 'to insure that fit people marry' and to 'check the production of unfit children'.[96] By 1937, a nullity clause appended the Commission findings and stated that a marriage would not be valid if 'either party was at the time of the marriage of unsound mind or a mental defective within the meaning of the Mental Deficiency Acts, 1913 to 1928, or subject to recurrent fits of insanity or epilepsy'. Mental 'defectiveness' was defined as 'a condition of arrested or incomplete development of mind existing before the age of eighteen years'. The petitioner had to start proceedings within a year of marriage, be unaware of the impediment at the time of the wedding, and 'marital intercourse' should not have taken place since the discovery of the impediment.[97] This inclusion of mental deficiency in the marriage laws would have satisfied many eugenicists, and it also reinforced the purpose of marriage as procreative.

The small amount of discussion about insanity during the passage of the Bill was gendered. In seeking clarification that the respondent was of 'unsound mind' at the time of the ceremony or had become so within a year of marriage, Lords Chelwood and Atkin each gave examples from a male point of view. Chelwood imagined an example of a man who was stuck in a marriage with a woman who 'was admitted to be quite mad'. The husband had noticed that during 'the courtship' that there was something 'rather strange in behaviour' but was assured that it 'was only due to her love for him'. Atkin added that 'unsound mind' was 'a not uncommon consequence of childbirth'.[98] Women here were more prone to being overly emotional, irrational and hysterical. This gendering was also visible in the new 'epilepsy' nullity clause, which was added to insanity to read

[96] Royal Commission on Divorce and Matrimonial Causes, *Minutes of evidence taken before the Royal Commission on Divorce and Matrimonial Causes, Vol.3* (London: HMSO, 1912), 71, 103–4, 106, 396, 398.

[97] William Latey and D. Rees, *Latey on divorce* (London: Street and Maxwell, 1943), 177–8.

[98] Hansard, Parliamentary Debates, House of Lords, *vol. 106 (7 July 1937), cols.* 69–190.

'bouts of insanity or epilepsy'.[99] As the Bill passed through parliament the only comment regarding this clause was made in the House of Lords by the Archbishop of Canterbury. The Archbishop stated that he 'had known of cases of great hardship, such as where working-class men had a wife who had epilepsy, or some incurable disease, which made it impossible for her to look after her children'.[100] The passage of the 1937 Act was against a gendered backdrop of male breadwinner and female homemaker and carer.

In a highly gendered post-war test case, a woman could have sexual agency and negotiate a particular type of marriage contract. The death of Robert Park on 17 March 1949 led to an inheritance battle over his will. *In the estate of Park; Park v Park* (1953) hinged on whether or not he was legally married to Wyn Blodwen two weeks before his death. This case clarified that even a person of 'unsound mind' could consent to marriage if he or she could understand its nature. The court heard how the seventy-eight-year-old widower wrote a new will on the afternoon of his wedding to a 'cashier at his club' whom he had met less than a month earlier. It was alleged that Mr Park had 'suffered from depression after the death of his former wife, to whom he had been married for 50 years' and furthermore, after a stroke 'he lost his grip on personal and business affairs and rapidly fell into a second childhood'. The defence lawyer summed up Park's mental state by saying that to 'use a colloquialism, he was hopelessly and completely "ga-ga"'. As evidence the lawyer said that 'he had proposed to a woman who was less than half his age' and that 'the day before the ceremony, the deceased was found by his valet struggling to get into his morning clothes in the belief he was being married on that day'. The next day he thought he had been already married for two weeks.[101] Against this, the court was told that from

> the moment Mr. Park made up his mind to marry the plaintiff... he never put a foot wrong in his pursuit and capture of her. His interest and will power were profoundly aroused.... Every step was sensible, calculated from

---

[99] Matrimonial Causes Act. 1937, s. 7 (i).

[100] 'Marriage Bill Changes', *The Times*, 8 July 1937, 8.

[101] 'High Court of Justice', *The Times*, 15 May 1953, 11.

the point of view of an old and physically unattractive man wooing a good-looking woman in her middle thirties.[102]

Citing *Durham*, the judge explained that the 'minds of the parties must also be capable of understanding the nature of the contract into which they were signing', and that in general 'the essence of the contract was an engagement between a man and a woman to live together and love one another as husband and wife to the exclusion of all others'.[103] The judge also stated that '[s]ubmission on the part of the woman may no longer be an essential part of the contract; but so far as the husband is concerned there is still the duty to maintain to protect'.[104] The judge did not annul the marriage because Park 'had obviously been proud of his achievement in winning the plaintiff's consent to his proposal of marriage'. In this law-changing[105] case, 'the deceased could and did understand the nature of the contract' and his active sexuality was the evidence. The marriage was therefore 'valid and binding'[106] and his second wife was due her inheritance. Here the husband's role is to 'protect' his wife, but it is the man's sexual desire that makes the marriage valid. Park was judged to have been behaving in the appropriate way by being 'profoundly aroused' by 'a good-looking woman'. His 'sensible' 'pursuit' and 'capture' of the woman showed, in social, cultural and legal terms, that he actively understood normative notions of sex and marriage.

The *Park* case also marked a change in the requirement of sexual relations within marriage. Although for a marriage to be legally complete it had to be consummated, the wife in *Park* successfully negotiated a non-sexual marriage that was legally binding. The court heard that at

some stage... the plaintiff made it clear to the deceased that the marriage was to be one free from any sexual relations between them. On this, she insisted and the deceased concurred, though possibly reluctantly, in abstaining from sexual intercourse with his intended wife. In fact no sexual

---

[102] 'High Court of Justice', *The Times*, 20 May 1953, 3.

[103] 'High Court of Justice', *The Times*, 13 June 1953, 9.

[104] Quotation not reported in *The Times*, see *In the estate of Park; Park v Park* [1953] 2 All ER 1411.

[105] 'Person of unsound mind can consent to marriage if at time entered marriage contract could understand its nature absent delusions', *Blackstone's Family Law*, 523.

[106] 'High Court of Justice', *The Times*, 13 June 1953, 9.

relations ever occurred between the parties either before or after the ceremony of marriage; nor did they after the ceremony of marriage share a common bedroom.[107]

As Hasson points out in his analysis of marriage consent, this case is 'an example of Mrs Park exercising autonomy... to agree that sex was not an essential component of *her* marriage contract'. Further, sex was 'thus no longer either an unspoken, or indeed inviolable requirement' since it was 'potentially open to negotiation'.[108] This should not be overstated, however, since most putative wives did not negotiate such a contract, and rape within marriage was not illegal until the 1990s.[109] The 'possibly reluctantly' still maintains a level of male sexual activeness and acquisitiveness.

In the 1950s, a Royal Commission confirmed that the principal concern of marriage and insanity was procreation. The first nullity case to test the 'unsound mind' clause of the 1937 Act, failed to define 'unsound mind' and instead legally conflated it with 'insanity'. 'Unsound mind' was intended to a temporal category distinct from the 'incurable' insanity. However, *Smith v Smith (otherwise Hand)* (1940) set a legal precedent that 'the words "insanity" and "of unsound mind" therein had the same meaning'.[110] Some contemporary legal scholars felt that, the 1937 Act notwithstanding, English law had not addressed 'the kind of insanity and its effect upon capacity to consent to marriage... specifically by legislation' and that 'incurably of unsound mind' was difficult to define.[111] Further clarity was not forthcoming from the Royal Commission on Marriage and Divorce in 1956. Instead, the Commission considered biological factors. Historian Sander Gilman argues during the nineteenth century there was a 'somaticization of madness' and that this 'increased across the twentieth century'. In the twentieth century there was, explains Gilman, a 'desire... to find more and more cases in which madness was the result of specific

---

[107] Quotation not reported in *The Times*, see *In the estate of Park; Park v Park*.

[108] Ezra Hasson, '"I Can't": Capacity to marry and the question of sex', *Liverpool Law Review* 31 (2010), 103.

[109] The landmark test case was *R v R* [1991] 3 WLR 767.

[110] Latey and Rees, *Latey on divorce*, 176.

[111] William McCurdy, 'Insanity as a Ground for Annulment or Divorce in English and American Law', *Virginia Law Review* 29, No. 6 (April, 1943), 786, 801.

biological, neurological or genetic factors'.[112] This can be seen in Royal Commission's consideration of physical and psychological illnesses. The Commission rejected a call for 'grave disease' at the time of marriage as a ground for nullity but only because 'it would create more difficulties than it would remove'. In a departure from 'compartmentalisation', the Commission

> recommend[ed] that the [legislation] should be re-drafted so as to make it clear that it refers only to a person who has gone through a ceremony of marriage with a full understanding of the nature of that ceremony and of what it imports but who nevertheless was of unsound mind at the time.[113]

This therefore suggested a slight gap between unsound mind and the earlier notion of insanity, now it was suggested that a *type* of person could not marry even if they understood the concept and contract of marriage. The Royal Commission concluded that the degree of mental defectiveness that would justify a nullity was 'that which makes a spouse unfitted for marriage and the procreation of children'.[114] This demonstrates the eugenicists' influence in defining marriage and barring those deemed unfit to breed, rather than the older notion of compartmentalisation and the ability to understand the purpose of marriage at the time of uttering the vows. The entire debate was underpinned however by social-class and gender assumptions about mental capacity and the emotions.

Eugenics discourses in this period defined which people were fit to procreate and therefore who should be able to marry legally. Categories of mental deficiency were heavily gendered before they were imported into marriage law in 1937, itself a legislative act that was twenty-five years in the making. In parliamentary debates and test cases, the definition of marriage was defined in terms of gender: women were to be child carers and homemakers, and men providers and protectors. Male sexuality was constructed as active, acquisitive and aroused by women,

---

[112] Sander Gilman, 'Madness as disability', *History of Psychiatry* 25, No. 4 (2014), 444–5.

[113] Royal Commission on Marriage and Divorce, *Royal Commission on Marriage and Divorce, Report 1951–1955* (London: HMSO, 1956), 80–1.

[114] 'Marriage and Divorce: Report of the Royal Commission', *British Medical Journal* 1, No. 4969 (March 31, 1956), 743.

but marriage was primarily procreative. There was however room, discursively and legally, for female sexual agency, and some women would have been able to negotiate their own marriage and sexual contract.

CONCLUSION

This exploration of marriage consent law during the period 1918 to 1960 has shown that changes in the law—whether through parliamentary legislation or precedent-setting nullity cases—followed sexed and gendered discussions that allow the historian to assess some of the ways in which marriage defined masculinity and male sexuality. Legal sources—legislative and judicial—possibly throw up exceptional cases, but this has been suggestive in showing some of the complexities of masculinity in relation to race, religion and social class. Parliamentary debates—apart from discussions about Indian child-marriage—were generally concerned with 'internal' issues regarding marriage, and show the class-based discussion during the passage of legislation. Case law however was brought into direct judgement of the non-White and the non-Anglican marriage. Sexual agency was complex and contradictory, but gender roles were static. English masculinity was to an extent defined against the Other, and marriage laws were set according to social-class assumptions.

We have seen that marriage consent laws assumed that a married couple would comprise a female homemaker and child carer, and a male breadwinner. The competing arguments in the affinity debates—that the wife's sister would be a good replacement mother, against the fear of sisterly rivalry—was premised on this gendered dichotomy. When this partnership was threatened by polygamy, the English woman was protected from the Otherness of Hindu and Muslim marital domesticity, but only if she had not been aware of all the facts before entering the marriage. The age of marriage debates reinforced gendered roles and stressed the protective role of the married man. This protective role was also a factor in considerations about mental capacity and marriage consent, in which women were posited as more emotional. To marry, a man had to have the capacity to protect a woman.

The marriage consent laws changed within the context of conflicting constructions of male and female sexuality. In all areas of marriage consent law, male sexuality was defined as active. Desire was generally subject to pragmatism. This was especially the case when men (re)married for child-care reasons. Women had sexual agency, as was demonstrated in affinity and age of marriage debates in which women were positioned as seductive, competitive and mendacious in order to capture a husband. Women could also actively negotiate a non-sexual marriage. This agency should not be overstressed since it has also been shown that marriage consent was, for the woman, perpetual sexual consent. When women had the most agency, it was in situations in which a woman could be categorised in a negative way such as deceitful teenage seducer, gold-digger marrying a richer older man, or trying to steal her sister's husband.

The comparison of companionate monogamous English marriage and masculinity with the polygamous Otherness of Hindu and Muslim marriage came at a time when India and Egypt were winning their independence from the British Empire. Parliament did not discuss polygamy in this context, but case law tested and set new boundaries. An affinity test case reinforced the notion that to be English in India was to be White and therefore White people were expected to remain within the bounds of Anglican-inflected affinity laws. English Law tacitly accepted polygamous marriage but only between Indian people in ceremonies in India. In parliament in the 1920s, Indian marriage was also depicted as backward and uncivilised because of the possibility of child-marriage, although the legal age of marriage consent at the start of this period was higher in India than in England. It was vital, at a time of Imperial uncertainty, for England, and English marriage and masculinity, to be able to compare favourably with those countries it wanted to identify with, chiefly countries that were White and Western.

Social class was rarely explicitly stated, but can be found below the surface. In age of marriage and mental capacity debates social-class norms, assumptions and prejudices played an important role in implicitly moving towards particular conclusions. In raising the age of marriage, the mainly middle- and upper-class parliamentarians would have been implementing age norms they were familiar with. Men and women in those social classes married later than did the working classes. The eugenics debate about mental deficiency and the desire of eugenicists to limit the ability of those deemed too defective to breed was inflected by class prejudice. In the widespread eugenics discourses circulating at the time, mental deficiency was linked disproportionately to the working class. By importing the categories of mental deficiency into marriage legislation, class prejudice found its way into this aspect of marriage consent law.

This chapter has concentrated on the restrictions of who could marry, but has not assessed what happened when a subject, male or female, said yes (or no) to an offer of marriage. The men and women here have not always known all of the facts before agreeing to marry, and have in some cases been allowed to retract that agreement through a nullity. The next chapter will assess codes of masculinity and engagement to marry by scrutinising breach of promise cases, public declarations of engagement such as the giving of an engagement ring, and the pressures men faced as they prepared to marry.

REFERENCES

Advisory Commission for the Protection and Welfare of Children and Young People (League of Nations). 1927. *The age of marriage and the age of consent*. Geneva: League of Nations.

Age of Marriage Act. 1929.

Anon (abridged by Jones, Philip). 2004. *Phillimore's Ecclesiastical Law (2nd edn 1895)*. Cardiff: Greenfach.

Anon. 1992. *The Book of Common Prayer*. London: Ebury.

Barrett, Maxwell (ed.). 1998. *Blackstone's family law index: Case precedents, 1900-1997*. London: Blackstone.

Barrett, Maxwell (ed.). 1998. *Blackstone's marriage breakdown law index: Case precedents, 1900-1997*. London: Blackstone.

Bingham, Adrian. 2004. *Gender, modernity, and the popular press in inter-war Britain*. Oxford: Oxford University Press.

Bourke, Joanna. 2007. *Rape: A history from 1860 to the present day*. London: Virago.

Brady, Sean. 2005. *Masculinity and male homosexuality in Britain, 1861–1913*. Basingstoke: Palgrave.

British Medical Journal.

British Nationality and Status of Aliens Act. 1914, s. 10 (1).

Brown, Judith M. and Wm. Roger Louis. 1999. *The Oxford history of the British Empire: Volume IV – The twentieth century*. Oxford: Oxford University Press.

Busfield, Joan. 1996. *Men, women and madness: Understanding gender and mental disorder*. Basingstoke: Palgrave.

Caplan, Lionel. 1991. Bravest of the brave. *Modern Asian Studies* 25(3):204–23.

Collins, Marcus. 2003. *Modern love: An intimate history of men and women in twentieth-century Britain*. London: Atlantic.

Cook, Matt. 2006. Law. In *Palgrave advances in the modern history of sexuality*, ed. Matt Houlbrook and H. G. Cocks, 64–86. Basingstoke: Palgrave.

Daily Express.

Daily Mirror.

Gillis, John. 1981. *Youth and history: Tradition and change in European age relations, 1770-Present*. London: Academic Press.

Gilman, Sander. 2014. Madness as disability. *History of Psychiatry* 25(4):441–9.

Haag, Pamela. 1999. *Consent: Sexual rights and the transformation of American liberalism*. Ithaca: Cornell University Press.

Hansard.

Hanson, Clare. 2013. *Eugenics, literature and culture in post-war Britain*. Abingdon: Routledge.

Hasson, Ezra. 2010. "I can't": Capacity to marry and the question of sex. *Liverpool Law Review* 31:1–16.

Hasson, Ezra. 2010. Capacity to marry: Law, medicine and conceptions of insanity. *Social History of Medicine* 23(1):1–20.

Holden, Katherine. 2007. *The shadow of marriage: Singleness in England, 1914–1960*. Manchester: Manchester University Press.

Houlbrook, Matt. 2005. *Queer London: Perils and pleasure in the sexual metropolis, 1918-1957*. London: University of Chicago Press.

Kuper, Adam. 2002. Incest, cousin marriage, and the origin of the human sciences in nineteenth-century England. *Past and Present* 174:158–83.

Langhamer, Claire. 2013. *The English in love: The intimate history of an emotional revolution*. Oxford: Oxford University Press.

Latey, William and D. Rees. 1943. *Latey on divorce*. London: Street and Maxwell.

Lexis database.

Light, Alison. 1991. *Forever England: Femininity, literature and conservatism between the wars*. London: Routledge.

McCurdy, William. 1943. Insanity as a ground for annulment or divorce in English and American law. *Virginia Law Review* 29(6):771–810.

Porter, Bernard. 1996. *The lion's share: A short history of British imperialism, 1850-1995*. Harlow: Longman.

Pugh, Martin. 2008. *'We danced all night': A social history of Britain between the wars*. London: Vintage.

Royal Commission on Marriage and Divorce. 1956. *Royal Commission on Marriage and Divorce, report 1951-1955*. London: HMSO.

Royal Commission on Divorce and Matrimonial Causes. 1912. *Minutes of evidence taken before the Royal Commission on Divorce and Matrimonial Causes, Vol.3*. London: HMSO.

Showalter, Elaine. 1987. *The female malady: Women, madness, and English culture, 1830–1980*. London: Virago.

Sinha, Mrinalini. 1999. Giving masculinity a history: Some contribution from the historiography of colonial India. *Gender and History* 11(3):445–60.

Stone, Lawrence. 1990. *Road to divorce: England 1530–1987*. Oxford: Oxford University Press.

The Times.

Van Ommeren, William. 1961. Mental illness affecting matrimonial consent. *Canon Law Studies* 415:whole vol.

Waites, Matthew. 2004. The age of consent and sexual consent. In *Making Sense of Sexual Consent* ed. Mark Cowling and Paul Reynolds, 73–92. Aldershot: Routledge.

Waites, Matthew. 2005. *The age of consent: Young people, sexuality and citizenship.* Basingstoke: Palgrave.

Welshman, John. 2013. First published 2006. *Underclass: A history of the excluded since 1880.* London: Bloomsbury.

Whiteside, Noel. 1991. *Bad Times: Unemployment in British social and political history.* London: Faber and Faber.

Yeo, Eileen. 2004. "The boy is the father of the man": Moral panic over working-class youth, 1850 to the present. *Labour History Review* 69(2):185–99.

CHAPTER 3

Engagement

'I love little Margery, her nose is so small, When she hides it in powder I can't see it all'. With this rhyming couplet, Arthur Crouch of Leeds was expressing a romantic masculinity in a love letter to his diminutively described fiancée, Marjorie Rose. Unlike most men, Crouch had his personal poetry made public in a court of law and in a national newspaper when his fiancée sued him for breach of promise to marry. In 1929, love letters were an expectation, even a requirement, of engagement, and the threat of public humiliation by revealing private intimacy hung over men who contemplated reneging on a promise to marry. Crouch, already divorced with children, had promised to marry Rose, but then married someone else. In his defence, Crouch claimed his fiancée's mother made his life 'a misery' and had beaten him with a 'horsewhip', bought especially for the purpose. Rose however stated in court that it was not a horsewhip, but a 'cane'. The ensuing breach of promise case sought a measure of control, and recompense, through the courts.[1] Although the description of violence in this case is unusual, the case is not exceptional in that it exposes the frequent tension between romance and love as legal contract, the blurring of public and private, the friction between prospective spouses, the pressure exerted by family members, and the gender asymmetry of courtship, commitment, engagement and marriage.

---

[1] 'Mother's cane', *Daily Mirror*, 11 October 1929, 2.

© The Author(s), under exclusive license to Springer Nature   69
Switzerland AG 2023
N. Penlington, *Men Getting Married in England, 1918–60*, Genders
and Sexualities in History, https://doi.org/10.1007/978-3-031-27405-3_3

This chapter will explore these themes, and in particular the 'interview' between a man and his prospective father-in-law, through newspaper reporting of breach of promise cases, and also oral history testimonies and etiquette manuals that discuss engagement to marry.

Throughout the period 1918 to 1960, it was possible for either party to sue the other for damages in the event of a cancelled engagement. The promise of marriage was binding: the law defined 'the promise to marry as a legal contract'. Although breach of promise cases were 'rare', they nevertheless 'haunted mid-century engagements' because 'the threat' of legal action 'still had power'.[2] The newspaper reporting of this legal action, breach of promise, will form the analytical core of this chapter. It helps us to understand the use of breach of promise and its effect on the men involved. More broadly, though, such coverage provides a glimpse into the experience, and expectations, of engaged men and is a useful tool in tracing changing notions of masculinity and male sexuality in relation to feelings of commitment, honour and intimacy.

Although in decline across the period, newspaper reporting of breach of promise cases reflected ideals of commitment, of intimacy and of masculinity. The origin of breach of promise lies in the ecclesiastical courts, but only after the Hardwicke Marriage Act (1753) did it become more typical for cases to appear before civil courts. Historian Ginger Frost explains that these cases were usually 'property disputes' and 'were often brought by men'. In the nineteenth century, though still 'theoretically open to both sexes', women became the dominant sex bringing breach of promise cases. Following law changes, many sued for 'wounded feelings'.[3] Historian Denise Bates argues that all 'classes of society' considered it 'ungentlemanly' for a man to sue for breach of promise and that in doing so he would compromise 'his own honour'.[4] This chapter will show some of the gendered contours of 'feelings' and 'honour' in the mid-twentieth century.

---

[2] Claire Langhamer, *The English in Love: The Intimate Story of an Emotional Revolution* (Oxford: Oxford University Press, 2013), 160–1, 164.

[3] Ginger S. Frost, *Promises Broken: Courtship, Class, and Gender in Victorian England* (Charlottesville: University Press of Virginia, 1995), 137, 142.

[4] Denise Bates, *Breach of Promise to Marry: A History of How Jilted Brides Settled Scores* (Barnsley: Pen and Sword, 2014), 155.

The number of cases declined from the mid-nineteenth century and men ceased to sue for breach of promise by the twentieth century. Historian Claire Langhamer argues that by 'the twentieth century breach of promise was widely viewed as a legal action out of step with modern intimacies'[5] and following a century of widespread opposition, the law was eventually abolished in 1970.[6] Legal scholar Saskia Lettmaier shows that the number of reports of breach of promise cases in *The Times* declined from 5.5 per month in 1870 to one case every two months by the 1930s, and that reporting of these cases in the *News of the World* halved after 1910. Though men could sue for breach of promise, very few did after 1800. Lettmaier analysed over 250 cases over a 300-year period and found that men 'had no scruples' in taking legal action in the seventeenth and eighteenth centuries. In her sample, Lettmaier found that only 3.7 per cent of cases were brought by men between 1800 and 1940.[7] The cases *Bower v Ebsworth* (1910), brought by 'a young draper's assistant',and *Vigier v Smith* (1917), in which the judge accused the wealthy 'French Viscomte [sic]' of 'wasting the time of a high court',[8] were exceptionally late cases involving a male plaintiff.

Despite the decline in the number of breach of promise cases from a high point in the mid-nineteenth century, the sample of over 1,000 articles from two newspapers used here demonstrates that breach of promise was still instantly recognisable throughout the period. As Bates dramatically points out, 'all but the most foolhardy or naïve men realised that breach of promise hung above their heads like the sword of Damocles'.[9] In the 1920s, *Daily Express* readers could expect to read about breach of promise every six weeks, and only slightly less often in the 1950s at every seven weeks. The *Daily Mirror* ran breach of promise articles every

---

[5] Langhamer, *English in Love*, 160.

[6] Frost, *Promises Broken*, 139.

[7] Saskia Lettmaier, *Broken Engagements: The Action for Breach of Promise of Marriage and the Feminine Ideal, 1800–1940* (Oxford: Oxford University Press, 2010), 10, 27–8, 172; Lettmaier points out that this was typical since Susie Steinbach and Frost each found the prevalence of male plaintiffs as 8% between 1780 and 1920, and 3% from 1830 to 1970, respectively. Lettmaier cites Ginger S. Frost, 'Promises Broken: Breach of promise in England and Wales 1753–1970', Unpublished PhD thesis: Rice University (1991), 98 and Susie L. Steinbach, 'Promises, Promises, Not marrying in England 1780–1920', Unpublished PhD thesis Yale University (1996), 210.

[8] Lettmaier, *Broken Engagements*, 28; Bates, *Breach of Promise*, 166.

[9] Bates, *Breach of Promise*, 169.

three weeks in the 1920s, and almost every six weeks in the 1950s. Newspaper reports of breach of promise cases spanned the social spectrum from Lords, world boxing champions and film stars to butchers, policemen, and a hairdresser suing an electrician.[10] Langhamer is right that breach of promise cases 'operated as a forum for the articulation of courtship rules and etiquette; an opportunity for the courts to remind the public how commitment was supposed to work'.[11] However, breach of promise newspaper articles also contained editorial or columnist opinion and show the type of gendered language that was circulating in the popular press regarding love, sex and commitment.

This chapter is concerned with codes of engagement, not just breach of promise cases. A similar legal action for a historian to consider would be 'seduction', but that lies beyond the scope of this book. Seduction was a legal action that could be initiated by the parents of the woman. As Bates explains, men 'could be sued for damages for seduction if they made a girl pregnant and refused to marry'. Seduction cases did not necessarily involve an alleged promise of marriage, but if there had been such a promise then the woman could sue in her own right for breach of promise. Although some individual cases of seduction and breach of promise could overlap, the legal frame of seduction is sex, and the legal frame of breach of promise is marriage. Ginger Frost points out that 'seduction was a separate legal action' but 'juries often gave awards to compensate for the loss of marriageability' following 'sexual intercourse' that had 'happened after the promise [of marriage] and on the faith of that promise'. Lettmaier explains that seduction cases were concerned with seduction as tort (injury to one party by another) itself whereas breach of promise cases focused on 'intended marriage' as a 'contract'.[12] To the historian, while an examination of seduction cases can tell us about illicit sexual intercourse, breach of promise cases are more useful for an assessment of conduct during engagement to marry.

---

[10] 'Beauty Queen to sue Peer pf 23', *Daily Mirror*, 10 April 1934, 1; 'Carnera and a London girl', *Daily Mirror*, 13 June 1934, 3; 'Sally meditates', *Daily Express*, 21 April 1934, 3; 'His name's just too romantic', *Daily Mirror*, 19 April 1934, 21; 'Other news in brief', *Daily Mirror*, 22 October 1924, 2; '£150 breach damages', *Daily Express*, 20 September 1934, 18.

[11] Langhamer, *English in Love*, 163.

[12] Bates, *Breach of Promise*, 8; Frost, *Promises Broken*, 18; Lettmaier, *Broken Engagements*, 8.

The oral history sample acts as a counter to both the unusual breach of promise cases and the formulaic, almost ritualistic, notions of engagement found in etiquette manuals. Etiquette manual authors wrote to emphasise, and in the process construct, 'tradition' and therefore it is a genre that changes very little over time. Publishers and authors aimed etiquette manuals at readers from the wealthier end of society and the manuals allow for historical analysis of gender, engagement and particular social-class aspirations. In contrast to etiquette manuals, oral history interviewees often described proposals or agreements to marry that were made for practical reasons, were spontaneous or simply long expected.

The codes of engagement shown here reflect and illustrate changes, continuities and contradictions in masculinity and male sexuality between 1918 and 1960. The chapter is in four sections: words, intimacy, things and pressure. The words of proposal and promise, perhaps spoken or written in a love letter, show some of the tensions within a masculinity that was expected to be at once stoical and romantic but was also less positively conceived as duplicitous and mendacious. What emerges here too is the frequent misunderstanding of words that often went with breach of promise and experiences of engagement more broadly. Sexual intimacy in breach of promise cases shows that intimacy often delineated different stages in a pre-marital relationship. A section on 'Things' looks at material cultural and will show that, to many couples, the engagement existed because of the presence, and ownership, of certain items, usually in the woman's possession. Engagement rings, trousseaus and collections of love letters made the engagement *real*; and allow the historian access to some of the gendered meanings of engagement and marriage, while exposing related power dynamics. The pressures on those marrying show that a prospective married couple did not exist in a vacuum, but had to negotiate relationships with family, and sometimes employers in order to become engaged to marry. Two relationships appear to be more prominent than others: that between the man and his mother, and between the man and his prospective father-in-law. This consideration of words, intimacy, things and pressure reveals some of the tensions and contradictions between masculine honour, feelings and intimacy experienced by, and expected of, engaged men during a period in which marriage was becoming more popular and entered into at a younger age.

Words

Words were an important element of an engagement, since for many the status of being engaged started with a written or verbal promise or agreement to marry. For others an engagement could be legally binding despite lack of (proven) verbal agreement. Evidence of these 'inferred engagements' could be love letters.

It is impossible to quantify the proportion of engagements that started with an explicit proposal of marriage. Half of the sample of oral history interviews give detail of the marriage proposal, but given the seeming reticence, especially among men,[13] to talk about such things in an oral history interview, the proportion could be higher.[14] On the other hand, the sample could be biased by selection towards those who started their engagement with a formal proposal. Such analysis does not seek to be statistically representative, but instead to show a range of subjectivities. Certainly, the authors of etiquette manuals were very clear that it was the man who had to ask the woman to marry him. Treading a fine line between masculine honour and romantic feelings, men were not expected however to find the words easily, and the words they chose had to make them appear to be manly. Writing in 1926, Lady Troubridge[15] considered that there was 'no time when the rules of etiquette need[ed] to be so strictly observed as during the period of courtship'. Troubridge advised that 'the proposal itself should be made in sincere and earnest language' since '[h]igh-flown terms and impassioned emotion are apt to appear ludicrous'.[16] Men's feelings and the words used to express emotion were perhaps therefore constrained by expectations of masculinity.

The onus was on the man to display honour and to propose, but women were supposed to play an active part. Etiquette manuals

---

[13] Of the ninety-five oral history interviewees cited in this thesis, fifty-six (59%) are men.

[14] This is in stark contrast to a study of weddings that were performed in 2006, in which 'it was the men who had the most to say about the proposal', Sarah Farrimond, 'Ritual and Narrative in the Contemporary Anglican Wedding', Unpublished PhD thesis: Durham University (2009), 198.

[15] Lady Laura Troubridge wrote 'seven society novels for Mills and Boon'. See Jay Dixon, *The Romantic Fiction of Mills and Boon, 1909–1995* (Abingdon: Routledge, 2016), 15

[16] Lady [Laura] Troubridge, *The Book of Etiquette* (London: Associated Bookbuyers' Company, 1931. First published 1926), 6, 8.

constructed a gendered set piece; a theatrical proposal based on assumptions of masculinity and femininity. In the 1929 *Wedding Etiquette*, Mary Woodman gave extensive advice on marriage proposals. Woodman advised couples that there were two parties and although 'it all depend[ed] on the man as to how the momentous question will be put', the 'girl' was not 'entirely passive'. Woodman further explained that the woman's 'duty lies in being prepared to help the man out of his troubles, should he flounder into difficulties'. This assumed that men naturally struggled with emotional language and behaviour, and further that there was a lack of meaningful communication between the two parties. Moreover, masculinity and femininity were constructed as opposite: where men were supposed to struggle with emotions, women were to excel. Invoking notions of psychological theories of gendered emotions and behaviour, Woodman explained that a 'word from [the woman] at the correct psychological moment may make all the difference, and spare her lover the mortification of appearing clumsy'. The word 'duty' was repeated since 'it is more or less their duty… to assist the man in bringing the matter to its proper climax' lest the man's honourable moment be undermined. The reason for a woman's actions was linked to the gendered investment in marriage: 'girls must marry, and some bachelors are slow'.[17] In the 1936 *Marriage Etiquette: How to Arrange a Wedding*, penned by a 'Best Man', the reader found that men 'are often reticent creatures, not given to talking of their past lives, their relations, or even their daily occupations when in the throes of a serious love-affair'. This assumption that men could not, or would not, adequately express their emotions led to an appeal to men to follow a course of action they could relate to: the workplace, specifically the class-biased 'business difficulty'. In acknowledgement that 'the sometimes difficult task of proposing marriage' can cause 'the utmost trepidation', those with a 'sensitive nature' were advised 'to tackle the task with the same courage and skill which he would use in any other emergency, and get it done thoroughly as he would if it were a business difficulty'.[18] After the Second World War, men were still to take the initiative and propose. In 1950, Ann Page affirmed that the 'man first approaches his girl and makes his proposal to her'. The proposal could

---

[17] Mary Woodman, *Wedding Etiquette* (London: W. Foulsham, 1929), 23–4.

[18] "Best Man", *Marriage Etiquette: How to Arrange a Wedding* (London: W. Foulsham, 1936. Revised 1949), 10–11.

be 'made verbally or in writing, but a verbal proposal is obviously best'.[19] In the sample of oral histories used here, only one had received a written marriage proposal. In the late 1950s, Freda Hall received a proposal from her future husband, Charles. It was in the form of a letter since he was stationed in Hong Kong.[20]

Some were concerned that women might take the initiative and propose to men, and claimed that breach of promise exacerbated this. Historian Joanna Bourke argues that, during the Great War and shortly after, there was a small, and ultimately, unsuccessful movement to encourage women to 'take the initiative in proposing marriage' to wounded men even though there were concerns that such a move 'would destroy all romance'.[21] The role of the man as the instigator of marriage was seen as being under threat from the supposed rise of sexual equality. In 1924, a St Valentine's Day opinion piece in the *Daily Mirror* blamed breach of promise, along with men and women meeting on 'equal terms', for killing romance.[22] The honourable role of the man as the pursuer was threatened. The writer of a 1929 letter opposed 'Sex Equality' 'nowadays' and appealed for the 'Abolition of breach of promise actions'.[23]

Rather than the formulaic proposal initiated by the man typical of etiquette manuals throughout the period, even a small sample of oral histories shows a range of proposals and, by implication, perhaps no proposal at all. Women were more likely to emplot[24] the proposal into a romantic narrative, whereas men tended to tell the story more casually. In 1935 in the North East, the parents of twenty-one-year-old Mary Potts allowed her to have 'a black dress' now that she had the 'key to the door'. Mary wore it to a 'ball' and received 'a very romantic proposal'

---

[19] Ann Page, *The Complete Guide to Wedding Etiquette* (London: Ward, Lock and Co., 1950), 3, 10–11

[20] C900/09075 interview with Freda Hall, Millennium Memory Bank, BLSA.

[21] Joanna Bourke, 'Love and Limblessness: Male Heterosexuality, Disability, and the Great War', *Journal of War and Culture Studies* 9, No. 1(2016), 10–11.

[22] 'Why women do not need Valentines', *Daily Mirror*,14 February 1924, 5

[23] 'As it strikes our readers', *Daily Mirror*,2 December 1929, 9.

[24] 'Providing the "meaning" of a story by identifying the *kind of story* that has been told is called explanation by emplotment'. One mode of emplotment is Romance. See Hayden White, *Metahistory: The Historical Imagination in Nineteenth-Century Europe* (Baltimore: John Hopkins University Press, 1973), 7.

from her future husband.[25] When Pam Portman married in 1947 at the age of nineteen she had been engaged for two years following a chance encounter with a soldier returning from the Second World War. Londoner Pam had been in the land army in Herefordshire and met her husband when she was out playing darts with friends and said to her friend 'he doesn't look bad'. He proposed three days later, leaning on a 'five bar gate with the moon shining', in the same week that she received a proposal from another man she was already 'courting'. This romantic narrative of chance, choice and moonlight is, however, cut through by a cognisance of the realities of war and she knew that 'the men coming home wanted to get married... everyone wanted to get married'. She rejected his initial proposal but married him two years later.[26]

Some women explained that the marriage proposal came as a surprise because they had known the man for a very long time, but this surprise was part of a romantic reminiscence. In the 1930s, Londoner Dorothy Grubb had been gradually getting to know a sergeant major in the Royal Highland Regiment but his eventual proposal 'came as a surprise'.[27] In 1930 in the North East, nineteen-year-old Harriet Scott received a surprise proposal. She had met Harry, who was two years her senior and a driver for the Co-op, when she was ten years old because the two families had a very close friendship. When one night, as they went out 'as usual', Harry started 'to talk seriously' and she roared with laughter. She rang him the next morning and 'fell into his arms'.[28] It is difficult to determine the man's view from these interviews with women, but possibly the surprise expressed by these women suggests that there was a lack of communication or a misunderstanding between the couple and that the man had not made his feelings and intentions clear and understood until the moment of 'surprise'. Beyond the possibility of misunderstanding, it is clear that men did not always perform a romantic, theatrical proposal, but instead that engagements often started pragmatically.

Other women retold the stories of their engagements as matter of fact, deliberately playing down the romantic and placing it within the

---

[25] C900/11134 interview with Mary Potts, Millennium Memory Bank, BLSA.

[26] C900/06567 interview with Pam Portman, Millennium Memory Bank, BLSA.

[27] C900/01071 interview with Dorothy Grubb, Millennium Memory Bank, BLSA.

[28] C900/11007 interview with Harriet Scott, Millennium Memory Bank, BLSA.

everyday.[29] Married in the 1920s, Lizzie Hartley remembered that her husband Robert simply asked her, 'Would you like to get married?', while she was in service in Blackpool. This had happened, for practical reasons, as soon as a cottage had become available to rent, since Lizzie's father had kicked her out and she had not anywhere permanent to live.[30] In the North East, Evelyn Macnamee married in the late 1930s after meeting her fiancé at the factory where they worked. Evelyn expressly narrated her engagement and marriage as one of being 'in love' but not romantic. When asked by the interviewer, Evelyn could not remember the proposal but said there was 'no romance about it'.[31] Within the narrative of the everyday, some women took the initiative to force a proposal from the man. In the 1950s, Yorkshire nurse Sheila Walker provoked her future husband into a proposal. He proposed after Sheila had had 'itchy feet' and threatened to take a job in Bridlington, a distance away.[32]

Male oral history respondents gave only very brief details about how they became engaged. Most men in these oral histories presented the supposedly nerve-wracking marriage proposal as casual, almost relaxed.[33] Even when pressed on the subject, Liverpudlian and son of a timber merchant, Arthur Ware placed his 1920s proposal to his wife within a larger, and perhaps, to him, more important life narrative. He simply stated that they were having a 'stroll' one evening on a 'grass bank between Mersey Road and Jericho Lane' where they 'sat down under a tree, and she said yes'.[34] For twenty-five-year-old Maurice Carter, there was 'no snap decision' to marry but they 'both felt [they] were meant'. He proposed while leaning on a five-bar gate during a bike ride in Essex. They married in 1949.[35] Only one of the men sampled confessed to being 'nervous', but this was told as a casual everyday story. Haulier Richard Ridgeway remembered how he proposed to his wife Enid, known

[29] For example, C900/10098 interview with Ellen Parry, Millennium Memory Bank, BLSA; C900/06036 interview with Florian Carr, Millennium Memory Bank, BLSA.

[30] C900/08012 interview with Lizzie Hartley, Millennium Memory Bank, BLSA.

[31] C900/11010 interview with Evelyn Macnamee, Millennium Memory Bank, BLSA.

[32] C900/07106 interview with Sheila Walker, Millennium Memory Bank, BLSA.

[33] For example, C900/15089 interview with Richard Gordon Perks, Millennium Memory Bank, BLSA.

[34] C900/10097 interview with Arthur Leslie Ware, Millennium Memory Bank, BLSA.

[35] C900/04009A interview with Maurice Carter, Millennium Memory Bank, BLSA.

as Bubbles. When he nervously proposed, in a car parked in a lay-by near a crossroads between Birkenhead and Chester, Bubbles second-guessed, played her part, and said that she could 'guess you want us to get married'.[36]

Newspaper coverage of breach of promise cases reveal that some engagements did not necessarily start with a proposal. Inferred engagements[37] were those that existed legally because of some form of behaviour other than a direct marriage proposal. Partly because written evidence is easier to demonstrate in a court of law than verbal evidence, love letters were 'often the star exhibit' of commitment to marry in breach of promise cases. In spite of the unromantic male oral history reminiscences, it was normal for engaged men to write love letters. The detailed newspaper reporting of love letters in breach of promise cases meant that the media and the threat of legal action potentially mediated men's outpouring of romantic words. Langhamer points out that the writing of love letters increased in the Second World War,[38] but this was also the case during the Great War, and it led to concerns about the content of men's letters. In 1919, an opinion piece in the *Daily Mirror* asked 'Does it seem fair, does it seem cricket, that love letters should be read in court?' The conclusion was that a '*real* love letter is never ridiculous, excepting to the loveless or those who have forgotten the glowing days of their youth and love'. The reading from the 'pages of the most secret thought of a man's life provid[ing] amusement for tittering women in the gallery' was seen as positive since it might prevent 'fickle young men... from being too ardent unless they are quite sure of their own fidelity'.[39] In a case that year, London clerk Alfred Grant had to pay damages to Nantes milliner Noely Normand. Many letters were read in court including:

What a happy day it will be when the war is over and we are indeed once and for all time in a bond of love. Darling, I save you many kisses, and the

---

[36] C900/15006 interview with Richard Morgan Ridgeway, Millennium Memory Bank, BLSA.

[37] Denise Bates dates this to the 1830s when letters were taken as evidence in lieu of a marriage proposal. Bates, *Breach of Promise*, 26

[38] Langhamer, *English in Love*, 118–20, 163.

[39] With original emphasis, 'Are the writers of love letters criminals?', *Daily Mirror*, 21 February 1919, 7.

most sincere love it is possible for any person living to send another who have but one single thought.[40]

Such cases show that men's words were not always to be trusted: they could be duplicitous or mendacious, or perhaps looking upon them more kindly, men simply were not allowed to change their minds once they had made a commitment. These letters also show that men were capable of expressing, and were expected to express, their romantic feelings in writing across the period.

Some commentators urged caution in the writing of love letters, but the absence of love letters was viewed with suspicion. A *Daily Mirror* editorial argued for a new legal category of '*conditional* engagements... freed from the threat of damages'. The editorial suggested that during a 'conditional engagement... the writing of terminable and unconditional love-letters would be prohibited'.[41] An opinion piece in the newspaper warned men against writing these types of letters. 'John Silence' wrote that the 'Law Courts are largely engaged in settling disputes that arise out of things thoughtlessly put into writing'. This included breach of promise cases. The columnist urged caution and gave the class-biased example of a 'shrewd businessman who left his mantle of acumen at the office' when he wrote the words 'Oh, my darling, how can I live without you?'[42] However, when a man did not send *any* love letters, he was an oddity. The case between poulterer Nathan Cole and 'Jewess' Esther Cohen was reported as unusual because 'the parties always communicated with each other by telephone'. The judge was told that he would 'not be troubled with ardent love letters'. The *Daily Mirror* reported that 'although fond of each other, [the parties] certainly kept an eye on the material advantage which each might hope to obtain from the marriage'.[43] Although Langhamer's comprehensive 'social history of heterosexual love' places the locus of change in the 1940s and 1950s,[44] this 1930s couple's relationship was seen as inferior because it was more about materiality than romance.

[40] 'A French milliner's romance', *Daily Mirror*,26 March 1919, 2.

[41] 'Long engagements', *Daily Mirror*,11 April 1924, 7.

[42] 'Dangerous things we put into writing', *Daily Mirror*, 2 December 1919, 7.

[43] '"No sentiment" breach suit', *Daily Mirror*, 20 March 1934, 9.

[44] Langhamer, *English in Love*, 4, 9.

Men were expected to propose, but not to be *too* emotional, with women doing their bit to be supportive and encouraging. Oral histories however show that many proposals were more matter of fact than 'romantic', with some coming as a complete surprise to the woman. This suggests some misunderstanding between couples, and especially perhaps that men did not convey their emotions and intentions. As breach of promise cases show, men did however write romantic letters across the period. Men's words were not always to be trusted and they could be manipulative or mendacious way in order to achieve pre-marital sexual intimacy.

INTIMACY

In the absence of words of commitment, newspaper reports from the 1930s gave gendered accounts of sexual intimacy as proof of a commitment to marry: the moment friendship or courtship became engagement.[45] Sex is presented in these cases as something given by the woman to the man in return for commitment, and that the man potentially promised to marry or at least gave the impression of intending to marry in order to achieve his sexual desires. In a 1929 case, the owner of a 'tobacco and confectionary shop' offered marriage to his employee rather than a pay rise so that she could afford to look after her children. The court heard that 'intimacy began' after the promise of marriage.[46] A decade later, 'gentleman farmer' Norman Varley successfully defended a breach of promise case in which Mary Stephens claimed that she had initially joined Varley as a housekeeper but over time 'they had lived together more as husband and wife than employer and housekeeper'.[47] Although the roles of housekeeper and housewife would have been similar, the relationship changed because of sexual intimacy. In these cases, sexual intimacy, not words of promise, marked a gendered and contestable boundary between different types or stages of relationship.

A defence against breach of promise used by some men was that the woman was not a fiancée but merely a 'mistress'. Whether a woman was a 'fiancée' or a 'mistress' was a war of words and this shows the

---

[45] For example, 'I should have shot him', *Daily Mirror*, 6 July 1934, 10; 'Woman, 60, sues for breach, says ex-M.P. besieged her', *Daily Mirror*, 28 June 1949, 5.

[46] 'Cigarette Shop Romance', *Daily Express*, 13 March 1929, 7.

[47] 'Woman stops breach suit', *Daily Express*, 24 March 1939, 9.

gender asymmetry in relation to marriage and to sexual intimacy.[48] Women needed to be married, but men could tacitly take a 'mistress' or sometimes several; thus revealing a further tension within masculinity: between honour and sexual acquisitiveness. A man could have more than one sexual partner, but he had to honour his commitments. In 1919, a Frenchwoman Adele Reynaud sued 'company promoter' John Martin ofAlbemarle Street, Piccadilly. Reynaud was working as a 'theatre' attendant at the time of their meeting. Although the couple lived together following a promise of marriage, Martin wrote to Reynaud saying that

> it would appear that you and I are two incompatible entities. I have always loved three or four women at the same time. There are three at present. How much they loved me you can judge according to your own feelings. Love depends solely on success and cash.[49]

In 1934, circus owner and naturalist, George Chapman defended a breach of promise case by claiming that his fiancée knew that he was already married. He denied claims that he had proposed but accepted that they had stayed together in hotels and that she was his 'official mistress'.[50] In a 1954 case, a fifty-five-year-old divorcee sued a seventy-two-year-old widower for breach of promise. The court heard that in 1952 Alexander Politi told Rayne Craven, 'You know [my wife] has not been a wife to me in the proper sense for many, many years' and that 'intimacy took place many times'. He refuted the claim that he had promised that 'If my wife dies, I shall marry you'.[51]

The reporting of lack of intimacy in breach of promise cases assumed that normal men were actively sexually desirous and sexually knowledgeable. As Langhamer points out, across this period sexual knowledge, if not experience was encouraged.[52] Lack of intimacy was used a defence by the Naval officer in the extensively reported 'Maid of Athens' case.

[48] For example, 'Widow's £20,000 suit collapses', *Daily Express*, 11 July 1924, 1; 'Lord Hewart questions Mrs Mendham', *Daily Express*, 11 July 1924, 3.

[49] 'My little darling Ju-Ju', *Daily Mirror*, 20 June 1919, 2; 'Darling angel Ju-Ju', *Daily Mirror*, 22 November 1919, 15.

[50] '"Breach" suit against a circus owner', *Daily Mirror*,12 June 1934, 6; see also, 'Girl's letters to circus owner in a breach of promise claim', *Daily Express*,12 June 1934, 7.

[51] 'Man of 72 in breach suit', *Daily Mirror*, 22 July 1954, 3.

[52] Langhamer, *English in Love*, 158.

Lieutenant-Commander Ridgeway claimed that he was 'justified' in his decision to cancel the engagement because of 'her intended refusal to consummate the marriage'. The jury of 'eleven middle-aged men and [one] matronly woman' found against him.[53] Women considered to be 'matronly'—older, stern and joyless—were an instantly recognisable stereotype long before the 'Carry On' era,[54] and the suggestion in this case is that a younger more virile jury may have been more sympathetic to the man. In 1949, telephonist Alec Bromnick could not afford to pay weekly damages to his fiancée, the 'midget' Trudy Peltz. Bromnick felt the case brought against him only to 'show [him] up' and that Peltz was 'still young' and would 'have plenty of chances to marry'.[55] The court heard, and the *Daily Express* told its readers, that she 'knew Alec had never had a girl before and she thought he "ought to know the facts of life – what it was to get married"'.[56] Here lack of sexual experience and knowledge undermines masculinity and is deployed by a woman to great effect.

Sexual intimacy became increasingly reported in newspaper coverage of breach of promise cases from the 1930s, perhaps reflecting a shift towards a more companionate view of marriage premised, in part, on sexual pleasure. In this discourse, sex was something a woman gave to a man, and marked the boundaries between different stages of a friendship/relationship. Wealthy men could use the category 'mistress' as a defence against breach of promise, and men generally were to be sexually desirous and knowledgeable.

THINGS

In additional to, or in the absence of words or intimacy, material objects were also important to many couples and could even be used as legal evidence of an engagement. For some couples, the engagement felt *real*

---

[53] 'Liana Maria weeps over a bunch of faded violets', *Daily Mirror*, 22 February 1949, 1.

[54] 'Matron' was not always used negatively but matrons were often assumed to be dourly dressed, 'comfortable' rather than 'demure', or simply old and unfashionable. For example, 'Cottons that rival silk', *Daily Express*, 5 April 1926, 4; 'To-day's Gossip', *Daily Mirror*, 9 January 1930, 11; 'Arding & Hobbs', *Daily Express*, 13 April 1935, 7

[55] 'Can't pay breach damages on £5 4 s. a week', *Daily Mirror*, 24 February 1949, 5.

[56] 'A midget with a big heart', *Daily Express*,23 February 1949, 5.

because of the presence of a collection of letters, an engagement ring, or a 'bottom drawer'. The presence and ownership of these items reveal gendered power relations and codes of engagement and marriage.

Love letters were not just written, sent, received and read, they were sometimes retained in large collections. Although these letters could be used in a court of law as evidence of a promise to marry, it is likely that the intention behind keeping a cache of letters would have been less legalistic for most couples. Although there is no direct evidence in the sources surveyed, it is entirely possible that keeping the letters to read and reread the words of a loved one, or perhaps just the very presence of the letters was a form of comfort during the engagement. Occasionally, the scale of the letter writing (affectionate letters written by man) and collecting was mentioned in breach of promise cases. The evidence of 'affection' and a promise to marry in a case a between Liverpool clerk and an 'ex-munitions girl' was a stash of '700 love letters' starting from when the defendant was 'going to France in 1915'.[57] One man, from over the water in Birkenhead, wrote 'voluminous correspondence' in rhyming couplets including 'Looking into your loving eyes/Teaches me how much your love I prize'. His commitment was as suspect as his poetry and the court ordered him to pay £75 damages.[58] Oral history interviewees remembered prolific letter writing from the 1950s. Jacko the Clown wrote to his fiancée every day when they were apart.[59] When her electrician fiancé was on National Service, chocolate 'enrober' Olive Wellings received six letters a week for eighteen months.[60]

The material object of chief importance as a sign of commitment was the engagement ring. The gendered buying and wearing of an engagement ring was an important demarcation between mere courtship and the status of engagement. The timing of the purchase was important and etiquette manuals advised against complacency at the moment of proposal. In 1919, etiquette manual author G. R. M. Devereux advised that the 'engagement ring should be given as soon as the engagement is

---

[57] '700 love letters!', *Daily Mirror*, 2 May 1919, 2.

[58] '"Poet's fickleness', *Daily Mirror*, 13 February 1924, 15.

[59] C966/05 interview with Jack Fossett (Jacko the Clown), Oral History of the Circus, BLSA.

[60] C821/07/01–07 interview with Olive Wellings, NLSC: Food: from source to Salespoint, BLSA.

a settled matter'.[61] The man was to wait until after proposing because it was not 'correct... to buy the ring without first consulting the lady as to the style she would prefer'.[62] As well as being gendered, the purchase of the ring was also a sign of wealth, class and status. In 1925, Eileen Terry encouraged men to splash out on an expensive ring: 'A man is fully justified in being extravagant over this token of his affection, which should be as valuable a gift as he can afford', she advised. The wearing of an engagement ring—displaying feelings and (prospective) marital status—was just as gendered as the choosing and buying was strictly for women, or a man would risk being unmanly. Terry was incredulous that it was 'becoming a custom nowadays for the girl to give the man a ring, which he [was] expected to wear'. This was beyond the pale since 'rings always make a man look so feeble... effeminate!'[63] Mary Woodman cautioned against a proposal in which the man 'fumbles in his pocket and produces a ring which he immediately begs his future wife to accept'.[64] Fumbling and begging would not have fitted with the ideal of married masculinity.

To be manly, a man was to be romantic and express his feelings within masculine constraints, but not to have any knowledge of jewellery or other wedding paraphernalia. In 1937, the Woods stated that it 'is the man's privilege to present his future bride with an engagement ring'. Unlike now, this should happen 'a few days after the romantic incident has taken place' when 'the engagement is an accepted fact'. The purchase of the ring was the 'man's affair' but he was to defer to the woman's 'special preferences' because 'most men know absolutely nothing about such things, and most girls know all about them' and the 'job is not one that a man actually enjoys'. This places 'man' and 'woman' within a narrative in which a 'girl' is simply waiting all her life to get married, whereas a man has less invested in the institution. Further, the binary of provider

---

[61] G.R.M. Devereux, *Etiquette for Women: A book of modern modes and manners* (London: C. Arthur Pearson, 1919), 86; Rev Exton advised that a 'showy ring' would not be 'good form', Rev. D. Exton, *Wedding Etiquette* (London: Universal Publications, 1935), 13.

[62] G. R. M. Devereux, *Etiquette for Men: A book of modern manners and customs* (London: C. Arthur Pearson, 1937. First published 1902), 72; similar advice is given in "Best Man", *Marriage Etiquette*, 14.

[63] Eileen Terry, *Etiquette for All: Man, woman, or child* (London: W. Foulsham, 1925), 123; most wedding ceremonies in the 1920s contained only one wedding ring, not two as is customary today.

[64] Woodman, *Wedding Etiquette*, 30.

86 N. PENLINGTON

and consumer is created: the woman knows how to shop, the man cannot 'actually enjoy' it. The man's ability to provide is dealt practically by the Woods, who suggested that he should visit the 'jeweller prior to the day of actual purchase and arranging with him to suppress all figures and tickets when the lady is present'.[65] It is at this point in the Woods manual, when the woman is choosing an expensive purchase with the man's money, that the 'girl' becomes a 'lady'.

Post-war etiquette manuals continued to give the same gendered advice. At the start of the 1950s, Ann Page claimed that the 'custom of the groom giving an engagement ring is very old, dating back hundreds of years' and further that the 'bride-to-be selects the ring' but should not wear it 'publicly until the engagement [has been] announced'. In contrast to advice given in other etiquette manuals, Page asserts that a 'diamond ring is chosen in most cases, but sometimes the girl will prefer a birth-stone'. All other manuals surveyed either do not state a preference or clearly state 'birthstone'. Page goes on to recommend that if 'the man's means are limited, he can arrange beforehand with the jeweller for a suitable selection of engagement rings to be produced when he and his fiancée enter the shop'.[66] Although, as Cele Otnes and Elizabeth Pleck argue, the diamond industry targeted advertising more directly at the 'love' market following the 'Great Depression', and diamond engagement rings featured in breach of promise cases across the period and across the social spectrum.[67] For example, the defendant stole the diamond ring belonging to 'cigarette girl' Violet Llewellyn in a 1924 case,[68] Sussex cricketer H. W. Parks bought his fiancée a diamond ring at Easter 1929,[69] and a 1937 case involved a 'wealthy leather merchant' who bought his fiancée a diamond ring.[70]

---

[65] Edgar and Diana Woods, *Planning your Wedding: A complete guide for all concerned and for all denominations* (London: Universal Publications, 1937), 14-15; Lady Troubridge advised a woman to 'consider her future husband's financial position', Troubridge, *Book of Etiquette*, 9.

[66] Page, *Complete Guide*, 18–19.

[67] Cele C. Otnes and Elizabeth H. Pleck, *Cinderella Dreams: The Allure of the Lavish Wedding* (Berkeley: University of California Press, 2003), 63.

[68] 'A Cigarette Girl's Broken Romance', *Daily Mirror*,14 October 1924, 16.

[69] 'County Cricketer Sued by Girl', *Daily Mirror*, 21 December 1932, 24.

[70] '"Cherie": I Shall Not Marry Now', *Daily Express*,2 March 1937, 9.

3 ENGAGEMENT   87

Newspaper coverage of breach of promise cases shows that the ring could be given conditionally and the wearing (or not) of the ring could be read in different ways. In a 1934 case, Spitalfields poulterer Nathan Cole made a counter-claim for the return of the ring, which he had given with conditions. Cole told the court 'I told her that I would buy a ring providing she promised to mind my stall, sell the poultry, look after the house, and be a second mother to the two girls'. The court decided that his ex-fiancée could keep the £95 ring.[71] Women could take control and defiantly wear the ring after the engagement had ended. In a 1939 case, Constance Potter was still wearing her engagement ring long after her fiancé had cancelled their engagement in 'order to show that I had something from him'.[72] The engagement ring could be the centre or signifier of conflict. The *Daily Mirror* reported on its front page that giving the ring back to the man 'in a huff' did not necessarily mean that the woman wanted 'the romance to end'.[73] One fiancée threw her engagement ring back at her fiancé during a 'quarrel',[74] while another was in possession of the ring even though in a 'tiff' she had once given it back to her fiancé.[75] Men defending breach of promise cases sometimes tried to claim that an 'engagement ring' was given as a birthday present.[76] In the 1949 case involving 'midget' Gertrude Peltz the court heard as evidence of her own lack of commitment to marriage that she 'went to a public dance and took her engagement ring off'.[77]

Given the importance of the engagement ring in both etiquette manuals and newspaper reporting of breach of promise cases, it is perhaps surprising that oral history interviewees seldom mention it. In the 1930s, Shropshire haulier, Richard Ridgeway bought his fiancée, Bubbles, an engagement ring, but only after she had accepted his marriage proposal. The ring was the first jewellery Richard had bought and he reminisced that the jeweller had allowed him to take five rings home to try.[78] Some

[71] 'Love over the telephone', *Daily Express*,20 March 1934, 7.

[72] 'In breach case, still wore ring', *Daily Mirror*, 6 December 1939, 9

[73] 'She gave it back in a huff', *Daily Mirror*, 17 December 1949, 1

[74] 'Jilted girl after buying £5 car', *Daily Mirror*, 10 March 1939, 5.

[75] 'Man prefers politics to marriage – so girl gets £25', *Daily Express*,20 June 1939, 8.

[76] 'Two cousins in breach case', *Daily Express*,8 March 1929, 7.

[77] '"Midget" girl says: Plot to stop wedding', 22 February 1949, 4.

[78] Interview with Richard Morgan Ridgeway.

88   N. PENLINGTON

men were later embarrassed by the modest ring they bought at the time of engagement. A retired Cumbrian bank manager, Harold Crowe's interview in the 1990s is full of references to banking and his own personal expenditure and investments. He felt that it was 'one of [his] terrible' regrets that he was 'poor' when he married his wife in the 1950s. He recounted that they were 'only friends' until he decided that she was the girl he wanted to marry when she turned twenty-one. He narrated the engagement story as hinging on a choice between buying her a twenty-first birthday present or an engagement ring. He felt that he had 'had' to buy the ring. He spent £27 but he reminisced from his wealthier retirement that 'it wasn't much of a ring, but she still prizes it'.[79]

The engagement ring was not always the only gift a man bought for his fiancée. An engaged man, foreshadowing his role as husband-provider, was expected to buy his fiancée gifts, but etiquette manuals drew a fine line between masculine generosity and unmanly profligacy, although there seemed to have been some change over time. In 1925, Eileen Terry explained that a man 'must be prepared to [give] presents, but again the lady should be easily content, and should not expect to find something in the unfortunate man's pocket every time he turns up'.[80] The woman's role here is to reign in the man's desires. A decade later, Rev. Exton also thought that gift giving from man to woman should be restrained during an engagement. He reminded the 'young man' that 'it is not permissible to give expensive gifts until very close to the wedding day' and that 'he must restrain his generous instincts, making a firm resolve to carry them out after the wedding'.[81] Here the man is placed very much into the position of provider. After the Second World War, etiquette advice changed. In 1950, Ann Page advised that when

> a man is saving up for the wedding, the girl should not allow him to spend money unnecessarily on presents, unless, of course, he is a man of means.... She should not allow him to buy her clothes... [or] anything that could be construed as "maintenance".... Flowers, confectionery and books are permissible.[82]

[79] C900/02589 interview with Harold Crowe, Millennium Memory Bank, BLSA.

[80] Terry, *Etiquette for All*, 124.

[81] Exton, *Wedding Etiquette*, 15–16.

[82] Page, *Complete Guide*, 19.

3 ENGAGEMENT   89

This perhaps reflects a change in attitudes and expectation as couples, and in this case the man, might pay for the wedding, rather than the bride's parents. The gender roles of male provider and female consumer are however reinforced and the woman is expected to exert some domestic control over finances.

Gendered materiality of romance and engagement extended to the 'bottom drawer', which was also taken as evidence of commitment in some breach of promise cases. The bottom drawer, or trousseau, was the collection of items such as linen, crockery and cutlery that a woman was assumed to need when she became a (house)wife. It was variously compiled by the woman herself or given as gifts, sometimes by her fiancé. In a class-biased intervention, etiquette advisor Eileen Terry stated that 'modern girls believe in quality and not quantity, when buying the trousseau'.[83] This gendered materiality of engagement and romance could also be used as evidence of a promise to marry in a breach of promise case. In a 1924 case, gardener Frederick Samuel Ball gave domestic servant Winifred Mary White 'a number of presents' for her 'bottom drawer'. This was taken as proof of engagement and White received damages. However, this case highlights a class and gender dimension to gift giving and the understanding of wedding preparations. The judge, Mr Justice Avery, did not understand the meaning of 'bottom drawer' and to 'laughter' in the courtroom asked for explanation. The plaintiff's counsel explained that 'he understood it was a symbolic term for the receptacle where people put things which would be useful after marriage'.[84] However, in another case five years later, the precise timing of commencing a 'bottom drawer' pointed in a different direction. When Wilhelmina Trebesiner of Hendon lost her breach of promise action against Adolph William Hart of Golder's Green, the jury decided that the central piece of evidence was a 'tea set' that had been given for her twenty-first birthday and was not necessarily a sign of engagement. The jury agreed with a witness who pointed out that a 'girl starts a bottom drawer long before her marriage'.[85] In this example, a 'girl' was expected

[83] Terry, *Etiquette for All*, 126.

[84] 'Judge's ignorance', *Daily Mirror*, 13 December 1924, 2; 'The bottom drawer', *Daily Express*, 13 December 1924, 2.

[85] 'Breach action fails', *Daily Mirror*, 22 June 1929, 4.

to prepare for marriage long before she met someone. Women therefore had far more invested in marriage than men.

On the cancellation of an engagement, pre-Second World War etiquette manuals were unanimous that all gifts should be returned.[86] The engagement ring was sometimes singled out for special consideration. This was probably due to both its relatively high financial value and its unique symbolic value. Etiquette manual authors were also against breach of promise, citing social-class reasons for avoiding such action. Terry claimed in 1925 that '[c]ases have been argued in the law courts upon the question of whether such a ring, and the subsequent presents, belong to the girl herself until she has ratified the implied legal contract by consummating the marriage'.[87] This reinforces the notion that a marriage is a financially unequal contract that is sealed only at the point of post-wedding penile-vaginal intercourse.[88] Terry however steered clear of legal arguments and stated that 'it is obvious that any decent-minded girl would return all presents, should the engagement be broken off'.[89] The term 'decent-minded' is clearly an allusion to social class. This advice had not changed in the 1930s. 'Best Man' declared that '[e]tiquette decides that all presents and letter should be returned immediately, although legally, only the engagement ring can be demanded'. Foreclosing any consideration of breach of promise action, the same author warned that '[o]nly an ill-bred person would take the course of writing to demand their return'.[90] As with 'decent-minded' above, 'ill-bred' is an allusion to social class. Post-war etiquette manuals did not mention the returning of gifts at all. There was therefore no consideration in later manuals of breach of promise and its potential impact.

There was a material element to engagement and men wrote many love letters and gave engagement rings as a sign of commitment to marry. The ring was more than a piece of jewellery and could be a contested symbol. Men could give the ring with conditions, but women could

---

[86] For example, Devereux, *Etiquette for Women*, 88–9; Devereux, *Etiquette for Men*, 74; Troubridge, *Book of Etiquette*, 15; Woodman, *Wedding Etiquette*, 35; Exton, *Wedding Etiquette*, 13.

[87] Terry was possibly referring to *Jacobs v Davis* (1917) in which the fiancée was ordered to return the ring.

[88] See Chapter 5, 'Non-Consummation'.

[89] Terry, *Etiquette for All*, 124.

[90] "Best Man", *Marriage Etiquette*, 15–16.

subvert the meaning of the ring and wear it defiantly. Prefiguring the role of husband-provider, engaged men gave other gifts, but subject to constraint before being actually married. The 'bottom drawer' suggests that men and women had a different relationship with the institution of marriage: marriage was an important element of masculinity, but women were to look forward to their wedding day from a young age.

PRESSURES

Although words, intimacy and things made an engagement, couples were part of larger, omnipresent family networks and these negotiated relationships affected the engagement according to a social-class-influenced gender asymmetry. Etiquette manuals gave extensive coverage to, and oral history interviewees placed importance on, the position of the woman's father in the process of getting engaged. In stark contrast, of the four parents, the man's father has the least presence in the sources surveyed. Although the woman had agency and could say 'no' to the marriage proposal, she was to an extent caught in a triangle of power with two men, as the father handed (symbolic, and in many cases economic) authority to the prospective husband. The man however had to seek an 'interview' with his prospective father-in-law and this shows gender asymmetry in both generations. It was to be a 'mere formality',[91] but was a site of masculine conflict between two men of different generations.

Throughout the period etiquette manuals stated that the man did not have to seek permission from the woman's father *before* proposing to her. He was however to speak to her father, man to man, as soon as possible after a successful marriage proposal.[92] Etiquette manual authors were obviously aware that this advice was *new*, since they either advised it tentatively or clearly made a comparison with an earlier period. For example, Eileen Terry pointed out that was 'no longer essential for a man to consult a girl's parents before he proposes to her'.[93] Edgar and Diana Woods stated that the 'old days are gone when the anxious swain was told by the lass to ask her father in reply to his question about being engaged'.[94]

---

[91] For example, "Best Man", *Marriage Etiquette*, 13.

[92] Woodman, *Wedding Etiquette*, 26.

[93] Terry, *Etiquette for All*, 123.

[94] Woods, *Planning your Wedding*, 8.

In 1919, G. R. M. Devereux suggested that it was 'still a moot point whether, when a man wishes to ask a girl to be his wife, he should speak first to her or to her father'. This was dependent upon social class since if the woman was 'a very wealthy young lady, or of somewhat higher social position, a man is duty bound to ask first [her] parents and guardians' permission'. At the very least, a man having secured the 'consent' of his fiancée should demonstrate the honour to 'face' her father 'and go through what is often a trying interview'. This placed the woman's future in the hands of men who were reasoned and unemotional enough to take responsible decisions since men 'do not gush at each other at any time, and a man naturally feels the risk and responsibility of trusting his child's whole future well-being in the hands of a comparative stranger'.[95] Terry went further and cautioned that 'a man should remember that a marriage is not only binding for life, but affects the lives of countless generations to follow'.[96] This constructed marriage as primarily procreative. The woman's father therefore performs a masculinity dependent upon marriage, head of household and paternity. He is also teaching this to the younger man, who could shortly be his daughter's husband and father to his grandchildren. By the third edition of Devereux's *Etiquette for Men*, published in 1937, the advice given was that the man was no longer 'called upon to "interview" the girl's father' but that it would be 'a compliment to him'.[97] Whether a compliment or formality, when approaching his prospective father-in-law, a man 'should mention in a manly way and not a gushing manner how a strong affection has sprung up'.[98] To become engaged, a man therefore had to control his emotions when facing another, perhaps more powerful man, and demonstrate a constrained manliness worthy of marrying the other man's daughter.

By the 1950s, etiquette manuals made comparison with previous eras but gender asymmetry still coloured their advice. In 1950, Ann Page made the comparison with 'Victorian days' and stated that, 'Nowadays many young couples announce their engagement without consulting their parents in any way'. Page however undermined this by advising that once 'the girl accepts, the man then approaches her father and asks his consent'.

---

[95] Devereux, *Etiquette for Women*, 85.

[96] Terry, *Etiquette for All*, 123.

[97] Devereux, *Etiquette for Men*, 72.

[98] Woods, *Planning your Wedding*, 9.

The pre-war language of the paternal 'interview' was still evident as Page suggested that 'a personal interview is best'. The advice was still gendered in that if 'the girl's father is dead, the man asks the consent of the girl's mother'.[99] In 1955, John and Mary Bolton claimed to be writing their etiquette manual in 'the present more free-and-easy times' and pointed out that

> it is no longer customary when the girl is over age for the man to approach her father for permission to marry his daughter, but it is only good manners and politic to see her father and mother or both before any formal announcement is made.[100]

This was still gender unequal since it gives more power to the man as the woman was treated like a child. Moreover, the woman was not expected to approach *his* parents in the same way. There is still a trace from a previous era of transfer of property between men.

Oral history interviewees gave a range of responses on the subject of paternal permission to marry before and during the Second World War.[101] Some men found that approaching their prospective fathers-in-law straightforward, but others were refused permission to marry, but either way the woman's father was usually the most important family figure. In Shropshire, navy medic Richard Perks asked for and received permission from her father who joked that he 'wanted a swede, a bag of potatoes and a rabbit in exchange!'[102] In 1930, nursemaid Harriet Scott received a proposal from Co-op driver Harry then he asked her father, himself a haulier, for permission by simply stating 'we'd like to get married', to which her father instantly replied 'of course thee can'.[103] Some men were however less fortunate. When Robert, who had been badly injured at the Dardanelles, proposed to Lizzie Hartley in the 1920s, she suspected that 'he was frightened to ask'. This was possibly with good reason since her 'strict' father, a herbalist, had kicked her out for seeing

[99] Page, *Complete Guide*, 3, 10–11.

[100] Mary and John Bolton, *The Complete Book of Etiquette* (London: W. Foulsham, 1955), 7, 114.

[101] There was no mention of asking permission to marry among those in the sample who married in the 1950s.

[102] Interview with Richard Gordon Perks.

[103] Interview with Harriet Scott.

Robert and eventually had to be locked 'in the house' on the day of the wedding, since he threatened to stop it.[104] In Birmingham, Alfred Bell met his future wife shortly after joining the army in 1937, having left his Yorkshire mining community. She was just finishing school and he did not therefore propose until 1944 when she was nearly twenty-one. Her working-class father initially refused permission but other family members pointed out that after her birthday she would not need parental permission. He relented and they married on Easter Saturday 1944.[105] Some parents foreclosed the possibility of a man asking for permission to marry their daughter. The parents of factory worker Evelyn Macnamee encouraged her and her siblings to take her friends, 'boys and girls', home because they wanted to know whom their children 'were mixing with'.[106]

Some fathers refused permission to marry for business reasons. Music Hall dancer Victoria McGill was 'engaged twice' but 'never made it'. Her father prevented both marriages because he 'didn't want the act to break up'.[107] When Jack Fossett—known as Jacko the Clown—married Connie, at the age of thirty-eight, it was after over twenty years of a relationship that had waxed and waned. Although there were many marriages between circus families, her father thought their marriage would lead to Jacko leaving the circus and splitting up the clown act. Connie dutifully returned the engagement ring, but they eventually married in 1960.[108] These examples, perhaps unusual because they concern music hall and circus entertainers, demonstrate the power that some fathers had, especially if they were influential in a family-run business. This power was not however complete since parents could be disobeyed. Giving judgement in a widely reported breach of promise cases in the 1930s, Lord Justice Swift made 'some pointed comments on the marriage contract and on the freedom of the modern girl' and claimed that 'daughters these days do not always do what their parents tell them'. Here a prominent judge was implying that in the 1930s young women had too much freedom and that this was problematic for the gender and generational order.[109]

---

[104] Interview with Lizzie Hartley.

[105] C900/18590 interview with Alfred Bell, Millennium Memory Bank, BLSA.

[106] Interview with Evelyn Macnamee.

[107] C486/19/01 interview with Victoria McGill, Vicinus Music Hall interviews, BLSA.

[108] Interview with Jack Fossett (Jacko the Clown).

[109] 'Verdict for Circus Owner', *Daily Mirror*, 15 June 1934, 14.

Oral history interviews also reveal that maternal influence was exerted, and sometimes resisted.[110] In 1930, when Harriet Scott became engaged her mother was delighted because Harry was the 'son [her] mother had never had'.[111] This gendered response shows that her mother greatly prized a male child. When Londoner Peggy Bowhay became engaged in the late 1940s, her mother did not approve of her fiancé because he was six months younger than her daughter was and therefore 'irresponsible'. Reminiscing fifty years later, Peggy felt that her mother 'probably wouldn't have approved of anyone'.[112] In contrast to Harriet Scott's mother gaining a son(-in-law), this mother could not bear to *lose* her child.

Breach of promise cases show that the influence of the woman's mother could also be felt by the male fiancé and could be a test of masculinity. This chapter opened with the 1929 breach of promise case against Arthur Crouch. Contesting generational and gender power relations, his prospective mother-in-law 'caned' him, possibly with a 'horsewhip'. The humiliating and emasculating experience of being physically beaten by an older woman would have been felt more keenly when the case went public through newspaper reports.[113] In 1960, Anthony Hall told his fiancée of three years, 'You'll have to choose between your mother and me'. He found his prospective mother-in-law, who had lent him £1,000 to buy a house, to have 'a generally intolerant and domineering attitude' and she forbade him to drink and threatened to live with the newly-weds and 'sit' with them 'in the evening'.[114] Hall, a university graduate earning 'a very substantial income' was ordered to pay £1,564 in damages because his fiancée, also aged 33, had lost 'the most important years of her young life' because he was 'not prepared to live under the same roof' as her mother.[115] Although this emasculated man lost his case and had to pay substantial damages, the judge and the newspapers did not treat him disrespectfully.

[110] For example, C900/16407 interview with Earnest and Phyllis Smart, Millennium Memory Bank, BLSA.

[111] Interview with Harriet Scott.

[112] C900/03542 interview with Peggy Bowhay, Millennium Memory Bank, BLSA.

[113] 'Mother's cane', *Daily Mirror*, 11 October 1929, 2.

[114] '"Your mother or me" he told her', *Daily Mirror*, 30 March 1960, 9.

[115] '£1,564 for a woman he jilted', *Daily Mirror*, 31 March 1960, 7.

The man's parents were also important in the process of becoming engaged. Etiquette manuals advised that once permission had been granted by the fiancée's father, she should be formally introduced to her new mother and father-in-law, but first-person testimonies show that many couples were already enmeshed in family and neighbourhood networks. For example, Rev. Exton suggested that 'the young man's family should, without delay, write or call on his fiancée and give her a welcome to their family circle'.[116] Devereux suggested that the man's parents 'should invite [her] to stay for a week or two'.[117] This obviously assumed that his parents had a home large enough to accommodate a houseguest and also that the woman was not lacking in leisure time. More importantly, this was a largely social-class-based assumption that the families did not already know each other. Many working-class and lower-middle-class oral history interviewees stressed that the two families were already close. They could be neighbours[118] or friends of an aunt,[119] or there was already a marriage[120] or close friendship[121] between the two families, or the families had known each other for many years[122] because they 'lived around the corner'.[123]

Breach of promise cases reveal that the man's father could exert pressure on his son to prevent an unfavourable marriage. In 1919, nurse Ethel Hey was awarded £600 for breach of promise against Richard Fawcett, a wool merchant and son of an ex-Lord Mayor of Bradford. The court heard that Fawcett had broken off the engagement previously and had written to his fiancée explaining 'there was trouble in his family over the engagement'. After pleading with her to 'take him back', he sent her for 'lessons in elocution in order to fit her for the position she would hold as

---

[116] Exton, *Wedding Etiquette*, 10; For similar advice see, "Best Man", *Marriage Etiquette*, 14.

[117] Devereux, *Etiquette for Women*, 87; Devereux reiterated the advice in a later edition of *Etiquette for Men*, that man's mother should 'invite the girl to stay with her for a convenient period', Devereux, *Etiquette for Men*, 73.

[118] Interview with Earnest and Phyllis Smart.

[119] C900/05101 interview with John Davis, Millennium Memory Bank, BLSA.

[120] Interview with Ellen Parry.

[121] Interview with Harriet Scott.

[122] Interview with Mary Potts.

[123] C872/25 interview with Gerry Davies, Book Trade Lives, BLSA.

his wife'. After spending £100 on Hey's education, he married 'another lady'.[124] Also in 1919, Fanny Whitard, a costumer from Clapham Junction, sued Hubert Renison, a bank clerk from Cheshire. His father did not want him to marry Whitard since 'he did not like her because she was a Londoner'. Instead, Renison's father wished him to marry 'the daughter of one of his [business] partners'. For his part, Renison told the court that 'he was twenty-four, and not yet old enough to know whether he was genuinely in love with the girl' and described his feelings towards her as merely 'a case of fascination'.[125]

The family member that undermined a man's masculinity more than any other relation was his mother.[126] Etiquette manual author Devereux warned that the man's mother may feel a 'little dethroned'.[127] Here the parent/child relationship is gendered suggesting that a mother is naturally closer to her children than the father, and that gender roles in the family were such that the mother's role would change considerably once her children left home. Newspapers presented men in breach of promise cases as being less than manly if they were 'influenced' by their mothers. Victor Jackson called off his wedding to a fellow musician even though his fiancée had made all of the wedding arrangements and had moved from London to Northampton to start married life. The *Daily Express* reported that this was 'influenced' by his mother, who had 'refused to allow him to be married', although he claimed that the reason was because he could not afford to marry. This suggested that for some men being under the 'influence' of a strong mother was more embarrassing than financial hardship.[128] In 1949, secondary schoolmaster, Enoch Cyril Frow felt pressed into marriage by his mother who 'had threatened to cut him

[124] 'Madly in love', *Daily Mirror*, 6 May 1919, 2.

[125] 'Special reports from the courts', *Daily Express*,17 October 1919, 9.

[126] For example, 'He got engaged out of love for me, says mother', *Daily Mirror*, 23 February 1949,1; 'Mother: We were wrong to press for engagement', *Daily Express*, 23 February 1949, 5; 'The Maid returns to Athens', *Daily Mirror*, 21 March 1949, 1; 'Jilted, gets £1,100', *Daily Mirror*, 4 May 1954, 3.

[127] Devereux, *Etiquette for Women*, 87; Devereux reiterated the advice in a later edition of *Etiquette for Men*, that man's mother should 'invite the girl to stay with her for a convenient period', Devereux, *Etiquette for Men*, 73.

[128] 'Wedding that did not take place', *Daily Express*,19 May 1934, 7.

out of her will unless he married a schoolteacher'.[129] Frow's humiliation was compounded as the judge contrasted him, a schoolmaster, with a 'schoolboy' who was 'expected to give a straight answer' in the classroom.[130] Although the case was dismissed, the judge found that Frow was 'evasive and exhibited no sort of moral courage' and was 'lacking in straightforwardness'.[131] This man was judged to have been lacking in the essential characteristics of masculinity and was therefore compared to a 'schoolboy'.

Oral history interviewees also told that the man's mother was overly possessive or too influential. Ian Kiek from a book-selling family in Purley was born in 1916 and remembered that his mother cried at the sight of his fiancée wearing an engagement ring. Ian recalled that his mother was protective of her three sons and that any 'lady' who visited the house 'wasn't good enough'. He thought this mother and son relationship was 'usual'.[132] Liverpudlian Mary Moore, known as Betty, never married but her reminiscences of the times when she 'only got so far' shed light on perceptions of masculinity. She was 'in love with one chap, John', who 'was [a] macho man, but he was very much under his mother's thumb'. Mary did not want to marry John because he thought the 'man should be the boss' and also because she saw how his father[133] treated his wife and daughter. John's sister 'never went out' and spent her time 'cleaning'.[134] This demonstrates that it was possible for a woman to resist an unpalatable masculinity by refusing to marry. This was however an isolated case in the oral history sample. It is also important to note that the 'macho man' in this case did get married to someone else five years later.

Grown-up children could try to intervene to prevent an engagement from turning into a marriage, thus leading to a breach of promise case. The married sons of poulterer Nathan Cole, aged fifty-one, did not want their father to marry a 'young girl' of twenty-eight. As well as the poultry business, Cole also owned 'various' properties.[135] The family of 'Jewish'

---

[129] 'Breach suit story: "He feared to lose legacy"', *Daily Mirror*, 25 October 1945, 3

[130] 'When a boy is asked about homework', *Daily Mirror*, 26 October, 1945, 3.

[131] 'Breach suit fails: Judge criticises man', *Daily Mirror*, 27 October 1945, 5

[132] C872/37 interview with Ian Kiek, NLSC: Book Trade Lives, BLSA.

[133] This is the only time the man's father is mentioned in the oral history sample.

[134] C900/08050 interview with Mary Moore, Millennium Memory Bank, BLSA.

[135] '"No sentiment" breach suit', *Daily Mirror*, 20 March 1934, 9.

Anthony Davis Shattock 'strongly objected' to his proposed marriage to 'Gentile' Henrietta Jacobs. Although, 'he was determined to go through with it' the pressure was too much to bear and Shattock cancelled the wedding by telegram on the day of the ceremony. Jacobs was shown the telegram as she arrived at the register office.[136]

Some men had to ask their employer, or senior officer, for permission to marry.[137] This had the potential to curtail a young man's masculine independence, but also allowed the senior man to exert authority—a type of paternal responsibility—based on age, education, rank or social class. Margaret Latimer recounted in an oral history interview that in the 1920s her parents had difficulty getting married in Northamptonshire. Her father was a policeman and his superior officer initially refused permission to marry because there 'weren't any available married quarters'. Only when suitable accommodation had been found did the senior officer grant permission.[138] In 1953, bank employee Anthony Akers had to ask his employer for permission to marry. He knew of one male colleague who had married without permission and had been denied a mortgage.[139] Men in National Service had to ask their senior office for permission to marry. In 1955, Harold Marshall wrote to his 'commanding officer' and received permission to marry.[140] Newspaper reports of breach of promise cases sometimes featured men who had to seek permission to marry from a senior officer. Corporal David McComish did not receive permission to marry from his superior naval officer, Lieutenant-Colonel Leslie Morris. Plaintiff Gloria Franklin tried to sue both her fiancé for breach of promise and the colonel 'for damages, alleging that he persuaded the corporal to change his mind'. For his part the colonel stated that on hearing that 'the girl was expecting a baby', he '"assumed the position of father" to the corporal in giving him advice'.[141] Social class and authority of a senior officer could combine to prevent men from defending breach of promise

---

[136] 'Jilted widow on wedding day', *Daily Mirror*, 26 April 1939, 25; '"Not to Wed" he wired', Daily Express, 25 April 1939, 4.

[137] For example, '£300 for breach', *Daily Express*, 20 July 1955, 9.

[138] C900/12092 interview with Margaret Latimer, Millennium Memory Bank, BLSA.

[139] C1367/14 interview with Anthony Akers, An Oral History of Baring's Bank, BLSA.

[140] C900/19547 C1 interview with Harold Marshall, Millennium Memory Bank, BLSA.

[141] 'A Shotgun Wedding', *Daily Mirror*, 21 February, 1956, 5.

cases. In 1949, army officer Major Sidney Chittenden appeared before a bankruptcy hearing and blamed his financial position on the damages and costs he had had to pay in a breach of promise suit, but was promptly told that it was not becoming for a Major to defend a breach of promise case. The Official Receiver told him, 'I don't want to use the word "chivalry," but it just is not done, is it?'[142] After the 'emotional watershed' of the Second World War,[143] perhaps some of the codes of masculine honour remained, but they were no longer called 'chivalry'.

Before chivalry had become old fashioned, newspapers could be scornful when they considered a man to have behaved in a less than manly way to his fiancée in a breach of promise case: they subjected him to trial by tabloid to add to his trial by jury. A man who cancelled a wedding by telegram shortly before it was about to take place was branded 'fickle' by the *Daily Mirror*.[144] The newspaper also chose the word 'fickle' to describe a man who cancelled his wedding on the day itself by sending a message to the best man, and he was cast a the cad or fairytale baddie. The vicar had to tell a church 'filled with guests and the public... the wedding would not take place'. The groom left the mining village of Chopwell and 'remain[ed] hidden for several days'.[145] Twenty-three-year-old invoice clerk Richard Baldock of Streatham was called 'blackguardly and hopelessly cruel'[146] for cancelling a wedding an hour before with a telegram that read 'Wedding cancelled'. The couple had known each other for three years before a year-long engagement. He had 'kissed his fiancée good night, and said he would see her the next day' but ruined 'the happiest day of this young woman's life'.[147] Although the reporting of breach of promise cases continued, this scornful reprimanding in the newspapers of men who had failed to live up to codes of chivalrous, masculine honour did not continue after the mid-1930s. This perhaps suggests that the remainder of this period can be seen as one of increasing romance and marrying for love, and that perhaps a man could now change his mind.

[142] '"Not done" for a Major to defend a breach case', *Daily Mirror*, 13 April 1949, 7

[143] Langhamer, *English in Love*, 9.

[144] 'Cupid's telegram rates', *Daily Mirror*, 24 April 1919, 13.

[145] 'It's all over', *Daily Mirror*, 20 December 1919, 2.

[146] Also cited in Langhamer, *English in Love*, 163.

[147] '"Breach" – by telegram', *Daily Express*, 7 December 1934, 11.

3 ENGAGEMENT **101**

A man was under pressure to keep a promise of marriage, and this pressure diminished culturally (if not legally) over time. Across the period men felt pressure from others as they sought to become married. Men had to ask the woman's father for permission to marry, and although etiquette manuals started to downplay this, the oral history sample shows that men typically did it. Women were caught in a triangle between her fiancé and her father, who had more power to decline if in an economically powerful position. This also applied to the influence the man's father had over his son. Men were assumed to be close to their mothers but had to be manly enough not to be too close, and they also had to hold respectfully their ground against a prospective mother-in-law. A man had to prove himself in the eyes of his prospective father-in-law, but some men had to seek permission to marry from an employer or senior officer.

Conclusion

By examining codes of engagement, this chapter has shown some of the changes, continuities and contradictions in masculinity between 1918 and 1960. Engagement to marry was technically a legally binding contract throughout the period, although there was a further and tentative shift towards a social and cultural view that engagement and marriage were primarily about 'modern constructs of true love and passion'.[148]

Different sources reveal different elements of engaged masculinity. Newspaper reports of breach of promise cases have shown some of the expected masculine behaviours of engaged men. The highly prescriptive etiquette manuals show some of the social-class-based expectations of commitment and manliness, while oral history testimonies reveal some of the variety of experiences of engagement. Engaged men were subject to an array of discourses, and social and familial pressures that shaped their experiences and expectations as men, and the way in which they performed masculine honour, feelings and intimacy.

Examination of the process of getting engaged—the proposal, asking paternal permission, love-letter writing, intimacy and gift giving—has

---

[148] Pamela Haag argues that this took place in the American context in the early twentieth century and that breach of promise laws were repealed in most states in 1931. This was almost forty years before the same changes were made to English Law. Pamela Haag, *Consent: Sexual Rights and the Transformation of American Liberalism* (London: Cornell University Press, 1999), 141.

shown some of the pressures on engaged men. By starting at the point of the marriage proposal, the focus is perhaps more on familial pressures than peer pressure. The latter may have been more evident by starting the narrative before the courtship to show how the couple met. This analysis has also not revealed the time engaged couples spent together or the time men spend fraternising with other men during engagement. A focus on courtship would have revealed the former; an assessment of workplace and leisure culture and would have shown the latter.[149]

Across the period and across social classes, men were expected to propose and seek permission from the woman's father, and each of these encounters was highly gendered. Men were to take the initiative and propose marriage. Although oral history testimonies show that the theatrical set piece proposal found in etiquette manuals did not always happen, the expectation that the man should be 'man enough' to propose was cross class. Another cross-class expectation was that the man should approach the woman's father—man to man—and ask his permission to marry his daughter. This sustained gender inequality by giving the men (father and prospective husband) more power than the women (mother and prospective wife). The man had the power and status to stand in his own right, whereas the woman was in the position of a child. Parents, especially fathers, could prevent a marriage from taking place especially if he was influential in a family business or held public office. Although, the woman's father did not have any legal power of granting or denying permission if his daughter was over twenty-one, he still had social, cultural and economic power. In the encounter between the two men of different generations, the older man had the opportunity to set a masculinity example to his prospective son-in-law. A similar encounter could also take place in another setting as some men had to ask an employer or senior officer for permission to marry.

---

[149] For example, Brad Beaven, *Leisure, Citizenship And Working-Class Men in Britain, 1850-1945* (Manchester: Manchester University Press, 2005), 171, 197; Andrew Davies, *Leisure, Gender and Poverty: Working-class culture in Salford and Manchester, 1900-1939* (Buckingham: Open University Press, 1992), 111; Juliet Gardiner, *The Thirties: An intimate history* (London: Harper Collins, 2010), 550; Adrian Horn, *Juke Box Britain: Americanisation and youth culture, 1945-60* (Manchester: Manchester University Press, 2009), 176; Claire Langhamer, *Women's Leisure in England, 1920-60* (Manchester: Manchester University Press, 2000), 113; Martin Pugh, *'We danced all night': A social history of Britain between the wars* (London: Vintage, 2008), 231.

Some gendered behaviours and expectations did not change over time. In those engagements that did not start with an explicit marriage proposal, other behaviour implied an 'inferred engagement'. Breach of promise newspaper reports shows that chief among the expected behaviours between prospective spouses was the writing of love letters. Despite the often unromantic oral history reminiscences, it was therefore normal for men across the period to express their feelings by writing romantic love letters. The gendered buying, giving and wearing of the ring constructed masculinity as providing and romantic without being too knowledgeable about the feminine world of weddings and consumerism. Femininity on the other hand was centred on consumption, rather than production, and women were expected to want to get married since they were girls. This life-long preparation could be seen in the bottom drawer. Some women were materially prepared for marriage long before meeting a man. Gift giving, sometimes towards the bottom drawer, reinforced the male breadwinner, female homemaker binary that the couple was expected to perform after the wedding ceremony. The sexual double standard was continuous during this period. Some wealthy men were able to claim, in some cases without shame, that a 'fiancée' was actually a 'mistress', whereas women were only allowed intimacy with the man to whom she was engaged, if at all.

There were some changes during this period, especially in newspaper reporting of breach of promise. Sexual intimacy in breach of promise cases was increasingly reported from the mid-1930s. Sex was gendered and presented as something that a woman gave to the men in return for commitment, something men could feign through manipulation or mendacity. The timing of sexual intimacy was crucial in a breach of promise case: if a woman did not *give* sex until after the engagement commenced, she had a stronger case. In the 1930s, the popular press ceased calling men 'fickle' for not honouring their promises to marry. This could have been an acknowledgement that men should be able to change their minds and that love was more important than honour. By the post-war period, etiquette manuals were less concerned with telling men to constrain their emotions.

We have seen some of the tensions and contradictions in masculinity during this period. Men wrote romantic letters during this period, in spite of warnings in the media to the contrary. However, proposals often came as a surprise to the woman, perhaps through misunderstandings or because the man had not adequately expressed his intentions before.

There were further tensions for a man within his social and kinship network. He was expected to be close to and respectful of his mother, but not be under her 'influence', and he also had to stand up to his prospective mother-in-law. He was supposed to take the initiative in the engagement, to be able to stand up for himself and represent himself independently of his parents, but he was subject to the will of the woman's father and sometimes of his employer. At a time when some young men were increasingly expressing themselves through a nascent youth culture, they were subject to negotiation with an older generation of men for the right to marry at a time when marriage was increasingly popular. Although working-class families were more likely to know each other, examples of parents expressing dislike of a prospective son or daughter-in-law can be found in any social class.

There was a wide variety of engagements, shown through a close reading of some narrow source bases. Men were subject to different engagement experiences according to social class, location and family or employment circumstances. Greater social mixing between men and women[150] did not go hand in hand with improved communication between the sexes, or specifically between prospective spouses. Men were caught between a need to show masculine independence and a web of social and familial ties. In the 'golden age of marriage', there were more gender continuities with the Victorian and Edwardian periods than changes for the engaged man. Although a woman legally had more freedom, tropes from an earlier economic and legal system influenced ritual and tradition to place her between her father and husband.

References

An Oral History of Baring's Bank, British Library Sound Archive Bates, Denise. 2014. *Breach of promise to marry: A history of how jilted brides settled scores.* Barnsley: Pen and Sword.

Beaven, Brad. 2005. *Leisure, citizenship and working-class men in Britain, 1850–1945.* Manchester: Manchester University Press.

"Best Man". 1936. Revised 1949. *Marriage etiquette: How to arrange a wedding.* London: W. Foulsham.

---

[150] See, for example, Matt Houlbrook, *Queer London: Perils and Pleasures in the Sexual Metropolis* (London: University of Chicago Press, 2005), 191.

3 ENGAGEMENT   105

Bolton, Mary, and John Bolton. 1955. *The complete book of etiquette*. London: W. Foulsham.

Book Trade Lives, British Library Sound Archive Bourke, Joanna. 2016. Love and limblessness: Male heterosexuality, disability, and the Great War. *Journal of War and Culture Studies* 9(1):3–19. *Daily Express. Daily Mirror*

Davies, Andrew. 1992. *Leisure, gender and poverty: Working-class culture in Salford and Manchester, 1900–1939*. Buckingham: Open University Press.

Devereux, G. R. M. 1919. *Etiquette for women: A book of modern modes and manners*. London: C. Arthur Pearson.

Devereux, G. R. M. 1937. First published 1902. *Etiquette for men: A book of modern manners and customs*. London: C. Arthur Pearson.

Dixon, Jay. 2016. *The romantic fiction of Mills and Boon, 1909–1995*. Abingdon: Routledge.

Exton, Rev, and D. 1935. *Wedding etiquette*. London: Universal Publications.

Farrimond, Sarah. 2009. Ritual and narrative in the contemporary Anglican wedding. Unpublished PhD thesis:

Frost, Ginger S. 1995. *Promises broken: Courtship, class, and gender in Victorian England*. Charlottesville: University Press of Virginia.

Gardiner, Juliet. 2010. *The thirties: An intimate history*. London: Harper Collins.

Haag, Pamela. 1999. *Consent: Sexual rights and the transformation of American liberalism*. London: Cornell University Press.

Horn, Adrian. 2009. *Juke box Britain: Americanisation and youth culture, 1945–60*. Manchester: Manchester University Press.

Houlbrook, Matt. 2005. *Queer London: Perils and pleasures in the sexual metropolis*. London: University of Chicago Press.

Langhamer, Claire. 2000. *Women's leisure in England, 1920–60*. Manchester: Manchester University Press.

Langhamer, Claire. 2013. *The English in love: The intimate story of an emotional revolution*. Oxford: Oxford University Press.

Lettmaier, Saskia. 2010. *Broken engagements: The action for breach of promise of marriage and the feminine ideal, 1800–1940*. Oxford: Oxford University Press.

Millennium Memory Bank, British Library Sound Archive National Life Stories Collection: Food: From source to Salespoint, British Library Sound Archive Oral History of the Circus, British Library Sound Archive.

Otnes, Cele C., and Elizabeth H. Pleck. 2003. *Cinderella dreams: The allure of the lavish wedding*. Berkeley: University of California Press.

Page, Ann. 1950. *The complete guide to wedding etiquette*. London: Ward, Lock and Co.

Pugh, Martin. 2008. *'We danced all night': A social history of Britain between the wars*. London: Vintage.

106   N. PENLINGTON

Terry, Eileen. 1925. *Etiquette for all: Man, woman, or child*. London: W. Foulsham.

Troubridge, Lady [Laura]. 1931. First published 1926. *The book of etiquette*. London: Associated Bookbuyers' Company. Vicinus Music Hall interviews, British Library Sound Archive.

White, Hayden. 1973. *Metahistory: The historical imagination in nineteenth-century Europe*. Baltimore: John Hopkins University Press.

Woodman, Mary. 1929. *Wedding etiquette*. London: W. Foulsham.

Woods, Edgar, and Diana Woods. 1937. *Planning your wedding: A complete guide for all concerned and for all denominations*. London: Universal Publications.

CHAPTER 4

The Wedding

'The world, in truth, is a wedding'—Erving Goffman (1959)[1]

Between 1918 and 1960, the typical wedding became more elaborate and extravagant. This period saw a shift from the majority of marriage ceremonies being small with the bride and groom wearing practical dress, to the spectacular 'white wedding' that became the aspirational norm by the 1950s. As sociologist Erving Goffman argued, the 'performance of routine' can 'incorporate and exemplify' the 'values of a society'.[2] This chapter examines masculinity during the rise in popularity of the 'white wedding'—a ceremony most young men went through— by looking at wedding etiquette manuals, newspapers and oral history testimonies to show the stories men (and women) constructed about weddings and marriage. The highly ritualised wedding ceremony and reception, which went beyond the utterances and actions legally and religiously required, performed and institutionalised normative masculinity, an identity inflected by class, race and Englishness.

---

[1] Erving Goffman, *The presentation of the self in everyday life* (London: Penguin, 1990. First published 1959), 45.

[2] Ibid., 44–5.

© The Author(s), under exclusive license to Springer Nature   107
Switzerland AG 2023
N. Penlington, *Men Getting Married in England, 1918–60*, Genders and Sexualities in History, https://doi.org/10.1007/978-3-031-27405-3_4

During this period, the 'white wedding'—a type of commercialised marriage ceremony that is now familiar to us[3]—became the 'proper'[4] wedding and included a white wedding dress and veil, a large and elaborate church ceremony with processions, bridesmaids and pageboys, and a reception with a seating plan, speeches and the ceremonial cutting of a white cake. The white wedding was, and is, a combination of old and new; an 'invented tradition' with a feeling of timelessness.[5] For most people, weddings before the Great War were usually small, without the ritual and theatricality of the 'white wedding'. As social historian John Gillis has shown, the nineteenth century was 'relatively barren of ritual activity' with urban working-class wedding ceremonies starting to show signs of becoming increasingly symbolical towards the end of that century. As the wedding ceremony underwent a 'reritualisation'[6] by the mid-twentieth century, it was usually followed by a reception, which in turn became more extensive and ritualised. In both the ceremony and the reception, the new husband and wife were learning and displaying gendered expectations of married life. The wedding also reproduced acceptable sexuality by delineating those who were married from those who were not and by drawing a distinction between male and female, masculinity and femininity. The gendered roles of the other important actors on the wedding day—the bride's father, the best man and bridesmaids—reinforced the institution of marriage. As literature scholar Elizabeth Freeman argues in the American context, the 'wedding purports to emplot bodies into linear time … the flower girls will grow up to be brides'.[7] Weddings present this generational iteration as natural and unquestionable. The unmarried were drawn into the ritual in such a way that created the expectation of marriage. In the theatricality of the 'white wedding', as Eve Sedgwick and Andrew Parker argued the 'I' becomes a 'we'—a sanctioned cross-gender

---

[3] Claire Langhamer, 'Afterword' in *Love and romance in Britain, 1918–1970* ed. Alana Harris and Timothy Willem Jones (Basingstoke: Palgrave, 2015), 246.

[4] Elizabeth Freeman, *The Wedding complex: Forms of belonging in modern American culture* (London: Duke University Press, 2002), 12.

[5] Eric Hobsbawm, 'Introduction: Inventing traditions' in *The invention of tradition* ed. Eric Hobsbawm and Terrance Ranger (Cambridge: Cambridge University Press, 1983), 1.

[6] John Gillis, *For better, for worse: British marriage, 1600 to the present* (Oxford, 1988), 260.

[7] Freeman, *Wedding complex*, 34.

dyad—constituted before a 'they' of silent witnesses.[8] This 'third person', the wedding guest (s), was not just a passive spectator. Their presence condoned marriage, constrained the wedding choreography through their expectations of an ideal wedding ceremony, and helped to circulate the notion of the ideal wedding (and marriage) long after the wedding day. The roles of the main wedding actors and the changing and expanding guest list will be considered to show how marriage was at the heart of masculinity, male homosocial interaction, and social and economic relations.

The discursive reach of the wedding extends far beyond the day itself. As sociologist Chrys Ingraham shows, 'weddings have served as a symbolic rite of passage for heterosexual men and women entering marriage' and therefore a gendered study of weddings demonstrates 'how heterosexuality is "institutionalised"'. This 'institutionalised heterosexuality constitutes the standard for legitimate and expected social and sexual relations'.[9] In the British context, sociologist Diana Leonard pointed out in her groundbreaking work that 'white weddings… make important statements about, among other things, the nature of marriage and family relations'. Between the First World War and the 1960s, the marriage rate increased and the age of (first) marriage decreased. Leonard argued that the usual explanation that this was because of higher incomes was too simplistic. Instead, Leonard analysed the 'social pressure to marry' in the post-war era, which included 'to become independent and adult; to be seen as normal, personally competent, attractive, and heterosexual'.[10] This chapter will unravel some of the different ways of narrating a wedding to reveal expectations of masculinity in England between 1918 and 1960.

The 'white wedding' also intertwined institutionalised gender and sexuality with normative notions of race and Englishness. Ingraham argues that the white wedding is 'a mechanism that secures whiteness as dominant and patriarchal heterosexuality as superior' and that the 'movie

---

[8] Andrew Parker and Eve Kosofsky Sedgwick, 'Introduction: Performativity and performance' in *Performativity and performance* ed. Andrew Parker and Eve Kosofsky Sedgwick (New York: Routledge, 1995), 10.

[9] Chrys Ingraham, *White weddings: Romancing heterosexuality in popular culture* (London: Routledge, 1999), 3, 17.

[10] Diana Leonard, *Sex and generation: A study of courtship and marriage* (London, 1980), 2, 8, 260.

industry' has used 'weddings as the main theme or as a plot device some-where in the film'.[11] Film studies scholar Richard Dyer argues that gender and race are 'ineluctably intertwined, through the primacy of heterosexuality in reproducing the former and defining the latter'. Following this argument, reproductive sexuality has to be carefully constrained to maintain racial boundaries and White superiority. Dyer also contends that since race is about embodiment one has to consider the dominant corporeal cultural form in the West: Christianity. Although Dyer is careful to point out that Christianity is not in 'its essence white', he shows the 'gentilising [sic] and whitening of the image of Christ and the Virgin in painting' and the 'ready appeal to the God of Christianity in the prosecution of racial superiority and imperialism'.[12] Using this Whiteness theory, Christian Socialist theologian Kenneth Leech argued that 'White Christians' in Britain are subject to the 'myth that "whiteness" is normative, dominant, central to Christian reality' and further that 'Anglicanism has promoted a white, often middle class and refined type of "Englishness"'.[13] As the visibility of church weddings increased during this period, more people were subject to the discourses and imagery of race that linked married masculinity to White racial superiority and Englishness.

To unpack the symbolism of weddings and the language used to describe them, we will look at three different sources: etiquette manuals, newspapers and first-person testimonies. Etiquette manuals with their inherent reliance on notions of tradition do not show change over time during this period but do reveal the elaborate and gendered planning and choreography of the idealised wedding. Newspaper coverage of weddings changed over time and therefore demonstrates the rise of the modern white wedding. Newspaper content shows that the presentation of weddings was highly gendered: the wedding was a woman's 'big day' with the man almost invisible. Oral histories however show that the lived experience of weddings varied enormously from the ideal and that men were often involved in the planning and preparation of the big day, and often strove to have the best wedding they could afford, even if it fell short of the big, white wedding. These sources combine to show a variety of ways of narrating a wedding and therefore how the increased popularity

[11] Ingraham, *White weddings*, 162 and for a list of 'Wedding Movies' see 177–83.

[12] Richard Dyer, *White* (London: Routledge, 1997), 14, 17, 20.

[13] Kenneth Leech, *Race* (New York: Church Publishing, 2005), 99, 102.

and availability of the romantic 'white wedding' placed institutionalised uxorious masculinity at the heart of personal, social and economic life. The performance at weddings and the language used to narrate them shifted over time and show how married masculinity changed during the period.

WEDDING ETIQUETTE MANUALS

A succession of etiquette manuals advised wealthier couples how to arrange and stage a 'traditional' wedding. Although these etiquette manuals did not have mass appeal it is important to understand the construction of gender and sexuality in these idealised weddings and further the implied definitions of class, race and Englishness. Since the purpose of etiquette manuals is to construct and appeal to a sense of 'tradition', they do not reveal change over time during this period. As it will be shown later in this chapter, society weddings were widely reported in the interwar period and the 'white wedding' as set out in these manuals became the aspirational norm after the Second World War.

Interwar etiquette manuals assumed that the typical wedding would be big, white, and Church of England.[14] In 1935, the term '"white" wedding' appeared in etiquette manuals. Although, a 'quiet' wedding with an afternoon dress could also 'be in perfectly good taste', it was posited as being inferior. The bride's dress defined the type of wedding and the whiteness of the dress could connote social class. Some etiquette manuals claimed that in 'the highest circles, she will wear a bridal robe of the whitest silk; but in many of the good class ceremonies… an afternoon dress or costume is considered in perfect taste'.[15]

Gender, in etiquette manuals, is defined by the interest and knowledge that men and women have of weddings. Men whose role is to be economically productive are not expected to know anything about weddings to the extent that 'a wedding to man is like a rainstorm on a summer's

---

[14] "Best Man", *Marriage etiquette: How to arrange a wedding* (London: W. Foulsham, 1936), 22, 28.

[15] M. Bee and S. Bee, *Weddings without worry: A modern and practical guide to wedding conventions and ceremonies* (London: Methuen, 1935), 2–3; Mary Woodman, *Wedding etiquette* (London: W. Foulsham, 1929), 45.

day since it usually catches him unprepared'.[16] In contrast, as sociologist Ingraham argues in the American context, the woman is expected to know about weddings since her role is invested in emotional production and has been 'socialised since childhood, as the domestic planner'.[17] As the Rev. D. Exton wrote in *Wedding Etiquette* (1935), '[to] the ladies... marriage and its customs have been part of their education since their cradle days'.[18] This is the narrative that the 'white wedding' is the biggest day in the life of a woman; something she has been 'dreaming' about since a little girl.[19] The impression that the wedding is the bride's dream day is further reinforced as her parents are expected to take ownership of the arrangements. Although the bride and groom should draw up the guest list together, wedding invitations were to be issued and received by the bride's family. The replies should be 'acknowledged immediately, gracefully, and personally by the bride'. Further, the bride's family were to place an announcement in a newspaper,[20] therefore communicating the family's good news, but also normalising big weddings and the institution of marriage.

The bride's decision about where to marry was not really a choice since etiquette manuals propagated the notion that a 'proper' wedding takes places in a church. Although it is the bride's 'privilege' that she 'chooses the day for her wedding', etiquette manuals rarely mention the choice of wedding venue. It could be inferred from this and from etiquette manual readership, that the typical wedding is one in which the bride is expected to be from an Anglican church-going family, and that naturally the wedding would take place in her parents' parish church. This is reinforced when the choice of venue is explicitly mentioned: the 'choice of church... is a matter for settlement by the bride and her parents'.[21]

---

[16] Rev. D. Exton, *Wedding etiquette* (London: Universal Publications, 1935), 7.

[17] Ingraham, *White weddings*, 74.

[18] Exton, *Wedding etiquette*, 8.

[19] For the American context, see Ingraham, *White weddings*, 39.

[20] "Best Man", *Marriage etiquette*, 20; Bee and Bee, *Weddings without worry*, 17, 27; Woodman, *Wedding etiquette*, 40 [republished in 1949, with minor revisions]; Exton, *Wedding etiquette*, 25; Diana Woods and Edgar Woods, *Planning your wedding: A complete guide for all concerned and for all denominations* (London: Universal Publications, 1937), 56, 96.

[21] Bee and Bee, *Weddings without worry*, 58; Woodman, *Wedding etiquette*, 58; Exton, *Wedding etiquette*, 30.

4 THE WEDDING 113

Etiquette manuals sought to assert gendered convention by restricting the role of men in the choices made before the wedding.

Etiquette manuals are very clear about who should do what, and a wedding *must* have a best man and bridesmaids. The best man should 'usually' be a 'bachelor' and 'of course' the 'chief bridesmaid... must be single'.[22] The other bridesmaids also should be unmarried.[23] The best man should be the epitome of masculinity: he should be 'a man who will not easily be flustered. The fussy, nervous, worrying individual is not wanted'.[24] In contradiction to the notion that men do not know about weddings and that the bride has control of her wedding day, the best man is responsible for much of the wedding's minutiae including booking the church and, on the day, 'the smooth running of the ceremony'.[25] The bridesmaids purpose was chiefly decorative. The roles of the bridesmaids and best man reinforce normative gender roles. The requirement that they should be single, those who would one day marry support the couple getting married.

The issue of who did what was not always visible on the day, as in who paid for what. The payment for different aspects of the wedding constructed gender roles and defined marriage. In keeping with the narrative that *her* wedding is the most important day of a woman's life, the bride's parents were to pick up the bill for most of the wedding costs. The bride symbolically paid for the bridesmaids' dresses, perhaps demonstrating that she was no longer part of their unmarried group. The groom however paid for bridesmaids' flowers, reinforcing notions of chivalry. The church fees were paid for by the groom who, with his best man, arrived early at the church to attend to such matters.[26] This ensured that at the start of the marriage, the husband secured his place as the 'head' of the household, the one who takes intelligent financial and legal decisions.

---

[22] Woods and Woods, *Planning your wedding*, 99, 103; "Best Man", *Marriage etiquette*, 54; Bee and Bee, *Weddings without worry*, 34, 40; Woodman, *Wedding etiquette*, 43; Exton, *Wedding etiquette*, 54; Ann Page, *The complete guide to wedding etiquette* (London: Ward, Lock and Co., 1950), 52.

[23] Woodman, *Wedding etiquette*, 43; Woods and Woods, *Planning your wedding*, 103; Page, *Complete guide*, 57.

[24] Woodman, *Wedding etiquette*, 43.

[25] Bee and Bee, *Weddings without worry*, 34; Woodman, *Wedding etiquette*, 82; Exton, *Wedding etiquette*, 54.

[26] Bee and Bee, *Weddings without worry*, 28, 58.

Etiquette manuals prescribe a type of dress for the bride and groom that created and reinforced normative femininity and masculinity. The wedding outfits, although in many ways twentieth-century inventions, are presented as timeless. From the 1930s, etiquette manuals advised that 'the conventional [female] dress is supposed to be of pure white silk or satin', but that the bride could wear an 'afternoon' dress if the wedding was to be 'small'. The white dress, connoting sexual purity, should not be worn by 'a woman marrying for the second time' since 'a white veil or orange blossom... being the special prerogative of maidenhood'. The groom 'should wear formal attire if his bride is in white', although in keeping with class-based codes of masculinity he 'should not wear much jewellery'.[27] He should dress to suit his bride. For example, if

> the bride is wearing white, and the bridegroom wishes to appear formally dressed, he must don a morning coat, usually of dark grey, a light lavender-coloured waistcoat, striped grey trousers, grey suede gloves, white wing collar with a puff tie or cravat usually of an unobtrusive grey... [and a]... silk hat.[28]

The 'formal' groom should also consider having 'the *soles* of his shoes blackened, in order that they look neat when he kneels at the altar'. A 'less formal' groom could wear 'black jacket and waistcoat, grey stripped trousers, white shirt with double collar and a knotted tie, and black bowler hat'. Although very prescriptive, etiquette manuals accepted that this 'equipment, however, is not necessarily followed, even in all church weddings'.[29] The groom's wedding attire supposedly sat outside of men's fashions since some etiquette manuals gave the same sartorial advice in revised editions twenty years apart.[30]

Although the focus at a wedding is typically on the bride in a dress that she would wear only once in her lifetime, it is important to understand that the man's suit is not an 'inexpressive' choice of clothing that

---

[27] "Best Man", *Marriage etiquette*, 22–3; Exton, *Wedding etiquette*, 73–4; Canning Town crane driver James Bushnell wore a signet ring bought by his fiancé when they got engaged in 1918. Interview with James Bushnell.

[28] Bee and Bee, *Weddings without worry*, 52.

[29] Page, *Complete guide*, 50; Bee and Bee, *Weddings without worry*, 52; Woodman, *Wedding etiquette*, 46.

[30] For example, Woodman, *Wedding etiquette*, 40 [and revised edition of 1949].

is 'supposedly an indicator of the most extreme uniformity'. The suit 'conveys very different meanings in different contexts and to different people' and can display 'sexuality' and 'confident adult masculinity', it is 'a potent symbol of success, virility and maturity... that looks incongruous on a boy'.[31] The suit became increasingly (hetero)sexualised in the first half of the twentieth century. Art historian Paul Jobling points out that the man who 'offers up his body for the delectation of women' in marketing campaigns for Austin Reed and The Fifty Shilling Tailors in the 1930s, and historians Frank Mort and Peter Thompson argue that there was a 'new emphasis on heterosexuality' in Burton's advertising aimed at male consumers in the 1950s.[32] For many men, and women, the men's suit became synonymous with the 'glamour and intense sexuality' of Hollywood idols such as Clark Gable and Cary Grant.[33] Under this Hollywood influence in the 1930s, it became more acceptable for the groom to replace the morning suit with a lounge suit.[34] On his wedding day, therefore, the man, dressed in the best outfit he can afford, is just as gendered and sexualised as his bride. Etiquette manuals state that the best man's appearance 'should resemble in attire a modest replica of the bridegroom'.[35] The dress of the main actors allows the gendered institution of marriage to reproduce itself. The unmarried best man and bridesmaids are 'replicas' of the marrying couple and could be the ones to marry next.[36]

The flow of the main weddings actors—bride, groom, best man, bridesmaids and bride's father—through the church during the ceremony performed gender and generation. The choreography for the wedding was considered by etiquette manuals to be especially important, with diagrams

[31] Anne Hollander, *Sex and suits: The evolution of modern dress* (London: Bloomsbury, 1994), 113; Tim Edwards, *Men in the mirror: Men's fashions, masculinity and consumer society* (London: Cassell, 1997), 9, 22.

[32] Paul Jobling, *Man appeal: Advertising, modernism and menswear* (Oxford: Berg, 2005), 5, 31–2; Frank Mort and Peter Thompson, 'Retailing, commercial culture and masculinity in 1950s Britain: The case of montague burton, the "Tailor of Taste"', *History Workshop* 38 (1994), 123.

[33] Edwards, *Men in the mirror*, 9, 20.

[34] Avril Lansdell, *Wedding fashions, 1860–1980* (Haverfordwest: Shire, 1983), 65–6, 69.

[35] Bee and Bee, *Weddings without worry*, 52.

[36] In some interwar weddings the bride and groom looked little different from the best man and chief bridesmaid, Lansdell, *Wedding Fashions*, 60.

116   N. PENLINGTON

provided for the uninitiated.[37] The only liturgical requirement was that the 'man should stand on the right hand; and the woman on the left'.[38] The processions into the church; then later into the vestry for the signing of the register; and, the recession from the church are all secular reinventions. The wedding was expected to start with the groom in the church and the bride outside, thus drawing attention to the bride as she finally entered and therefore creating the impression that it was *her* big day; that women are more emotionally invested in marriage and the home. The groom took 'his place on the right of the chancel steps with the best man at his right hand, a little behind him'. The bride then '[took] the right hand of her father' and entered the church with a procession of bridesmaids in pairs following. The man is already socially and economically established, and she is being given to him by another man. The bride 'moves forward through the ranks of the bridesmaids, who fall in behind two be two'. This moment of theatricality symbolises the bride's transition from girlhood to womanhood, and the 'ranks' of the unmarried she is about to leave behind. This procession should be performed to 'the thrilling strains of the Bridal March'. The procession culminates with the formation of a symmetrical arrangement at the front of the church. The bride 'takes her place on [the groom's] left, with her chief bridesmaid, a little behind her'. The bride's father stands to her left, 'a trifle in the rear'.[39] The bride and groom, dressed accordingly, perform the idealised and sexualised male and female. The groom and the bride's father form a symmetrical position, which can be seen the handing over of patriarchal authority. The unmarried best man and the bridesmaids perform the potential for heterosexual iteration. The relative position (further forward) of the best man and the fact that the bridesmaids outnumber him (since all other men are removed from the ceremony) demonstrate the relative power of male and female, and, further, demonstrates that women should *compete* for a male spouse.

The 'giving way' further reinforced active masculinity and passive femininity. Some etiquette manuals erroneously claimed that 'Who giveth this

---

[37] For example, Ann Page, *Complete guide*, 71–7.

[38] For example, Anon., *The book of common prayer with the additions and deviations proposed in 1928* (Cambridge: Cambridge University Press, 1928), 432.

[39] "Best Man", *Marriage etiquette*, 29–30; Bee and Bee, *Weddings without worry*, 58–9; Exton, *Wedding etiquette*, 33; Woodman, *Wedding etiquette*, 47; Bee and Bee, *Weddings without worry*, 59.

woman to be married?' was an 'essential clause'. It was not a legal requirement. According to etiquette manuals, if the bride was 'fatherless', the 'giving away' could 'be performed by a brother, uncle or any male relation or friend' In contrast to the important role of the bride's father (or substitute male) in the ceremony, the bride's mother does not have any role on the day but advises the bride during the preparation. Another married female relative could do this if the bride is 'motherless'.[40] Although the bride's mother has been important before the wedding during the arrangements, she is virtually redundant on the day. It is her husband, the bride's father, who is seen to be more important as their daughter leaves home to start life with another man.[41]

Following the ceremony, a second procession takes place as the 'chief bridesmaid and the best man, as well as the parents of the couple, also follow [the newly married couple] into the vestry' to sign the marriage register. Some etiquette manuals encourage the active best man to '[offer] his left arm' to the passive chief bridesmaid, thus reproducing institutionalised coupledom by creating a replica of a married couple. Following the signing of the register by the couple and witnesses, the 'bridegroom then offers his left arm to his bride... and they leave the church, passing down the aisle' commencing on the 'rousing crash of the opening chords of the Wedding March'. The bride, who entered the church veiled, should now have her veil 'thrown well back and billowing out behind her' as the 'happy couple walk briskly down the main aisle to the church doors'.[42]

The wedding celebrations continue at the reception and so does the gendered performance. Social class and masculine chivalry are demonstrated at the reception, since the 'gentlemen attend to the ladies, and the servants assist'. Only men gave speeches, especially the bride's father, the groom and the best man. The groom should start his speech with 'My wife and I'.[43] This shows that he and the woman have become a

---

[40] Bee and Bee, *Weddings without worry*, 59; Alfred May, *Marriage in church, chapel or register office* (London: Longmans, 1920), 46; Exton, *Wedding etiquette*, 47; Woodman, *Wedding etiquette*, 48.

[41] For father's permission for marriage, see Chapter 3.

[42] "Best Man", *Marriage etiquette*, 31, 35; Exton, *Wedding etiquette*, 56–7; Woods and Woods, *Planning your Wedding*, 78; Bee and Bee, *Weddings without worry*, 60.

[43] "Best Man", *Marriage etiquette*, 62–6; Bee and Bee, *Weddings without worry*, 70; Woodman, *Wedding etiquette*, 48, 51; Woods and Woods, *Planning your wedding*, 92–5.

'cross-gendered "we"'[44] with an active-male, passive-female binary. If the wife speaks at all, she 'adds a simple expression of thanks to everybody' but 'more often' she is 'confined to smiling approval at her husband's efforts' The groom could also take this opportunity to reproduce married coupledom by 'express[ing] his wonder at the best man's single state, where there are so many attractive and eligible young ladies awaiting a fate similar to that of his wife'.[45]

The cutting of the wedding cake is the final ceremonial act of the reception; this simple action was suffused with gendered cultural symbolism. Social anthropologist Simon Charsley argues that a variety of 'meanings and interpretations' circulated from the late nineteenth century as the white-iced wedding cake became popular among those who could afford it. The joint 'plunging' of the knife into the cake was considered by some to be a metaphor for 'taking the plunge' into married life. The white cake could stand in for the bride, dressed in virginal white, and cutting symbolic of her losing her virginity.[46] Etiquette manuals clearly stated that the bride cuts the wedding cake, but 'with the assistance of the husband'.[47] This is the most *active* role for the bride during her wedding day as she takes charge of cutting the cake. During the rest of the ceremony and reception, the man has been active and the woman passive, but here in the realm of food, of domestic labour, the wife's position, relative to her new husband, as homemaker is suggested.

The 'traditional' wedding was something that transcended religious belief and practice. Although the writers of etiquette manuals assumed that most readers were Anglicans and that most weddings would take place in Church of England churches, they did cater for those readers of other faiths and denominations.[48] In the 1935 *Weddings without Worry*, 'other dominations' were told to follow the same advice as that given for the majority, Anglican wedding. In 'Nonconformist ceremonies' the etiquette for 'dress, bridesmaids, the best man, "giving away the bride",

[44] Parker and Sedgwick, 10.

[45] Bee and Bee, *Weddings without worry*, 70–71; Woodman, *Wedding etiquette*, 51.

[46] Simon R. Charsley, *Wedding cakes and cultural history* (London: Routledge, 1992), 31, 124–6.

[47] "Best Man", *Marriage etiquette*, 60; Woodman, *Wedding etiquette*, 49.

[48] For example, "Best Man", *Marriage etiquette*, 45–6; Woods and Woods, *Planning your wedding*, 26, 33–8.

and customs and formalities' were to be the same as outlined for Anglican weddings. In Roman Catholic weddings the 'bride and her bridesmaids will be attired in a similar fashion [to Anglican counterparts], with veil train, according to taste'. Likewise, Roman Catholic men were expected to assume the same roles as Anglicans such that the 'bridegroom has his best man to assist him'. Quakers were to follow the 'usual customs appertaining to bridesmaids and best man, and white wedding gown for the bride, are observed according to individual taste'. In Jewish weddings, the advice was that the 'dress of the bride and her bridesmaids, the bridegroom, and best man does not differ from that' in Anglican weddings.[49]

Weddings encouraged the reproduction of further weddings. An invented tradition appeared at the end of the wedding that passes on the baton to the next bride. In 1948, *The Good Housekeeping Bride's Book* emphasised an 'old custom' in which 'the bride tosses her bouquet among the bridesmaids, and the bridesmaid who secures the largest part will be first to marry'.[50] This is the earliest example in the sample of etiquette manuals. In 1950, Ann Page posited the 'custom of throwing the bouquet' to be 'a very old one' and the 'bridesmaid who catches it is supposed to be the next bride!'[51] The bridesmaids, all unmarried, are invited to stand and try to catch the bouquet under the primarily male gaze.

Etiquette manuals narrated weddings for a particular audience with particular expectations. Primarily aimed at a wealthy readership, they narrated the *ideal* 'white wedding'. Rather than seeking a 'comparison of prescription and practice',[52] this examination of etiquette manuals shows that they were an influential literary source that affected the way that weddings were seen. At each stage of the idealised 'white wedding', notions of masculinity and femininity were iterated and reinforced. Etiquette manuals presented the idealised 'traditional' white wedding in a Church of England church, with other faiths and denominations copying, as quintessentially English. Etiquette manuals seek to show that wedding

---

[49] Bee and Bee, *Weddings without worry*, 99–101, 103, 106.

[50] *Good housekeeping bride's book*, 30.

[51] Page, *Complete guide*, 45.

[52] Philip Carter, *Men and the emergence of polite society, Britain 1660–1800* (Harlow: Longman, 2001), 35.

120 N. PENLINGTON

ceremonies, and other forms of etiquette, are timeless and unchanging. It is unsurprising, therefore, that the manuals here did not change over time.

NEWSPAPERS

Unlike etiquette manuals, newspapers narrated weddings for a mass audience and between 1918 and 1960 there was a change in the way weddings were reported. Increasingly, newspapers depicted the ideal wedding as big, white and in a church. Reflecting, but also promoting changes in wedding fashions, the term 'white wedding' became normal and combined with the assertion that anyone could have access to a big wedding. Whereas in etiquette manuals the roles of the male wedding actors—the groom, best man and bride's father—received attention and advice, newspapers were comparatively silent on the role of men in weddings. Newspapers presented the romantic wedding as the biggest day in a woman's life leading to a marriage set around procreation and roles of male breadwinner and female homemaker.

White became the colour worn by most 'traditional' brides by the end of the period, but there was confusion in the 1920s as to whether white was new or traditional. The white wedding dress had earlier roots: Ingraham argues that Queen Victoria's wedding in 1840 caused many middle-class 'Western' women to adopt the 'white wedding gown'.[53] In 1925, the *Daily Express* asked 'Is the traditional white wedding passing into ancient history?' The newspaper went on to say that 'Brides should not change these customs',[54] implying that the woman had the final say on *her* big day. Opinion was divided with some arguing that a bride should 'not submit' to white if it does not suit her.[55] There were contradictory opinions on whether a bride should wear white and whether it was traditional or new. In 1928, the *Daily Mirror* reported the conflicting views that brides 'seem to have grown tired of wearing white',[56] but that a bride was 'new-fashioned enough to have an all-white wedding'.[57] The

---

[53] Ingraham, *White weddings*, 34.

[54] 'Modern brides and the colour mania', *Daily Express*, 23 January 1925, 6.

[55] 'Rainbow bridal dresses', *Daily Express*, 08 June 1926, 9.

[56] 'As I see life', *Daily Mirror*, 30 June 1928, 6.

[57] 'As I see life', *Daily Mirror*, 29 October 1928, 6.

4 THE WEDDING 121

newspaper announced in 1932 that the 'all-white wedding has become fashionable again'.[58] Newspapers presented wedding fashions and colour choices as feminine; masculinity was tacitly assumed to be something 'other'.

As with wedding etiquette manuals, newspapers defined weddings according to the bride's dress and the arrival of the term 'white wedding' created an expectation of a particular type of wedding. Although the Oxford English Dictionary dates the term 'white wedding' to 1840 (the year of Victoria's wedding), it was not used in newspapers in this period until the late 1920s.[59] The *Daily Mirror* typically defined a wedding by the bride's dress. A wedding could be 'a very pretty pink and white wedding',[60] an 'All-White Wedding',[61] 'a gold and white wedding',[62] 'All-Gold Wedding'[63] or 'Red and White wedding'.[64] The term 'white wedding' became normal during the 1930s. Although newspapers occasionally referred to a big wedding as an 'all-white wedding',[65] increasingly the term 'white wedding'[66] was used. In 1939, the *Daily Express* ran an etiquette advice article entitled '"Marry at Leisure" feature for spring

[58] 'To-day's Gossip', *Daily Mirror*, 21 July 1932, 11.

[59] The term 'white wedding' appeared in *The Times* four times in the nineteenth century, and did not become frequent until the 1930s.

[60] 'To-day's Gossip', *Daily Mirror*, 11 August 1920, 4.

[61] 'The Social Round', *Daily Mirror*, 1 November 1920, 13.

[62] 'Golden bridesmaids', *Daily Mirror*, 25 April 1923, 2; similar in 'Tennis wedding', *Daily Mirror*, 4 July 1932, 5.

[63] 'All-gold wedding', *Daily Mirror*, 10 March 1926, 21.

[64] 'As I see life', *Daily Mirror*, 20 November 1929, 6.

[65] 'Lord Iddesleigh weds', *Daily Mirror*, 15 May 1930, 2; 'As I see life', *Daily Mirror*, 26 June 1930, 16; 'As I see life', *Daily Mirror*, 02 July 1930, 16; 'To-day's gossip', *Daily Mirror*, 21 July 1932 11; 'All-white wedding "guest"', *Daily Mirror*, 10 February 1933 12; 'Miss Halsey's all white wedding', *Daily Mirror*, 27 May 1933, 1; 'Ivor Lambe's Tales', *Daily Mirror*, 7 June 1939, 11; 'Talk of London', *Daily Express*, 19 January 1933, 15; 'Lady Diana plans all-white wedding', *Daily Express*, 8 April 1939, 7.

[66] 'As I see life', *Daily Mirror*, 25 January 1929, 6; 'White wedding of Miss V. French', *Daily Mirror*, 22 April 1931, 6; 'I've had SIX husbands', *Daily Mirror*, 19 December 1935, 12; 'Our live letterbox', *Daily Mirror*, 25 February 1938, 24; 'Eileen Ashcroft's sanctuary', *Daily Mirror*, 12 May 1938, 11; 'Cinderella's wedding day', *Daily Mirror*, 03 June 1938, 29; 'What "£ s. d.s" would do', *Daily Mirror*, 20 August 1938, 1; 'Brides' "Lucky sign"', *Daily Mirror*, 7 August 1939 4; 'Going away', *Daily Express*, 21 March 1939, 13.

brides'. The article advised readers that if the ceremony is not a 'white wedding' it should still follow the 'same etiquette'. The '[b]ridesmaids are dropped, as are ushers, choir and awning at the church door' but there is 'usually a best man', the bride is still 'given away preferably by her father' and 'the ceremony follows the same course but without hymns or psalms'.[67] On this basis, a small wedding was bigger and more theatrical than a big wedding a generation earlier. It became a joke that the new 'white wedding' made a groom 'horribly nervous' because of the required 'amateur theatricals'.[68]

The narration of weddings during this period shifted from the 'white wedding' being only for Society circles to society in general. In the 1920s, a wedding could be reported as being 'a mid-season crowd'.[69] A decade later, readers were given details of 'the first all-white wedding of the season'.[70] Although religious denomination was not mentioned explicitly in newspaper articles, coverage was given also to Roman Catholic, Society weddings taking place in Westminster Cathedral, Brompton Oratory and St James' Spanish Place.[71] Newspaper coverage during the 1930s, an era of growing celebrity and cinema culture, started to open the possibility of a 'white wedding' to other people, including speedway stars,[72] and tennis and rugby players.[73] It was not until after the Second World War that the 'white wedding' was presented as being normal for all social classes. After the Second World War, a newspaper typically used the term 'white wedding' to describe a wedding that is instantly recognisable as a church wedding in which the bride wears white and is attended to by bridesmaids.[74] Church weddings were normalised as brides were reported

[67] 'Going away', *Daily Express*, 21 March 1939, 13.

[68] 'Our live letterbox', *Daily Mirror*, 25 February 1938, 24.

[69] 'To-day's gossip', *Daily Mirror*, 11 August 1920, 4.

[70] 'As I see life', *Daily Mirror*, 2 July 1930, 16.

[71] For example, 'Tea table talk', *Daily Express*, 21 November 1919, 3; 'A diary of to-day', *Daily Express*, 17 January 1922, 6; 'A diary of to-day', *Daily Express*, 3 May 1922, 8; 'Famous beauty weds marquis', *Daily Mirror*, 20 March 1923, 2; 'Lord Manton's wedding', *Daily Mirror*, 19 April 1923, 1; 'Party to see a trousseau', *Daily Mirror*, 17 February 1933, 7.

[72] 'Cinderella's wedding day', *Daily Mirror*, 3 June 1938, 29.

[73] 'Tennis wedding', *Daily Mirror*, 4 July 1932, 5.

[74] For example, 'Viewpoint', *Daily Mirror*, 31 May 1947, 2; 'She's flying the Atlantic to a white wedding', *Daily Mirror*, 23 June 1947, 1; 'Edna had her white wedding after

4 THE WEDDING   123

as 'doing the Christmas rush to the altar'.[75] By the 1950s, there was 'nothing unusual' about a 'white wedding [with]... five bridesmaids, a matron of honour and a pageboy'.[76] By the 1950s, newspapers were using the language of earlier etiquette manuals: the *Daily Mirror* asked 'Should a wedding be - WHITE or QUIET?'[77] The big white wedding had become so normal that other weddings were derided. The *Daily Mirror* expressed shock that in Russian weddings, unlike the English equivalent, there were 'NO cars, No confetti, No wedding ring and NO ONE TO GIVE THE BRIDE AWAY'.[78] In 1960, the *Daily Express* claimed that '72 per cent of this country's brides marry in church. And that means a big boost in the white wedding'.[79] The era of the white wedding had fully arrived.

The language used to report weddings reinforced the wedding as the biggest day in a woman's life: it was *her* day. Some brides felt that the wedding is 'not the bride's day at all' and that it 'belongs to ALL her female relatives'.[80] The coverage of Diana Mitford's 1929 wedding stressed that the 'bride... is having a white wedding'.[81] A decade later, brides were quoted as saying 'the dream of every girl, [is] a "white wedding"' and to be '"princess" for a day' on 'the greatest day of her life'.[82] When the *Daily Mirror* invited readers to fantasise about how to spend a £20,000 inheritance, one woman wrote that she would 'have

all—Thanks to victor', *Daily Mirror*, 29 December 1947, 3; 'Her bridal bouquet will be wreath', *Daily Mirror*, 30 August 1948, 5; 'And an extra ten shillings for the topper', *Daily Mirror*, 02 February 1949, 5; 'Pin-up page for a lovely EASTER BRIDE', *Daily Mirror*, 25 March 1949, 4; 'A white wedding—"fair's fair"', *Daily Express*, 10 August 1951, 5; 'Tito will hear of this wedding', *Daily Express*, 7 August 1953, 5, 'One little drop of oil saves rainy day', *Daily Express*, 08 June 1954, 5; 'A white wedding, mother pleads', *Daily Express*, 18 August 1955, 5; 'Do you take this man?', *Daily Express*, 29 December 1955, 5; 'So June, the bride, wears gumboots', *Daily Express*, 14 February 1956, 5.

[75] 'No! No! says the bride', *Daily Mirror*, 15 December 1948, 2.

[76] 'Claire, 15, plans her wedding', *Daily Mirror*, 22 April 1955, 3.

[77] 'Should a wedding be WHITE or QUIET?', *Daily Mirror*, 07 October 1957, 17.

[78] 'All you need at a Russian wedding is A MAN, A WOMAN', *Daily Mirror*, 12 September 1957, 13.

[79] 'Today's bride has a double life', *Daily Express*, 2 March 1960, 9.

[80] 'No! No! says the bride', *Daily Mirror*, 15 December 1948, 2.

[81] 'As I see life', *Daily Mirror*, 25 January 1929, 6.

[82] 'Cinderella's wedding day', *Daily Mirror*, 3 June 1938, 29.

124   N. PENLINGTON

a white wedding instead of a register office ceremony'.[83] The white wedding was still presented as the biggest day for a woman even during wartime. One bride exclaimed 'My ambition was realised, it was a white wedding',[84] while another who got married in a register office vowed that she would 'have a white wedding later'.[85] The end of rationing was framed as an opportunity for a woman to have her dream wedding because with 'everything off coupons...the Easter bride' can 'replan and have a white wedding after all'.[86] In the 1950s, newspapers reminded readers of the dark days of war 'when clothes rationing spoiled many brides' hopes of a white wedding' and even offered the chance for a lucky competition winner, a '28 year-old housewife' from Portsmouth, to have 'a photograph in a [white] wedding dress nine years later courtesy of the Daily Mirror'.[87] Men in comparison were absent from much of this newspaper coverage, implying that masculinity was something other than fashion, frivolity and consumerism, and instead perhaps sensibleness and long-term solidity.

The white wedding could be a masculine aspiration. Some grooms were determined to provide a romantic, white wedding for their brides. One groom borrowed a white wedding dress and three bridesmaids white dresses so that his bride would have 'the wedding of her dreams'.[88] Some men risked being mocked by writing to the letters pages asking 'Serviceman, getting married, urgently requires White Wedding veil'.[89] Another groom, a Lance Corporal from Walworth, borrowed a dress from 'a London film wardrobe' to give his bride a 'surprise white wedding'.[90] These men could not produce the money required for a white wedding through conventional breadwinning but were prepared to go to extraordinary lengths for the sake of romance and status. Such examples from

---

[83] 'What "£ s. d.s" would do', *Daily Mirror*, 20 August 1938, 1.

[84] 'Offered to free Fiancee', *Daily Mirror*, 22 February 1940, 3.

[85] 'There *Was* a wedding', *Daily Mirror*, 27 May 1941, 8.

[86] 'Pin-up page for a lovely EASTER BRIDE', *Daily Mirror*, 25 March 1949, 4.

[87] 'Her dream wish came true', *Daily Mirror*, 06 October 1954, 9.

[88] 'Edna had her white wedding after all—Thanks to victor', *Daily Mirror*, 29 December 1947, 3.

[89] 'Live letters', *Daily Mirror*, 31 March 1948, 6.

[90] 'A tall story, but it will all end in a white wedding', *Daily Mirror*, 2 February 1948, 5.

newspapers may be few, but they demonstrate that romantic codes of chivalry and masculinity could extend to providing a dream wedding.

Some lucky couples could win a white wedding in a competition and some competitions reinforced gender roles and expectations. By the late 1950s, such competitions were more common. Some jewellers offered competition prizes of a 'Free Continental Honeymoon' or 'Free White Wedding'. The cost of entry was the purchase of a diamond ring.[91] The *Daily Mirror* offered the chance to win 'a slap-up white wedding' and 'a glamorous honeymoon'.[92] The winners' wedding photographs appeared in the newspaper.[93] Some brides won the honour of being the 'Daily Express Easter Bride'. The newspaper invited readers to '[f]ollow her on this page as she puts through the immense organisational job needed for a white wedding'. The photograph of the 1953 Easter Bride showed her 'without the romantic aura of a wedding veil' but she reassured readers that 'we are definitely having a white wedding. Partly because of the glamour, but mainly because I'm a member of the Church'.[94] With ten days to go until the big day, readers were informed that a 'bride cannot turn her back on the kitchen, even in all the excitement of a white wedding only ten days off' as the twenty-two-year-old is pictured wielding an impossible amount of modern kitchen equipment.[95]

As well as presenting the white wedding as the start of (gendered) domestic bliss, newspaper reporting defined the real purpose of marriage as starting a family. While etiquette manuals focused on the ideal characteristics of the best man and bridesmaids, newspapers were more interested in the rise of the 'child attendant'. The increased involvement and visibility of children in wedding ceremonies created procreative sexuality as normal, natural and timeless, and a central purpose of marriage In 1930, the *Daily Mirror* reported that in 'recent society weddings... a regular crocodile of bridesmaids ha[d] followed the bride up the aisle'. There would be, typically, six or eight bridesmaids.[96] A wedding with

---

[91] 'Lawrence Seder Goldsmiths and Silversmiths', *Daily Mirror*, 7 March 1957, 4.

[92] 'Up in the air!', *Daily Mirror*, 23 March 1959, 12–13.

[93] 'Dream dress day', *Daily Mirror*, 6 April 1959, 12–13.

[94] 'Follow her from now until Easter', *Daily Express*, 16 March 1953, 3.

[95] 'Even a bride can't turn her back on the kitchen', *Daily Express*, 26 March 1953, 3.

[96] '3 generations at wedding', *Daily Mirror*, 08 June 1935, 7; 'Ivor Lambe's Tales', *Daily Mirror*, 07 June 1939, 11.

126   N. PENLINGTON

'only two attendants' had become unusual.[97] When a Conservative MP married in St Martin-in-the-fields in 1931, there were ten bridesmaids dressed in white, like the bride.[98] Bridesmaids could be sisters of the bride or groom[99] or fellow 'debutants' of the bride.[100] As the number of bridesmaids grew, the ages decreased. In the 1920s, some society weddings had children as 'attendants'. A wedding may have 'six little bridesmaids... in white'[101] or adult bridesmaids and child 'trainbearers'.[102] A key feature of the white wedding became bridesmaids dressed in white.[103] Bridesmaids were replicas of the brides by increasingly wearing the same colour dresses[104] and could be as young as two years old.[105] Boys were increasingly included as 'pages'[106] and men could be trainbearers.[107] More and more brides entered the church followed by a procession of child bridesmaids. Sometimes an age distinction was made between 'grown-up bridesmaids' and 'child attendants'.[108] The 'Etiquette Replies' page of the *Daily Mirror* advised that the 'two children should walk behind you [into church], and the two grown-up bridesmaids should follow them'.[109] By 1960, an article in the *Daily Express* claimed that '[c]hild attendants have come into their own' and that 'the

[97] 'As I see life', *Daily Mirror*, 17 July 1930, 16.

[98] 'First new M.P. to marry', *Daily Express*, 30 October 1931, 11.

[99] 'W. Lipscomb gave a party ... in two continents', *Daily Mirror*, 26 March 1936, 9.

[100] '3 generations at wedding', *Daily Mirror*, 08 June 1935, 7.

[101] 'The social round', *Daily Mirror*, 1 November 1920, 13.

[102] 'Golden bridesmaids', *Daily Mirror*, 25 April 1923, 2.

[103] 'White wedding for Miss V. French', *Daily Mirror*, 22 April 1931, 6; 'W. Lipscomb gave a party ... in two continents', *Daily Mirror*, 26 March 1936, 9.

[104] 'All-gold wedding', *Daily Mirror*, 10 March 1926, 21; 'As I see life', *Daily Mirror*, 26 June 1930, 16.

[105] 'Lord Iddesleigh weds', *Daily Mirror*, 15 May 1930, 2.

[106] 'Tennis wedding', *Daily Mirror*, 4 July 1932, 5; 'Live letters', *Daily Mirror*, 20 May 1961, 19.

[107] 'W. Lipscomb gave a party ... in two continents', *Daily Mirror*, 26 March 1936, 9.

[108] 'Lady Diana plans all-white wedding', *Daily Express*, 8 April 1939, 7.

[109] 'Etiquette replies', *Daily Mirror*, 23 August 1939, 22.

4 THE WEDDING   127

most popular sound in the aisles of England is the patter of tiny, white-clad feet'.[110] The trope 'patter of tiny ... feet' would have been instantly familiar to readers as a reference to the 'natural' purpose of marriage: reproduction.

Away from cosy domesticity, the normality and romance of the white wedding combined with a newspaper mainstay: the elopement story. Stories of couples eloping to Gretna Green were regular newspaper fare in the mid-twentieth century and the stories were typically presented romantically 'as testament to the power of love'.[111] The *Daily Express* claimed, somewhat exaggeratedly, that '[e]lopement now is just about as common place as the traditional church wedding over in the little church around the corner'.[112] By the mid-1950s, these elopement stories increasingly posited the 'white wedding' as a 'proper' wedding. Romantic stories of runaway elopers could be embellished by reporting that the Gretna Green ceremony will be a 'white wedding'.[113] Such elopements fulfilled the gendered ideal that the wedding is the biggest day in a woman's life. One sixteen-year-old 'runaway bride' was reported as saying 'I had my heart set on a white wedding' and that her 'dream of a white wedding had come true'.[114] The promise of a respectable 'white wedding' was used to encourage elopers to return home. One mother appealed to her sixteen-year-old daughter via the *Daily Express* 'Come back home Moira, and make it a white wedding'.[115] Parents of 'teenage elopers' made a television appeal: 'We'll give Carol a white wedding if that is what she wants'.[116] There was bewilderment when couples ran away *from* a 'white wedding' to Gretna.[117] Although the bride is typically the centre of these

---

[110] 'Today's bride has a double life', *Daily Express*, 2 March 1960, 9.

[111] Elopements to Gretna Green continued throughout the period even though irregular marriages ceased in Scotland in 1939. Claire Langhamer, *The English in love: The intimate history of an emotional revolution* (Oxford: Oxford University Press, 2013), 172, 174.

[112] 'But some many come to grief in Gretna...', *Daily Express*, 18 November 1954, 8.

[113] 'Puzzled mothers say: Why elope?', *Daily Express*, 19 June 1956, 3.

[114] 'Denise has her white wedding—At Gretna', *Daily Express*, 23 September 1954, 5; 'The bride aged 16', *Daily Mirror*, 23 September 1954, 6.

[115] 'A white wedding, mother pleads', *Daily Express*, 18 August 1955, 5.

[116] 'The TV appeal couple on way home', *Daily Mirror*, 4 April 1959, 5.

[117] 'All set for a white wedding—Then they dash to Gretna', *Daily Mirror*, 1 October 1955, 4.

stories, the role of the groom is important. He, too, was risking a conflict with parents, employers and possibly the police in order to strike out defiantly, escape parental clutches and romantically marry the woman of *his* choice. Amid the apparent recklessness, the groom is able to position himself according to codes of masculinity honour and independence.

In newspaper narration of weddings between 1918 and 1960, the 'white wedding' became normal, but the man is almost invisible in this media presentation of the 'white wedding'. The big church wedding became something that could, and should, be achieved, by all and not just the Society set. Reinforcing the notion that masculinity is concerned with economic production, and femininity with emotional production, the 'white wedding' is posited as being the biggest day is a 'girl's' life. Newspapers placed the white wedding within a complex of consumerism and domesticity, spheres from which men were conspicuously absent. Men were therefore to be producers and providers. Some men wanted to provide a romantic, white wedding for their brides and some fathers were able to exert power by agreeing to pay for a wedding. The generative purpose of marriage was emphasised by attention to the rise of 'child attendants' at weddings, but the more romantic, companionate ideal of marriage could be found in white wedding elopement stories.

First-Person Wedding Narratives

First-person accounts of wedding days give a different perspective from either etiquette manuals or newspapers. Men tended not to mention their wedding at all in their autobiographies. In oral history interviews, however, men are more likely to give details of their wedding day, but usually only in response to a direct question from the interviewer. This absence in first-person testimonies demonstrates that the same 'socialising mechanism' that taught girls that the wedding will be 'the happiest day of their lives' is absent in boys' and men's lives. In becoming masculine, boys and men learn that 'their "work" is other than that'.[118] Men's reminiscences do however show that, through the wedding, institutionalised coupledom appeared at the heart of masculinity and allowed men to demonstrate their privileged position at once within a nexus of home,

[118] Ingraham, *White Weddings*, 81.

work and 'all-male association'.[119] Men were often keen to have the best wedding they could, even if it fell short of the idealised white wedding of etiquette manuals and the popular press. This first-person evidence adds to the etiquette manuals and newspapers to show that the discourses on which men could draw to tell stories of weddings and marriage were varied, and complicated by class, locality and race.

Most women remembered their wedding days as one of the most important events in their lives, but not all had a white wedding. When asked about the 'high points of life', Angela Baker replied that 'the most obvious one would have to be my [1950s] wedding'.[120] In Humberside, wartime bride Ella Thompson had a 'nice little wedding' and expressed the feeling of many women about their wedding days: 'I came from Sproatley in a taxi and I felt like a queen... all in white and I was proud of myself'.[121] In Liverpool, tobacco stripper Barbara Harrison 'had the most wonderful wedding' in 1953.[122] Some women found that the aspiration of a white wedding was curtailed by gendered notions of sexual purity before marriage. In Northumberland, a colliery worker's daughter Mary Anderson stated that 'I didn't want any man before I was married because I wanted a white wedding'. She married in 1945 and had 'a true white wedding'.[123] In Norfolk, Hazel Glaister's father threatened her that she could not have a 'white wedding' if she 'ran around with the boys'; but she did anyway and still had a white wedding.[124] Nellie Rowson, in Shropshire, was pregnant and therefore 'didn't have white wedding or nothing but it was a very happy day for me'. Reminiscing over sixty years later, her 1933 register office wedding was a 'red letter day' in her life.[125]

[119] Tosh, 'What should historians do with masculinity?', 187.

[120] C1029/40 interview with Angela Baker, Down to Earth: An Oral History of British Horticulture, BLSA. Also see C1029/43 interview with Gilly Drummond, Down to Earth: An Oral History of British Horticulture, BLSA.

[121] C900/07043 C1 interview with Ella Thompson, Millennium Memory Bank, BLSA.

[122] C900/10029 C1 interview with Barbara Harrison, Millennium Memory Bank, BLSA.

[123] C900/11088 C1 interview with Mary Anderson, Millennium Memory Bank, BLSA.

[124] C900/11549 interview with Hazel Glaister, Millennium Memory Bank, BLSA.

[125] C900/15073 interview with Nellie Rowson, Millennium Memory Bank, BLSA.

While some women could only 'vaguely'[126] remember their wedding, others could recount detail about the day and the dress, music and other arrangements, but women did not mention the bridegroom's involvement in wedding preparations. Norfolk woman Stella Ringwood could vividly describe the detail of her 1928 wedding, especially her blue and black dress, seventy years later.[127] Also in Norfolk, Kathleen Kiddle recounted detail of her dress sixty years after her 1939 wedding.[128] Edith Evans, married in a Methodist church, surprised her husband by wearing white. Her groom was 'voicing his surprise at seeing his bride in white' because he had 'expected an everyday hat and coat!' Edith however wanted a white wedding because as she explained, 'I guessed that it would be the only wedding I was likely to have so I might as well have the real thing'.[129] Liverpudlian Veronica Jeffers could give very close detail of her dress and the process of making it over sixty years after her 1944 church wedding.[130] Married in 1942 in Dulwich, Betty Judge could remember the bomb damage to the church but also that she 'marched in to Purcell's *Trumpet Tune*, and out to Mendelssohn's *Wedding March*'.[131] Margaret Gillin's account of her brother-in-law queuing in T. J. Hughes for a table-cloth on the morning of his wedding stands out in her memory,[132] but also stands out among oral history accounts. Women do not mention the role of the men in wedding preparations.

Women's personal testimonies reveal the range of interwar weddings: from those attended by a couple of witnesses[133] to the large extravagant weddings. Interviewed fifty-two years after her 1919 wedding, 'house-wife' Mrs Deacon of Torpoint, Cornwall, remembered that even though she and her fiancé were engaged for four months, the wedding was organised only a couple of weeks before because 'you didn't have to have so long in those days as they do now'. This interviewee repeatedly drew a

---

[126] C900/11568 interview with Christine Peach, Millennium Memory Bank, BLSA.

[127] C900/11507 interview with Stella Ringwood, Millennium Memory Bank, BLSA.

[128] C900/11545 interview with Kathleen Kiddle, Millennium Memory Bank, BLSA.

[129] Edith Evans, *Rough Diamonds* (Bognor Regis: New Horizon, 1982), 214–5.

[130] C900/10023 interview with Veronica Jeffers, Millennium Memory Bank, BLSA.

[131] C464/40/01-16 interview with Betty Judge, NLSC: General, BLSA.

[132] C900/10038 interview with Margaret Gillin, Millennium Memory Bank, BLSA.

[133] For example Michael Katz wedding in 1940. C821/70/01–07 interview with Michael Katz Food: From Source to Salespoint, BLSA.

comparison between her small wedding and the later big, white weddings. The wedding reception was small and informal 'cos we only had the few friends at home you see… [with] just – you know, [a] one tier-cake in our day of course'. There was no announcement in the local newspaper because it 'wasn't done in them days'. She wore her wedding suit many times after the day and although there were bridesmaids, they did not have special outfits, 'nothing terrific like that'. Mrs Deacon framed the wedding day in modesty: 'I don't like a lot of show really'.[134] Small weddings are also a theme in working-class autobiographies covering the same period. Shortly after the First World War, Nellie Hoare's wedding in the Bournemouth register office was attended by only her brother and his wife, and after the ceremony 'Reg and Glad went home'.[135] In 1925, Goole teacher Alice Bond 'invited only the immediate families to our wedding simply on account of the expense'.[136] However, not all working-class weddings in the 1920s were small. In London's East End Grace Foakes's family set up 'a money club within the family' with each member of the family contributing four shillings a week until there was enough to give Grace a wedding dress of 'white crepe-de-Chine' complete with white veil. To complete this 1929 wedding there were four brides-maids in 'saxe blue calf-length dresses' who 'carried yellow tea roses'.[137] In terms of style and tropes of 'tradition', this working-class wedding would not have been out of place in the Society pages of the popular press. Although it seems that men did not get involved in wedding preparations, the whole family, including the men, pulled together financially to put on a big wedding.

When reminiscing about their weddings, many men set the day within the wider social context by describing the types of guests and the scale and importance of the wedding, and reception, as a social event. Rather than narrating the wedding as the greatest day of their lives, weddings to these men were as important as social functions as they were a rite of passage when remembered later in life, and this was the case for men who married across the period. Many had smaller less formal weddings. In Canning

[134] C707/346/1-3 C1 interview with Mrs Deacon, Family Life and Work Experience before 1918, BLSA.

[135] Nellie Hoare, *A Winton story* (Bournemouth: Bournemouth Local Studies, 1982), 36.

[136] Alice Bond, *Life of a Yorkshire girl* (Hull: Bradley, 1981), 69.

[137] Grace Foakes, *My life with Reuben* (London: Shepheard-Walwyn, 1975), 25.

132   N. PENLINGTON

Town, crane driver James Bushnell did not have speeches at his reception.[138] Over in Hampstead Road, Frederick Allen had a small reception in his family home. Some 'white weddings' were small. When Frederick married in 1918 in a London Anglican church, his bride wore white and there were bridesmaids. The wedding was however 'very quiet' with only 'two or three' in attendance.[139] Some had a function in a pub.[140] In Humberside, farm-worker Doug Grant was married in a church in 1938 but had his reception at the bride's parental farm.[141] London-based clerk George Henry Evers, married in 1926, had 'only' twelve guests at his Church of England wedding, but they gave a 'fair amount' of presents.[142] In 1950, Artist John Ward had a small wedding in Somerset with 'not many guests'.[143] Some had twenty-four guests, 'mostly family', at the reception.[144] In contrast to women's reminiscences, in which the interviewee places herself at the centre of the wedding, men tend to talk in a more detached way, almost as if it could have been anyone's wedding.

While some men stressed the family members present at their weddings, others drew attention to the wedding as an important event to which to invite (male) work colleagues.[145] As sociologist Chrys Ingraham argues in the American context, 'weddings are viewed as innocuous' but they give people 'significant advantage in the workplace and are anything but benign'. Through a mix of symbolism and a varied guest list, weddings 'signify that the couple is normal, moral, productive, family-centred, upstanding, and most importantly, appropriately gendered'.[146] This places institutionalised heterosexuality at the heart of economic and social relationships. Middle-class men in the post-war era of the 'career

---

[138] Interview with James Bushnell.

[139] Interview with Frederick Allen.

[140] Interview with John Higgens.

[141] Interview with Doug Grant.

[142] C707/223/1-2 C1 interview with George Henry Evers, Family Life and Work Experience before 1918, BLSA.

[143] C466/208A interview with John Ward, NLSC: Artists' Lives, BLSA.

[144] Interview with James Bushnell.

[145] Women mention work colleagues as wedding guests only occasionally. For example, C900/18509 C1 interview with Renee Kingston, Millennium Memory Bank, BLSA and C821/188 interview with Janet Farrow, Food: From Source to Salespoint, BLSA.

[146] Ingraham, *White weddings*, 18.

manager', as Michael Roper argues, increasingly self-identified with a masculinity in which married status was essential for a successful career. Roper found that '[m]arriage was frequently an informal prerequisite for promotion' and that the 'most demanding jobs went to married men'. The wedding was *the* occasion for a man to overcome the 'cultural separation of work and home'[147] and to straddle visibly the organisational hierarchy, post-war affluent consumerism and married sexuality. Banker Philip Hatch attended many of his colleagues' weddings.[148] In 1958, engineer Jim McMahon married in a Roman Catholic Church in Enfield. His 'boss and co-workers' attended but his family did not because they were in Australia.[149] When future Tesco boss Ian MacLaurin married in 1961 aged 24, many of the Cohen Tesco family were among the eighty guests.[150] Grooms made sure that their male friends were well catered for. Following a wedding in a Methodist Church in Preston in 1946, Sam Kilburn had a reception in the church; but because it was a 'dry do' (his father-in-law was in the Sons of Temperance Bowling Club) he had to make other arrangements so that his army friends could have an 'alcoholic drink'.[151]

Some men placed their wedding reminiscences within the context of the local community, perhaps stressing their work, social or political connections. In 1937, when Middlesbrough steelworker Dickie Seymour married Olwyn in South Bank Primitive Methodist church, he was careful to fit the time of the wedding around men's shifts.[152] In 1946, Lincolnshire steelworker Harry Taylor married Barbara in a church before a congregation of sixty, the church was full. The reception at a hotel had 'no end of guests' because they were 'both well-known local families'. On returning from honeymoon, they had a party in the church hall and 'anyone passing could come in'.[153] Away from working-class

[147] Michael Roper, *Masculinity and the British organisation man* (Oxford: Oxford University Press, 1994), 1, 13, 84.

[148] Interview with Philip Hatch.

[149] C464/58 interview with James McMahon, NLSC: General, BLSA.

[150] Interview with Ian MacLaurin.

[151] C821/166 interview with Samuel Kilburn, NLSC: Food: From Source to Salespoint, BLSA.

[152] C532/032 interview with Dickie Seymour, NLSC: Lives in Steel, BLSA.

[153] C532/008/01-07 interview with James Henry (Harry) Taylor, NLSC: Lives in Steel, BLSA.

134   N. PENLINGTON

weddings, there were perhaps different notions of status within the local community. After the Second World War, when banker Anthony Akers married at a church in King's Lynn, the reception with 'a lot of guests' was in the Town Hall. His father-in-law was a 'very generous man' who knew the Mayor and gave the town hall 'as a gift'.[154] Steelwork manager Les Peirson also had political connections and remembered that at his wedding in the 1930s, his wife was given away by a member of parliament and the M. P.'s daughter was a bridesmaid. There was a 'hell of a good do there' in the church hall and 'a cine' was made of proceedings. He claimed it was 'like any other decent wedding'.[155] During the war, on Teesside, wagonwright Thomas Harper and his bride held their reception in the 'Con Club' where they had met. They hired a caterer for the 'wedding breakfast'.[156] This steelworker and his fiancée perhaps placed their community loyalty with the Conservative Club rather than the more expected context of a steelworks community. In narrating their wedding day, men are more likely than women to place the day within the context of community and social networks, perhaps emphasising the masculine privilege of being able to more freely between home, work and all-male association.

Following the convention found in both etiquette manuals and newspapers, oral history interviews reveal that the women did most of the wedding preparation, especially the mothers. In some cases, it was the woman's mother, as posited in the 'traditional wedding'. Reminiscing about his 1930s wedding, Peirson said that he could not really remember who made the wedding preparations but suggested it was his fiancée's mother who 'made all the arrangements'.[157] In Lincolnshire, Frank Flear was keen to 'stress that this is a working-class family' and remembered that his fiancée's mother arranged his church wedding and reception in the church hall in 1956. She also prepared a 'cold dinner', with 'others helping', for 100 guests and made a huge three-tier cake because 'they did their own catering and baking in those days'. In his interview, Frank was conscious of his own social class and that 'middle-class would have been

---

[154] Interview with Anthony Akers.

[155] C532/002 interview with Leslie (Les) Peirson, Lives in Steel, BLSA.

[156] C532/022 interview with Thomas Harper, NLSC: Lives in Steel, BLSA.

[157] Interview with Leslie Peirson.

totally different' according to 'affordability and custom'.[158] Across the period, however, the man's mother could be in charge of arrangements. In 1927, Middlesbrough steelworker Harold Leech's mother 'put the meal on' because his bride did not have a mother.[159] In 1946, steelworker Harry Taylor's mother made the three-tier wedding cake' but he did not explain why.[160] In 1953, dairy owner's son Desmond Moseley's mother made all the dresses. This was possibly because of the wealth and status of the family. Desmond's aunt made the cake and it was baked and iced at the dairy.[161] It was however possible for a man to feel 'pretty involved' in the wedding preparations. Poet Anthony Thwaite and his bride had 'discussions' with her parents before their 'rather grand' wedding at their parish church, St Martin-in-the-Fields, and a reception on Northumberland Avenue in 1953.[162] The 'white wedding' perhaps required some of the groom's time before the wedding day. In the 1930s, Les Peirson had a full wedding rehearsal, with bridesmaids and the best man and much consideration given to 'who's gonna propose a toast... that kind of thing'.[163] Overall, the wedding day was some thing the groom simply turned up to after other people, mostly women, had done the preparation, especially the apparently feminised tasks of cooking and catering.

Men were more likely to contribute financially to their wedding than to get involved with the minutiae of preparation. The intertwining of marriage and the masculine position of breadwinner also intersects with discourses of class. Although there was an increased emphasis on the aspirational wedding in the popular press and an expectation in etiquette manuals that the bride's father would pay, working-class men prided themselves on paying for their own weddings across the period. The scale of these working-class weddings was bound by economic circumstances: these men strove to have the best wedding they could. James Bushnell was in the army when he married in a church in Canning Town in 1919. They walked to the church to save the taxi fare, and he paid for

---

[158] C821/113 interview with Frank Flear, NLSC: Food: From Source to Salespoint, BLSA.

[159] C532/025 interview with Harold Leech, NLSC: Lives in Steel, BLSA.

[160] Interview with James Henry (Harry) Taylor.

[161] Interview with Desmond Moseley.

[162] C1276/15 interview with Anthony Thwaite, Authors' Lives, BLSA.

[163] Interview with Leslie Peirson.

the reception, a 'good old knees up' and a cold dinner of corned beef, cheese and pickles.[164] Ken Lynham's father-in-law paid for the 'wedding breakfast'—a restaurant meal—but he and his bride paid for 'everything else'.[165] Married in 1949, Frank Davies and his bride had 'a very small wedding' because they had 'paid all out on the house'.[166] Also in 1949, John Watts saved up to pay for his wedding while he was in the army.[167] Ted and Doris Knight both saved for their 1939 wedding. She looked after lodgers in her parents' home while he worked as a coachman with his family.[168] These working-class men were pragmatic about who could achieve a proper wedding, but they were doing it on their own terms. They were not expected to pay for the wedding but wanted to, and, if necessary, were prepared to share the cost with their working fiancée. This is in contrast to the expectation after marriage that the man would be the breadwinner with a stay-at-home wife.

Men's personal testimonies reveal that although posited as being the bride's big day, some grooms exercised power and made the decision on where to get married. Rather than allowing the bride a choice, some men chose venues with their own family connection. Liverpool telegraphist Frederick Allen chose the church for his wedding in 1919 because 'the parson was a relation'.[169] In the early 1950s, bank employee Peter Norris's parents got married in Sandhurst with 'considerable pomp' and 'mass bands and honour guards and crossed swords' because his father was an instructor there.[170] Artist Anthony Eyton chose to marry at a particular church because his friend was a priest there and 'so that was it really'.[171]

---

[164] Interview with James Bushnell.

[165] Interview with Ken Lynham.

[166] Steve Humphries and Pamela Gordon, *A man's world: From boyhood to manhood, 1900–1960* (London: BBC Books, 1996), 169.

[167] C821/190 interview with John Watts, NLSC: Food: From Source to Salespoint, BLSA.

[168] Doris Knight, *Millfield memories* (London: Centerprise, 1976), 35.

[169] C707/107/1-2 C1 interview with Frederick Allen, Family Life and Work Experience before 1918, BLSA.

[170] C1367/15 interview with Peter Norris, An Oral History of Barings, BLSA.

[171] C466/213A interview with Anthony Eyton, NLSC: Artists' Lives, BLSA.

4 THE WEDDING   137

Etiquette manuals and newspapers assumed that couples would marry in church, typically the church attended by the bride's parents, but oral history testimonies depart from the idealised wedding of etiquette manuals and newspapers to suggest otherwise. Many couples wanted to marry in the church through religious conviction or because of a belief that the marriage would not be 'proper' otherwise. The choice of church is something that lingered long in the memory of some men. For Christians, like Doug Grant, it was important to get married in a church.[172] Some were simply married in the village church,[173] while other men were married at the church attended by their wife's family,[174] even if the man was not a churchgoer himself.[175] Rather than a sign of weakness, the decision to hold the wedding in the woman's church could be an act of chivalry, especially for a very religious man. On the Wirral in the early 1950s, fruit seller Douglas Kemp ceded to his bride's wish to marry in the Church of England even though he was a 'strong Presbyterian'.[176]

If the couple attended the same church then the decision was simple,[177] but many couples had to make practical wedding venue decisions. When Anglican and banker Anthony Akers married his second wife, a Roman Catholic, they had their wedding in a non-Conformist chapel because of his divorce. Despite these prohibitions from their own denominations, they thought it was 'important to get married in church because they both believed in God'.[178] John Glen married in a Church of England church in Birmingham in 1960, although his bride was Presbyterian. Interviewed some years later he claimed, 'I thought I wouldn't be properly married otherwise'.[179] Painter Leslie Marr married in Hampstead Methodist Church because the Church of England church would not

[172] C900/07122A C1 interview with Doug Grant, Millennium Memory Bank, BLSA.

[173] C466/212/01-09 interview with John Higgens, NLSC: Artists' Lives, BLSA.

[174] C1154/02/01-07 interview with John Brushfield, An Oral History of the Wine Society, BLSA.

[175] Interview with Leslie Peirson; Interview with Thomas Harper.

[176] C821/189 interview with Douglas Kemp, NLSC: Food: From Source to Salespoint, BLSA.

[177] Interview with Harold Leech; C960/33/01-05 interview with Ivor Robinson, NLSC: Crafts Lives, BLSA.

[178] C1367/14 interview with Anthony Akers, An Oral History of Barings, BLSA.

[179] C1379/26 interview with Dr John Glen, An Oral History of British Science, BLSA.

marry his bride because she had not been 'christened'.[180] Some Anglican vicars were less strict. In the late 1930s, Workington steelworker Stan Hullock had to get married at twenty-four because he and his partner had 'made a slip'. Despite the pregnancy, they were able to marry in the Anglican church.[181] In the 1950s, Lancashire bookbinder Philip Smith married his 'open-minded Christian' fiancée in an Anglican church near Letchworth. Although Philip was a Quaker, the vicar was 'happy' to marry them after 'interviewing' them 'about attitudes to religion'.[182]

These couples did not seriously consider marrying in a register office, but some interdenominational couples ended up settling for a register office. Fisherman Ken Lynham married in a register office in Weymouth because he was Methodist and his bride Roman Catholic.[183] A register office was a last resort for Bristol sausage factory worker Michael Katz, who in 1940 went to the local synagogue, but was asked for £20. That 'ended' his and his fiancée's 'relationship with organised religion' and they married in a register office.[184] For many couples, therefore, the wedding in the bride's family church simply did not hold true. This sample suggests the variety of discussions and negotiations men entered into when helping to pick a wedding venue. Although invisible during the rest of the arrangements, the wedding venue, and therefore the type of wedding, mattered to many men.

Some middle-class men, in their oral history interviews, cast their wedding venue within the discourse of conventionality, as if to attempt to mock ironically their own class status, while bolstering their masculine status of marriage. At Easter 1950, Kent-born artist Andrew Forge had a 'regular marriage of that kind' in St Mary's Bryanston Square, even though he 'didn't like the bourgeois orthodoxy of it all'.[185] Writer John Carey married in Balliol College chapel in 1960 and wanted his bride to use the *Book of Common Prayer* 'obey' because he was 'rather conventional in that respect' and 'sure' that his 'mother would have promised to

---

[180] C466/291A interview with Leslie Marr, NLSC: Artists' Lives, BLSA.

[181] C532/042 interview with Stan Hullock, NLSC: Lives in Steel, BLSA.

[182] C960/36/01-13 interview with Philip Smith NLSC: Crafts Lives, BLSA.

[183] Interview with Ken Lynham.

[184] Interview with Michael Katz.

[185] C466/36/01-18 interview with Andrew Forge, NLSC: Artists' Lives, BLSA.

obey' his father. His bride however refused to 'obey'.[186] Trying to bridge the gap of generational expectations could end in a strange outcome. When architect Oliver Cox married in the late 1950s, he wanted to get married in the 'conventional way' so that 'we could say our vows in front of everybody'—the 'whole family' and 'friends'. So, they married in at 'Battersea old church'[187] although they were 'not really church people'. He reminisced that several friends who were 'non-believers' marched around outside the church instead of coming into the service.[188]

Once the wedding venue was agreed upon, men had to find something to wear. Men's dress was often very important; it lived on in grooms' memories for decades and is a sign of the lengthy preparation men put into looking the part on their wedding day. In the Bournemouth register office after the Great War, Nellie Hoare's groom 'had a new suit, made to measure which was a surprise to [Nellie], with a nice white shirt and tie and new shoes' and the bride wore 'a new navy costume and white silk blouse'.[189] This shows the level of masculine pride the groom's had in their appearance and the importance of the wedding day. Despite the focus on etiquette manuals and newspapers on the bride's dress, men were able to remember details of their own dress many years after the wedding day. For example, fisherman Ken Lynham wore a new suit and a flowery tie. His outfit was 'quite expensive'. His bride simply wore blue.[190] Married in 'white weddings' across the period and across the social classes, men could remember the style of suit,[191] the colour[192] or whether the suit was bought[193] or hired.[194] Choosing a suit was perhaps more masculine than being involved in cooking and catering. This ability

---

[186] C1276/49 interview with John Carey, NLSC: Author's Lives, BLSA.

[187] Presumably St Mary's, Battersea.

[188] C467/80/01-07 interview with Oliver Cox, NLSC: Architects' Lives, BLSA.

[189] Perhaps he was keen not to wear army uniform, Hoare, *A Winton story*, 36; Many men would have worn their uniform on their wedding day. For example, interview with James Bushnell.

[190] Interview with Ken Lynham.

[191] Interview with Leslie Peirson; Interview with Frank Flear.

[192] Interview with Ivor Robinson; Interview with Ian MacLaurin.

[193] Interview with Samuel Kilburn.

[194] C1046/09/01-12 interview with Percy Savage, An Oral History of British Fashion, BLSA.

140   N. PENLINGTON

and willingness to recount detail of the wedding suit, shows the importance men attached to their wedding day when given the opportunity to speak about it.

Not all 'white weddings' were White, some 'West Indian' communities prided themselves on hosting large, white weddings, although this may have passed unnoticed by the majority population. Historians of gender and sexuality have rightly considered race in this period.[195] However, oral historians have often used, perhaps unintentionally, white-only cohorts.[196] First-person accounts of weddings involving Black or Asian people in Britain between 1918 and 1960 are hard to find. This could be because non-White weddings were statistically very few.[197] However, it is clear from impressionistic sources that large white weddings did take place in some Black Caribbean communities. In Jamaica, a wedding was 'likely to be an elaborate, and therefore an expensive affair'.[198] In Brixton in the 1950s 'migrant' weddings were marked by their 'lavishness' and were 'usually performed in a church' with the bride expressing a desire to 'do it properly' and not to have a 'seven-and-six (sic) registry marriage'. Although dressed in 'elaborate white' and 'attended

[195] For example, Frank Mort, *Capital affairs: London and the making of the permissive society* (London: Yale University Press, 2010); Matt Houlbrook, *Queer London: Perils and pleasures in the sexual metropolis* (London: University of Chicago Press, 2005); Langhamer, *English in love*, 71–5.

[196] For example, Simon Szreter and Kate Fisher, *Sex before the sexual revolution: Intimate life in England, 1918–1963* (Cambridge: Cambridge University Press, 2010).

[197] The *fear* of immigration in the 1950s is not matched by the overall *numbers* for England and Wales. Home Office estimates suggest that net inward migration between 1955 and 1960 was 161,450 from the 'West Indies', 33,070 from India and 17,120 from Pakistan. (Source: R.B. Davison, *Black British: Immigrants to England* (London: Oxford University Press, 1966), 3) By 1961, only 7.1 per 1,000 of the England and Wales population were 'Coloured'. (Source: E. J. B. Rose, *Colour and citizenship* (London: Oxford University Press, 1969), 97). The majority of immigrants from the Commonwealth were men, many of whom were not in a position to marry. (Sources: Sheila Patterson, *Dark strangers: A sociological study of the absorption of a recent West Indian migrant group in Brixton, South London* (London: Tavistock, 1963), 417 and Rose, *Colour and Citizenship*, 105) Government agencies did not, and do not, collect data on 'ethnicity' from marriage certificates; but even if we assume that the marriage rate for immigrants was roughly 70 per thousand for men and 50 per thousand for women as in the general population (Source: *Vital Statistics: Population and Health Reference Tables*, ONS), we must conclude that the number of Black and Asian weddings was a very small fraction of the overall number of weddings in the 1950s.

[198] Davison, *Black British*, 32.

by a number of bridesmaids' the bride cannot compete with the groom who 'outshines' her by 'wearing an American-style draped dinner jacket and ballooning peg-top trousers in pale blue, Bordeaux, or some other gay colour'. The bride would 'usually be given away by an older male friend if no male relatives [were] in England'. The ceremony would be followed by a large reception at which the guests were 'those kinfolk and former friends and acquaintances who [were] in London, neighbours, work-mates, and new friends'.[199] Although these weddings were hugely important to those involved, most of the majority White population would have been unaware that these weddings were taking place. Only a small proportion of the population encountered Black immigrants face-to-face, and newspapers covered only White 'white weddings'. Moreover, the mainly male West Indian migrants in the 1950s, tended not to attend regularly the 'white-led Anglican, Catholic, and Free Churches' as they had in 'their homelands' because of 'the often ambivalent attitudes which these mainline Churches adopted towards the first waves of Commonwealth immigrants'.[200] As historian Marcus Collins argues, '[u]ndertstandings of West Indian masculinity were affected by, but had no discernible effect on, evolving norms for white men in this period'. Further, Collins shows that 'West Indians went unmentioned in the wider debate on companionate marriage taking place outside the race relations literature'.[201]

Men talking about their wedding day in oral history interviews rarely mention specific guests, but when they do, it is the best man. This further demonstrates that the ritualised white wedding was a site for demonstrating and emphasising male–male friendship. When choosing a best man, it seems that many men made a practical choice from a small pool rather than giving it the careful consideration advised by etiquette manuals. Some grooms chose a team-mate from the village cricket club[202] or an old school friend[203] to be best man while others chose from within

[199] Patterson, *Dark strangers*, 436–7.

[200] Clive Field, *Secularization in the long 1960s: Numerating religion in Britain* (Oxford: Oxford University Press, 2017), 72.

[201] Marcus Collins, 'Pride and prejudice: West Indian men in mid-twentieth-century Britain', *The Journal of British Studies* 40, No. 3 (July, 2001), 417.

[202] Interview with John Higgens.

[203] Interview with Ian MacLaurin.

the family.[204] During the Second World War, Anthony Akers was the best man at his sister's wedding because her bridegroom did not have any friends in Cornwall, the wedding location. Akers himself chose his own brother to be best man at his wedding.[205] After the Second World War, some grooms chose a best man from outside of their faith group. Philip Hatch was the best man to many of his Roman Catholic friends although he himself was not Catholic.[206] In 1952, Ivor Robinson could not reciprocate and invited his friend Paul to be the best man because the latter was away in the army.[207] In the mid-1950s, Oliver Cox chose fellow architect Gabriel Epstein as his best man.[208]

Reminiscences of weddings that took place later in the period stress the mix of generations at weddings. This partly shows the distance between the larger later weddings and the smaller earlier weddings, but also that the white wedding was a site of iterated gender and generation. In the early 1950s, fruiterer Douglas Kemp had a 'good turnout' at his wedding. There were grandma, aunties, cousins and friends from work, home and 'digs'.[209] In 1953 in Scarborough, Desmond Moseley's wedding 'was something special because we had a very big guard of honour with the guides and the scouts'.[210] This type of guard of honour, especially provided by one's service or police force colleagues, became popular during the Second World War.[211] Here the use of girl guides and boy scouts would have placed the wedding at the centre of civic respectability and also provided another way, alongside 'child attendants', of involving gendered children in wedding ceremonies and thus can be seen as an example of iterative and generative heterosexuality. In 1961 in Surbiton, John Brushfield had a big wedding. He felt that 'it was considered quite important to have a full selection of young people there'.[212]

[204] Interview with Dickie Seymour.

[205] Interview with Anthony Akers.

[206] Interview with Philip Hatch.

[207] Interview with Ivor Robinson.

[208] Interview with Oliver Cox.

[209] Interview with Douglas Kemp.

[210] Interview with Desmond Moseley.

[211] Lansdell, *Wedding fashions*, 72.

[212] Interview with John Brushfield.

First-person testimonies show the variety of stories men and women tell about weddings. Men tended to reminisce about the wedding day as a social function, rather than as an emotional life event to mark the start of a romantic and companionate marriage. This supports the notion that 'the division of emotional labour'[213] was unequally shared in marriages. Men remembered the all-male elements of the day such as the best man and co-workers. There was a distance between the idealised weddings of the etiquette manuals and the feminised white weddings of the newspapers, and the lived experience of groom's during this period. Men tried to have the best wedding they could, even if only some elements of the 'white wedding'. Men were concerned about being dressed appropriately and that the wedding should be 'proper'. Although women performed most of the weddings preparations, especially catering tasks, men were as concerned as their brides about the wedding venue, and therefore the type of wedding.

CONCLUSION

English weddings changed dramatically during the period from 1918 to 1960. At the start of the period, most weddings were small, quiet and practical, but over time the choreographed 'white wedding'—complete with processions, a range of suitably dressed actors and guests, and a formal reception—became more the norm. The normality of weddings in daily life placed institutionalised coupledom at the centre of economic, emotional and social life. We can see, through the three different sources of narrating weddings, that idealised marriage ceremonies reinforced masculinity and femininity intertwined with class, race and Englishness, but that the lived experience of oral history interviewees reveals tensions and negotiations across a range of weddings. Although the wedding was supposed to be the bride's 'big day', men were able to demonstrate their privileged position of being able to move freely between domesticity, economic production and homosocial interaction.

Etiquette manuals aimed at a wealthy audience narrated weddings to create the ideal 'traditional' wedding. The term 'white wedding' first appeared in etiquette manuals in the 1930s and encapsulates the popular notion of a 'traditional' wedding recognisable today—the white dress, the

---

[213] Roper, *Masculinity and the British organisation man*, 163.

144 N. PENLINGTON

bridesmaids (often children) in white, the suited-and-booted groom and best man, the church, the processions, the best man, the 'giving away' and the lavish reception. The 'white wedding', a combination of old and new, performed 'natural' gender and sexuality as timeless and unchanging. Throughout the preparations and the wedding day itself, sex, gender and sexuality were crystallised around the binaries of male breadwinner and female homemaker, and biological father and mother. The new 'traditional' wedding also reinforced social-class distinctions and normative notions of Englishness. Despite the existence of big Black Caribbean 'white weddings', the wedding was White; normative masculinity was White.

Etiquette manuals may not have had a wide readership, but they influenced the expectations of weddings presented in newspapers. The way in which newspapers narrated weddings changed between 1918 and 1960 increasingly making the 'white wedding' appear normal. In the interwar period, newspapers reported mainly Society weddings; weddings that were similar to the 'traditional' weddings as set out in etiquette manuals. Newspapers increasingly gave etiquette advice and the term 'white wedding' appeared in newspapers in the 1930s. This 'traditional' wedding was posited as available to all. A 'proper' wedding was in a church and the romantic 'white wedding' was the biggest day in a 'girl's' life. The increased attention to weddings in newspapers made marriage central to all aspects of daily life. Men were largely invisible in newspaper coverage of weddings. Masculinity was therefore not concerned with consumerism and homemaking, but instead with a steadier, stoical breadwinning. Although they were not required in the preparation of the wedding, men were however part of the romantic choreography. Newspapers combined elopement stories with the 'white wedding' to demonstrate the futility of trying to stop romantic love, and the determination of some young couples to achieve a wedding and marriage on their own terms, including the masculine status of independence. The iterative reproduction of institutionalised coupledom was reinforced as newspapers helped to make the involvement of children in weddings appear normal and widespread. Longer guest lists, at bigger weddings, helped to reinforce the institution of marriage and would have reminded unmarried guests of the normality of being part of a married couple.

Although newspaper proprietors, editors and most journalists were male, men gave a different take on weddings in personal testimonies than in etiquette manuals or newspapers. Weddings are absent in men's autobiographies and are only mentioned in response to direct questioning in oral history interviews. This demonstrates that, although marriage was an important element of masculinity, the man's 'work' was other than emotional. Women tend to talk about the wedding day as an important life event. Men's reminiscences about their weddings day are as important social gatherings rather than romance. Contrary to depictions of weddings in etiquette manuals and newspapers, men were often involved in choosing the wedding venue and therefore the type of wedding. They were also concerned about dressing for the occasion and working-class grooms were prepared to contribute towards the wedding if necessary, to have the best wedding possible given the circumstances. Some working-class men strove to provide a big wedding, but some middle-class men self-consciously tried to be 'unconventional' or deliberately 'conventional'. It was however the women who did most of the work required to stage a big wedding. Men's personal testimonies show that the new, romantic 'white wedding'—with the groom just as sexualised as the bride—was an important site of homosocial interaction. Men were able to affirm and reaffirm their 'gender privilege'[214] by fraternising with competing and overlapping kinship, friendship and occupational networks to place married masculinity at the heart of personal, social and economic life.

REFERENCES

An Oral History of Barings, British Library Sound Archive.
An Oral History of British Fashion, British Library Sound Archive.
An Oral History of British Science, British Library Sound Archive.
An Oral History of the Wine Society, British Library Sound Archive.
Anon. 1928. *The Book of Common Prayer with the additions and deviations proposed in 1928*. Cambridge: Cambridge University Press.
Authors' Lives, British Library Sound Archive.
Bee, M., and S. Bee. 1935. *Weddings without worry: A modern and practical guide to wedding conventions and ceremonies*. London: Methuen.
"Best Man". 1936. *Marriage etiquette: How to arrange a wedding*. London: W. Foulsham.
Bond, Alice. 1981. *Life of a Yorkshire girl*. Hull: Bradley.

[214] Tosh, 'What should historians do with masculinity?', 187.

146 N. PENLINGTON

Carter, Philip. 2001. *Men and the emergence of polite society, Britain 1660–1800.* Harlow: Longman.

Charsley, Simon R. 1992. *Wedding cakes and cultural history.* London: Routledge.

Collins, Marcus. 2001. Pride and prejudice: West Indian men in mid-twentieth-century Britain. *The Journal of British Studies* 40(3):391–418.

Daily Express.

Daily Mirror.

Davison, R.B. 1966. *Black British: Immigrants to England.* London: Oxford University Press.

Down to Earth: An Oral History of British Horticulture, British Library Sound Archive.

Dyer, Richard. 1997. *White.* London: Routledge.

Edwards, Tim. 1997. *Men in the mirror: Men's fashions, Masculinity and consumer society.* London: Cassell.

Exton, Rev. D. 1935. *Wedding etiquette.* London: Universal Publications.

Family Life and Work Experience before 1918, British Library Sound Archive.

Field, Clive. 2017. *Secularization in the long 1960s: Numerating religion in Britain.* Oxford: Oxford University Press.

Foakes, Grace. 1975. *My life with Reuben.* London: Shepheard-Walwyn.

Food: From Source to Salespoint, British Library Sound Archive.

Freeman, Elizabeth. 2002. *The wedding complex: Forms of belonging in modern American culture.* London: Duke University Press.

Gillis, John. 1988. *For better, for worse: British marriage, 1600 to the present.* Oxford.

Goffman, Erving. 1990. First published 1959. *The presentation of the self in everyday life.* London: Penguin.

Hoare, Nellie. 1982. *A Winton story.* Bournemouth: Bournemouth Local Studies.

Hobsbawm, Eric. 1983. Introduction: Inventing traditions. In *The invention of tradition* ed. Eric Hobsbawm and Terrance Ranger, 1–14. Cambridge: Cambridge University Press.

Hollander, Anne. 1994. *Sex and suits: The evolution of modern dress.* London: Bloomsbury.

Houlbrook, Matt. 2005. *Queer London: Perils and pleasures in the sexual metropolis.* London: University of Chicago Press.

Humphries, Steve and Pamela Gordon. 1996. *A man's world: From boyhood to manhood, 1900–1960.* London: BBC Books.

Ingraham, Chrys. 1999. *White weddings: Romancing heterosexuality in popular culture.* London: Routledge.

Jobling, Paul. 2005. *Man appeal: Advertising, modernism and menswear.* Oxford: Berg.

Knight, Doris. 1976. *Millfield memories*. London: Centerprise.

Langhamer, Claire. 2013. *The English in love: The intimate history of an emotional revolution*. Oxford: Oxford University Press.

Langhamer, Claire. 2015. Afterword. In *Love and Romance in Britain, 1918–1970* ed. Alana Harris and Timothy Willem Jones, 245–253. Basingstoke: Palgrave.

Lansdell, Avril. 1983. *Wedding fashions, 1860–1980*. Haverfordwest: Shire.

Leech, Kenneth. 2005. *Race*. New York: Church Publishing.

Leonard, Diana. 1980. *Sex and generation: A study of courtship and marriage*. London, 1980.

May, Alfred. 1920. *Marriage in church, chapel or register office*. London: Longmans.

Millennium Memory Bank, British Library Sound Archive.

Mort, Frank and Peter Thompson. 1994. Retailing, commercial culture and masculinity in 1950s Britain: The case of Montague Burton, the "Tailor of Taste". *History Workshop* 38:106–27

Mort, Frank. 2010. *Capital affairs: London and the making of the permissive society*. London: Yale University Press.

National Life Stories Collection: Artists' Lives, British Library Sound Archive.

National Life Stories Collection: Crafts Lives, British Library Sound Archive.

National Life Stories Collection: General, British Library Sound Archive.

National Life Stories Collection: Lives in Steel, British Library Sound Archive.

Office for National Statistics. *Vital Statistics: Population and Health Reference Tables*.

Page, Ann. 1950. *The complete guide to wedding etiquette*. London: Ward, Lock and Co.

Parker, Andrew and Eve Kosofsky Sedgwick. 1995. Introduction: Performativity and performance. In *Performativity and performance* ed. Andrew Parker and Eve Kosofsky Sedgwick, 1–18. New York: Routledge.

Patterson, Sheila. 1963. *Dark strangers: A sociological study of the absorption of a recent West Indian migrant group in Brixton, South London*. London: Tavistock.

Roper, Michael. 1994. *Masculinity and the British organisation man*. Oxford: Oxford University Press.

Rose, E. J. B. 1969. *Colour and citizenship*. London: Oxford University Press.

Szreter, Simon and Kate Fisher. 2010. *Sex before the sexual revolution: Intimate life in England, 1918–1963*. Cambridge: Cambridge University Press.

Tosh, John. 1994. What should historians do with masculinity?—Reflections on nineteenth-century Britain. *History Workshop Journal* 38:179–202.

Woodman, Mary. 1929. *Wedding etiquette*. London: W. Foulsham.

Woods, Diana and Edgar Woods. 1937. *Planning your wedding: A complete guide for all concerned and for all denominations*. London: Universal Publications.

CHAPTER 5

Non-consummation

To complete the legal process of getting married, the marriage has to be consummated by a single act of coitus. From the point of view of the man, and those historicising masculinity, the new husband had to perform a particular sexual act with his putative wife in order to become fully married and achieve full masculine status. In 1937, 'wilful refusal' to consummate a marriage became a ground for nullity. Moreover, changes to the law in 1937 and again in the 1950s made each act of coitus a *re-consummation* of marriage by disallowing nullity or divorce on a variety of grounds if a married couple had performed penile-vaginal intercourse since the matrimonial dispute. Although the number of annulled marriages due to non-consummation was small, discussion about the meaning of consummation and the purpose of marriage intensified, especially after the Second World War, as the established Church lost ground to an increasingly secular State during an era of increased acceptance of contraception, artificial insemination and the notion of sexual pleasure as essential to a happy marriage. The 1956 Royal Commission heard from numerous experts that 'wilful refusal' should enforce regular coitus throughout the marriage. The repeated *linguistic* performative redefinition of 'sex' and the corresponding repeated *corporeal* performative action of 'sex' inflected the shifting norms of masculinity and male sexuality.

© The Author(s), under exclusive license to Springer Nature   149
Switzerland AG 2023
N. Penlington, *Men Getting Married in England, 1918–60*, Genders
and Sexualities in History, https://doi.org/10.1007/978-3-031-27405-3_5

150   N. PENLINGTON

For most of the last millennium, Christian teaching directly defined marriage in England, and it is for this historical reason that the requirement to consummate marriage exists in English Law. Early Christians debated the 'presence or absence of sex in the Garden [of Eden]' and the relationship between Adam and Eve's consummation and the 'fall'.[1] Well-known New Testament unconsummated marriages—for example, that of Saint John the Evangelist,[2] and Mary and Joseph—inspired some 'chaste marriages in the Middle Ages'.[3] In the eleventh and twelfth centuries, debate raged in the Western Church as to the definition of marriage and the precise relationship between consent and consummation. If consummation was required for valid marriage, it followed that 'if the man were impotent the marriage was either invalid or should be annulled'.[4] After the Reformation, the Church of England adopted the Roman Catholic requirement of consent and consummation, and stated that the purpose of marriage was 'procreation of children', a 'remedy against sin, and to avoid fornication'.[5] The requirement of consummation through coitus still stood throughout the period 1918–1960.[6] Although the act of coitus was presented as natural, as influential sociologist Jeffrey Weeks argues, a '*historical* approach to sexuality is one that seeks to understand it as a product of shifting historical circumstances rather than biology or nature'.[7] This chapter will ask what a continual redefinition of coitus meant for masculinity.

[1] Gary Anderson, 'Celibacy or consummation in the Garden? Reflections on early Jewish and Christian interpretations of the Garden of Eden', *The Harvard Theological Review* 82, No. 2 (April 1989), 148.

[2] John T. Noonan Jr., *Power to dissolve: Lawyers and marriages in the courts of the Roman Curia* (Cambridge MA: Harvard University Press, 1972), 82.

[3] Elizabeth Abbott, *A history of celibacy* (Cambridge: Lutterworth, 2001), 146.

[4] Noonan, *Power to dissolve*, 80; Angus McLaren, *Impotence: A cultural history* (London: University of Chicago Press, 2007), 31.

[5] *The Church and the law of nullity of marriage: The report of a commission appointed by the Archbishops of Canterbury and York in 1949 at the request of the Convocations* (London: SPCK, 1955) [Hereafter 'Church Commission'].

[6] It is still a requirement for male–female marriages today. 'Same-sex' couples are not required to consummate under the Civil Partnership Act (2004) or The Marriage (Same Sex Couples) Act (2013).

[7] Jeffrey Weeks, *Sex, politics and society: The regulation of sexuality since 1800* (Harlow: Longman, 2012. First published 1989), 2.

5 NON-CONSUMMATION   151

Historians have almost entirely ignored annulments in favour of statistically larger divorces. Although research on divorce has shed light on social and political trends, and relations between men and women, it is important to uncover the changing definitions of consummation since nullity law defines both marriage and 'normal' married sex. While divorce law breaks marriages, nullity law 'shapes the existence of all marriages because it defines the pre-requisites of all valid marriages'.[8] Although in comparison to divorce cases the number of nullities was small, it is still helpful to consider the statistics. The *proportion* of nullities to divorces was small and ranged between 2.5% and 3.5% but the *number* of nullities for non-consummation increased 15-fold from an average of 40 a year after the Great War to nearly 600 annually by the 1950s. There was perhaps a latent demand for the new nullity grounds and the changes in 1937 led to a big increase in the number of petitions. Figures 5.1 and 5.2 show that the number of nullity decrees granted rose in tandem with the number of divorces, but the number of petitions grew significantly more. The lower success rates of nullity cases in comparison with divorces (see Fig. 5.3) can perhaps be explained by the higher burden of proof required in nullity cases for non-consummation than for divorce cases.[9] The demand for 'wilful refusal' is shown visibly in Fig. 5.4 and it seems that most of these cases were brought by husbands. In Fig. 5.5, it is shown that after 1937 most nullity petitions were filed by husbands and this remained the case after the expansion of legal aid in 1949 when most divorce cases were initiated by wives. The increased likelihood that husbands would take advantage of the new ground of 'wilful refusal' perhaps reflects the greater sexual expectations of men and the continued reticence by many women to express publicly a dissatisfaction with sex.

Historians have studied changes in divorce law and the parliamentary processes involved in each change, and further, the impact of law changes on divorce rates. Lawrence Stone's otherwise authoritative study of

---

[8] Cordelia Moyse, 'Reform of marriage and divorce law in England and Wales 1909–37', Unpublished PhD thesis: University of Cambridge (1996), 193; For other examples of nullity law, see Chapter 2.

[9] Lord Penzance stated in *X v Y* (1865), 34 LJ (P) 81, 86 that the 'media of proof [of impotency] are threefold - medical inspection of the parties; medical testimony as to the conclusions to be drawn therefrom; and, finally, the examination upon oath of both parties as witnesses'. Joseph Jackson, *The formation and annulment of marriage* (London: Butterworth, 1969), 314.

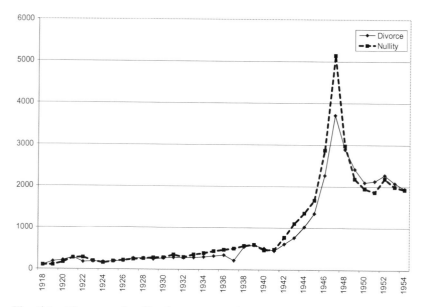

Fig. 5.1 Divorce and nullity decrees granted in England and Wales, 1918–1954 (1918, $n = 100$)

divorce does not assess twentieth-century debates surrounding nullity,[10] which is something that is taken up by Cordelia Moyse, who rightly makes the connection between changes in sexual attitudes and expectations, and changes in the nullity law in 1937.[11] Moyse does not however consider the post-war era when debates about non-consummation became more voluminous and significant. Legal scholar Richard Collier's analysis of family law provides a close reading of divorce and nullity legal test cases to show legal representations of male heterosexuality in family law in the post-war era.[12] This important contribution makes extensive use of

---

[10] Lawrence Stone, *Road to divorce: England 1530–1987* (Oxford: Oxford University Press, 1990), 394–405.

[11] Moyse, 'Reform of marriage', 193; Weeks incorrectly states that the 'grounds of nullity were extended to cover non-consummation' in 1937. Weeks, *Sex, politics and society*, 271.

[12] Richard Collier, *Masculinity, law and the family* (London: Routledge, 1995), 138–74.

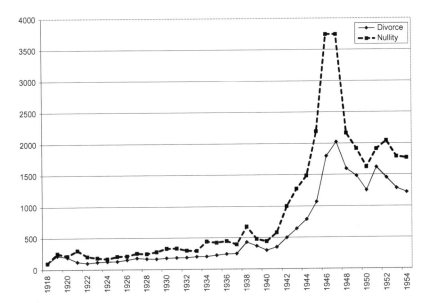

Fig. 5.2 Divorce and nullity petitions filed in England and Wales, 1918–1954 (1918, $n = 100$)

legal cases but does not adequately consider wider sources, such as newspaper reporting or the 1956 Royal Commission on Marriage and Divorce, which as will be shown, provides an important analytical intersection of legal, medical and theological discourses in the post-war era.

Male impotence is an established field of historical enquiry. Lesley Hall's study of male sexual anxiety briefly covers a range of unconsummated marriages, some of which lasted for nine, ten and twelve years before one of the parties wrote to sex advisor Marie Stopes (who claimed to have had an unconsummated marriage herself) for advice. More typically, most of 'the surprising number of correspondents' sought help after a few months. Hall found that there was a range of reasons for failing to consummate a marriage including 'ignorance', 'abstinence' and 'pain'. Angus McLaren's cultural history of impotence from Ancient Greece to Viagra shows that during the twentieth century impotence was increasingly seen as psychological, not physical, as 'commentators began to blur the purportedly clear line separating the impotent and nonimpotent [sic]'

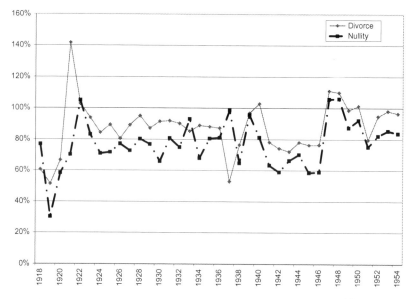

Fig. 5.3 Approximate success rate (%) in divorce and nullity cases[13]

male.[14] The outcome of this chapter, using entirely different sources, agrees with Hall that there was a range of experiences of unconsummated marriage, and with McLaren that medico-legal opinion on impotence shifted to a more psychological definition.

The under-researched subject of nullity for non-consummation allows for an examination of a number of intersecting and competing discourses based on a variety of sources. By analysing medical, legal and theological journals, books and pamphlets, and parliamentary papers it is possible to show how 'official' discourses defined and redefined sex and marriage, and therefore masculinity. Newspapers show how these discourses were presented to the wider public. In a society in which 'normal' men were expected to marry, debates about consummation of marriage are debates about what it meant to be a 'normal' man. To interpret these sources, it is

---

[13] Quotient of decrees in year and petitions from same year, so not therefore the same cases. Results over 100% possibly due to lag between petition and decree.

[14] McLaren, *Impotence*, 168, 176; Lesley Hall, *Hidden anxieties: Male sexuality, 1900–1950* (Cambridge: Polity, 1991), 102–3.

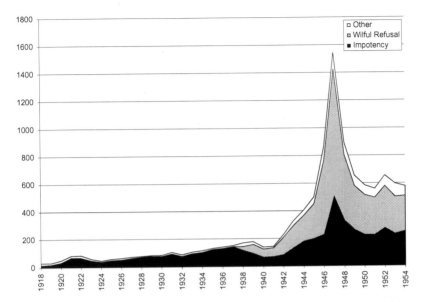

Fig. 5.4 Nullity decrees granted in England and Wales by type, 1918–1954

important to consider the performativity both of linguistic utterances and bodily actions. Here it is instructive to follow the theoretical lead set by feminist scholar Heather Brook. Brook shows in reference to Australian marriage and civil partnership law that although consummation is discursively performative, the 'act' of 'sex' is performative too. Building on the performativity theory of J. L. Austin and Judith Butler, Brook argues that the repeated performative of inserting the penis into the vagina iteratively (re)validates the marriage and (re)creates the 'act' of true 'sex' itself.[15] This approach links law, cultural norms and sexual actions and will be applied to legal changes in England between 1918 and 1960.

This chapter follows the changes over time in the definition of (non)consummation to show how married male sexuality was an 'ever

---

[15] Heather Brook, 'How to do things with sex' in *Sexuality in the legal arena* ed. Carl Stychin and Didi Herman (London: Athlone, 2000), 140.

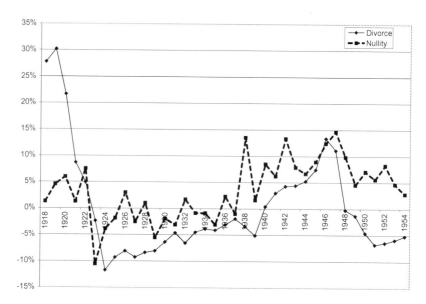

Fig. 5.5 Divorce and nullity petitions filed in England and Wales by husband or wife, 1918–1954 (Source: Royal Commission on Marriage and Divorce, Royal Commission on Marriage and Divorce: Report, 1951–1955 [London, 1956], 357–61)[16]

moving' norm.[17] The first of four sections considers the discussion of non-consummation during the 1912 Royal Commission and the subsequent introduction, in the 1937 Matrimonial Causes Act, of the clause of 'wilful refusal' to consummate a marriage. This discussion increasingly placed sexual pleasure at the heart of legal definitions of marriage, albeit in tension with procreation. The next section shows that this new clause led to a discursive eruption about sex and the purpose of marriage after the Second World War. The ability and willingness to consummate marriage was increasingly framed in psychological terms and the discussion about

---

[16] Detailed nullity data for years 1954–1961 are not available.

[17] For a more recent discussion on (anti)normativity as an 'ever moving' norm, see Robyn Wiegman and Elizabeth A. Wilson, 'Introduction: Antinormativity's queer conventions', *differences* 26, No. 1 (2015), 16.

'wilful refusal' defined a normal married man as one who is the regularly penetrative sexual partner in a heterosexual marriage. The subject of the third section is sex as condonation, a legal category that made every act of coitus an act of forgiveness for a marital offence. This effectively made coitus an act of *re*-consummation. The final section considers the proof needed in a non-consummation nullity case and shows the unequal expert view of the penis and vagina in penile-vaginal intercourse and therefore the gender asymmetry in consummation of marriage. It will be shown that by looking at the larger debates about consummation and nullity, historians can reveal changing official and personal attitudes to, and expectations of, sex, sexuality and marriage. For individual couples, nullity law begins to matter when their marriage breaks down, but for society as a whole, nullity law matters because it contains, in tension, the dominant theological, legal, medical, political and cultural definitions of sex and marriage: the purpose of marriage, the definition and purpose of 'sex', and (fe)male sexuality.

NON-CONSUMMATION, THE 1912 ROYAL COMMISSION AND THE 1937 ACT

The changes in the nullity law for non-consummation, including 'wilful refusal', enacted in 1937 were a long time in coming; parliament finally enacted the recommendations of the 1912 Royal Commission after a gap of twenty-five years. The small amount of discussion about non-consummation and nullity in the interwar period did however contain a rise in the ideal of mutual sexual pleasure within marriage and a shift from physical to psychological definitions of impotence.

The Royal Commission on Divorce and Matrimonial Causes started hearing evidence in February 1910 and eventually recommended changes to nullity law without much discussion. The resulting Majority and Minority Reports in 1912 unanimously recommended extensions to the nullity law including 'wilful refusal to consummate the marriage'.[18] However, very few witnesses to the Royal Commission expressed a desire for a clause regarding 'wilful refusal' to consummate a marriage, and the Commissioners questioned only a few witnesses about nullity since they

---

[18] H. Gorell Barnes and J. E. G. Montmorency, *The Divorce Commission: The Majority and Minority Reports summarised* (London: S. King and Son, 1912), 69.

158   N. PENLINGTON

were primarily concerned with the statistically larger 'problem' of divorce. Arguing from a eugenics standpoint, Dr Robert Jones, on behalf of the British Medical Association, was concerned about 'bodily incapacity' because the most important element of marriage was the 'procreation of healthy children for the State'. A rare voice to espouse that 'the presence of bodily desire' was important to marriage was writer Maurice Hewlett.[19] Barrister R. E. Moore wanted to see 'persistent refusal' made a ground for nullity for reasons of legal expediency and consistency. Moore stated, based on his experience in the divorce courts and hinting at a psychological definition of impotence, that refusal was often taken as evidence of incapacity and that changing the law would remove 'subterfuge'.[20] Certainly, Moore's summary was correct; although the Royal Commission did not cite any nullity test cases there were two almost on the eve of the Commission: *W v W*,[21] incapacity inferred from the refusal of sex; and *S v S (otherwise M)*,[22] persistent refusal to consummate the marriage.[23] This echoes historian Lawrence Stone's explanation of divorce law changes: a three-stage process in which, first, clients themselves sought to push the boundaries of the law; secondly, lawyers and judges attempted to narrow the gap between legal theory and human practice; and finally, the law changed when 'duplicity and hypocrisy became intolerable'.[24]

Masculinity was central to an early attempt to guide the Royal Commission's recommendation through parliament. In 1920, Lord Buckmaster's unsuccessful attempt to steer the recommendations of the Royal Commission through parliament initiated some discussion in the newspapers regarding nullity, non-consummation and 'wilful refusal'. In April 1920, *The Times* supported the whole package of reform, including nullity for 'wilful refusal', and pointed out that even the 'revolutionary'

---

[19] Royal Commission on Divorce and Matrimonial Causes, *Minutes of evidence taken before the Royal Commission on Divorce and Matrimonial Causes, Vol. 3* (London: HMSO, 1912), 17, 524.

[20] Royal Commission on Divorce and Matrimonial Causes, *Minutes of evidence taken before the Royal Commission on Divorce and Matrimonial Causes, Vol. 1* (London: HMSO, 1912), 203.

[21] *W v W* [1905] 74 LJP 112 HC PDAD.

[22] *S v S* (Otherwise M) (1907–8) XXIV TLR 253 HC PDAD.

[23] Maxwell Barrett (ed.), *Blackstone's marriage breakdown law index: Case precedents, 1900–1997* (London: Blackstone, 1998), 164.

[24] Stone, *Road to divorce*, 19–20.

Minority Report supported the reform. This editorial however struck a sexually conservative line by quoting the Lord Chancellor's 'apt' words that the 'spiritual and moral sides of marriage were incomparably more important than the physical side'.[25] In response, 'provocative' Anglo-Catholic clergyman and writer T. A. Lacey called *The Times'* use of such a quotation 'harmful' and reminded readers that 'corporal union... is essential to the constitution of marriage' and that 'unwholesome prudery, characteristically English... undervalue[ed] this element'. Lacey told readers that a 'marriage of souls'[26] is not a 'real marriage'.[27] In parliament, the husband was posited as having sexual rights, but the wife none. Buckmaster urged his Peers to reconsider by pleading that if 'the woman absolutely denied her husband access?... Was he to beat her and rape her?'[28] The Bill's sponsor therefore defined sex from a male point of view. Masculinity has at its core not just (hetero)sexual desire but sexual rights within marriage.

Mutual sexual pleasure entered the debate more prominently in the 1930s, but alongside eugenic concerns. Different Christian denominations stated their position on sex and consummation of marriage. In 1927, the National Council of the Evangelical Free Churches celebrated the 'importance and sanctity of sex in marriage'.[29] In the same year, a public argument erupted between Lord Buckmaster and Westminster Cathedral in which the latter emphasised the Catholic stance that husband and wife become 'one flesh'.[30] In 1930, the established Church also restated that 'intercourse between husband and wife as the consummation of marriage had a value of its own' and hinted that sex could be about more than procreation, that it 'enhanced... married love' and that 'complete abstinence might induce nervous disorders and injuries to the body and mind'.[31] By 1935, the Convocations of Canterbury and York agreed that 'wilful refusal to consummate the marriage' should be a ground for

---

[25] 'Divorce', *The Times*, 14 April 1920, 15.

[26] The well-known 'marriage of souls' case followed the following year. See, for example, 'Marriage of souls', *Daily Express*, 16 June 1921, 1.

[27] 'Marriage and divorce', *The Times*, 16 April 1920, 10.

[28] 'House of Lords', *The Times*, 9 June 1920, 10.

[29] 'Free Church assembly', *The Times*, 10 March 1927, 9.

[30] 'Letters to the editor', *The Times*, 16 November 1927, 10.

[31] 'Commonwealth of Churches', *The Times*, 14 November 1930, 11.

nullity,[32] since there are 'natural physical rights and duties of the spouses as regards *coitus*'. The Church was as interested in eugenics and 'race' as mutuality and 'sexuality' since it stated that 'the obvious and natural purpose of marriage is the maintenance of the race, and, therefore, the procreation and nurture of children'.[33]

Few campaigners actively pushed for a change in the nullity legislation, but case law had already moved the definition of impotence in a more psychological direction. Privy Councillor and former Conservative MP Sir Ellis Hume-Williams was a lone voice in calling for the ground of 'wilful refusal'[34] because 'many unhappy persons are left without remedy'[35] when 'one party wilfully refuses to carry out one of the duties for which marriage was instituted'.[36] Hume-Williams pointed to two important test cases since the Royal Commission in which the wife had refused the husband sex. The judgment in *Dickenson v Dickenson otherwise Philips* (1913) 'held that the wilful refusal of a wife to permit consummation was a sufficient ground for nullity'. This was overturned in *Napier v Napier* (1915) when the Court of Appeal judged that 'wilful refusal' could be accepted as a ground only if there was proof of 'invincible repugnance' (towards the sexual partner in question), or 'hysteria or nervous condition equivalent to impotence'.[37] The latter case marked a significant change in the legal view that sexual dysfunction was more likely to be psychological rather than physiological—something 'wrong' with the mind, not the body.

The eventual passage through parliament was virtually unnoticed. When, in 1937, the independent Member of Parliament A. P. Herbert successfully championed the Matrimonial Causes Act, there was no discussion in parliament regarding the extensions to the nullity law and no coverage in the newspapers. Herbert, who was invited to stand as a

---

[32] 'Convocation of Canterbury', *The Times*, 6 June 1935, 11; 'The Church and marriage', *The Times*, 7 June 1935, 18; and restated the following year in 'The Church and divorce', *The Times*, 29 May 1936, 19.

[33] Church of England, *The Church and marriage: Being a report of the Joint Committees of the Convocations of Canterbury and York* (London: SPCK, 1935), 5, 75.

[34] 'The Church and divorce', *The Times*, 6 June 1936, 8.

[35] 'Petitions to annul marriages', *The Times*, 7 December 1933, 10.

[36] 'Law report', *The Times*, 8 June 1935, 10.

[37] William Latey, *The Matrimonial Causes Act 1937* (London: Sweet & Maxwell, 1937).

5 NON-CONSUMMATION 161

Conservative parliamentary candidate, was able to sell the recommendations of the Royal Commission as 'conservative' and hence secure wide support. Herbert himself admitted that his job was to 'give the picture a new frame, hang it in a new light – and sell it' in order to implement the twenty-five-year-old proposals. To his dismay, few in either house of parliament understood the importance of nullity and although there was intense debate over the minutiae of the divorce law, the new nullity clauses, including 'wilful refusal', were passed unchallenged—with the exception of Lord Elton who opposed the changes[38]—and without discussion. As Herbert characteristically put it, 'those who strain at a gnat of divorce will swallow eagerly a camel of nullity'. Although few considered that the new clause fundamentally changed the requirements of marriage, it was now the case that 'capacity to marry was required not only on the day of marriage but throughout its existence'.[39]

The passing of the 1937 Matrimonial Causes Act may have marked a victory for those who had wanted a substantial change in divorce law for the first time in eighty years, but it was only the start of a new era of debates about nullity and non-consummation, and therefore the married man. The origins of 'wilful refusal' were inflected with eugenics, but increasingly during the interwar period the debate enshrined male sexual pleasure as a right, and, further, case law defined impotence as psychological. Church historian Cordelia Moyse concludes that the Act moved away from the Church's teaching that 'consent not consummation made marriage' by enshrining in law the 'centrality of sexual intimacy to a valid modern marriage' and that this was 'a final parting of the ways between Church and State on divorce and marriage law'.[40] In 1937, Alfred Fellows, barrister and Vice-Chairman of the influential Divorce Law Reform Union, saw the 'wilful refusal' clause as 'largely non-controversial' since 'wilful non-consummation ha[d] hitherto often been accepted as evidence of impotence' in nullity cases.[41] However, others pointed out that the term 'wilful refusal' was contestable, or that the

---

[38] 'Political notes', *The Times*, 6 July 1937, 16.

[39] Moyse, 'Reform of marriage', 224, 381; A. Herbert, *The ayes have it: The story of the Marriage Bill* (London: Methuen, 1937), 3–4, 59, 66–7, 140.

[40] Moyse, 'Reform of marriage', 191, 227.

[41] Alfred Fellows, *The popular divorce guide: A guide to the Matrimonial Causes Act, 1937 (Mr A. Herbert's Marriage Bill)* (London: Watts, 1937), 36.

162   N. PENLINGTON

relationship between con(tra)ception and consummation was unclear.[42] These points of contention—including the inconsistency between 'wilful refusal' *after* marriage and impotence *at the time* of marriage—were the basis for the debates that erupted after the Second World War, during which the Church lost further its influence over marriage, and consummation and married masculinity became redefined subject to 'secular' medico-legal discourses.

'Wilful Refusal' and the Purpose of Marriage

After the passage of the 1937 'Herbert Act', the seemingly insignificant 'wilful refusal' clause eventually became a catalyst to an eruption of discourse about the purpose of marriage, the definition of sex, and in turn married masculinity. The most important test cases on the 'wilful refusal' clause appeared in 1945 towards the end of the Second World War.[43] During the following decade, there was an explosion of important legal cases, theological disputes and a Royal Commission. At the heart of this debate was the purpose of sex in marriage and the potential for both pleasure and procreation in penile-vaginal intercourse. This therefore follows Weeks' mandate that a 'history of sexuality must be concerned with the shifting exigencies of reproduction but also the diversity of sexual needs and practices that flourish alongside the pattern of procreation'.[44] Although the 'wilful refusal' debate started as a discussion about consummation of marriage, it moved on to focus on continual 'sex' throughout marriage. Unlike the interwar period, these debates were played out in the newspapers, often on the front pages of the popular press.

A legally important series of cases in the late 1940s tested the 'wilful refusal' clause in relation to contraception. This sparked a debate about the purpose of marriage and sex, and therefore dominant, but competing, notions of married masculinity. At the heart of these cases was the *normal* sexually active man based on a definition of *natural* sex. *The Times* reported at length the findings of *Cowan v Cowan* (1945),[45] in which

---

[42] S. Seuffert, *The Matrimonial Causes Act, 1937* (London: Solicitors' Law Stationery Society, 1937), iv, 18.

[43] This is also the case for polygamy nullity test cases, see Chapter 2. Both seem to be part of the post-war spike in nullity and divorce cases.

[44] Weeks, *Sex, politics and society*, 1.

[45] *Cowan v Cowan* [1945] 2 All Eng. 197.

5 NON-CONSUMMATION   163

'their Lordships... were of opinion that sexual intercourse could not be said to be complete when a husband deliberately discontinued it before it reached its natural termination'. Consummation had not been performed since 'one of the principal ends, if not the principal end, of marriage was intentionally frustrated'.[46] This finding was in keeping with Church teaching, but led to a fear of a 'flood of nullity petitions'. The *Daily Mirror* reported an increase in the 'numbers of inquiries to solicitors by childless wives'.[47] This judgement was however reversed two years later in *Baxter v Baxter* (1947),[48] a case in which the husband unsuccessfully applied for nullity on the ground that his wife refused to have sex without contraception, a sheath in this case. The *Daily Mirror* placed *Baxter* on the front page under the headline 'Important case "affects status of marriage"'[49] and followed the case closely.[50] The newspaper reported that the husband's case was that 'every textbook agreed that consummation meant ordinary complete intercourse',[51] a definition that dated back to Dr Lushington's famous, and infamously vague, pronouncement in 1845.[52] The husband stated 'that he was not prepared to deprive himself of intercourse' (without a sheath) but the Court found that he could not invoke the 1937 'wilful refusal' clause since 'he had unsuccessfully brought to bear such tact, persuasion, and encouragement as an ordinary husband would use in the circumstances' and had therefore 'failed' to take 'all reasonable steps to effect the consummation'.[53] The husband,

---

[46] 'Law report', *The Times*, 17 July 1945, 2; 'The childless wife', *Daily Express*, 17 July 1945, 3.

[47] '"No-baby" marriages', *Daily Mirror*, 23 July 1945, 3; The *Daily Mirror* reported one straight away *Hamlet v Hamlet*, 'Wife's plea that she didn't refuse children fails', *Daily Mirror*, 23 May 1946, 3.

[48] *Baxter v Baxter* [1948] AC 274.

[49] 'Important case "affects status of marriage"', *Daily Mirror*, 14 December 1946, 1.

[50] For example, 'Man whose wife refused to have a child appeals against "no divorce" ruling', *Daily Mirror*, 25 January 1947, 7; 'Husband "acquiesced," judge says—Loses appeal', *Daily Mirror*, 18 February 1947, 3.

[51] 'Contraceptives case: Lords delay judgment', *Daily Mirror*, 11 November 1947, 5.

[52] The famous case *D-e v A-g (falsely calling herself D-e)* [1845] 1 Rob Ecc 280, in which Lushington stated, 'Sexual intercourse, in the proper meaning of the term, is ordinary and complete intercourse'. Cited in Collier, *Masculinity, law and the family*, 152.

[53] 'Law report', *The Times*, 18 February 1947, 2; See also Margaret Puxon and Sylvia Dawkins, 'Non-consummation of marriage', *Medicine, Science and the Law* 4 (1964), 15.

164 N. PENLINGTON

though asserting his right to regular sex, had failed as a 'reasonable' man and acquiesced in his wife's decision not to conceive and therefore his nullity petition was dismissed. His acquiescence was crucial since similar front-page 'birth control marriage' cases went the other way.[54] Baxter had failed as a man through his submission. Sexual pleasure and paternity were both important elements of masculinity, but a man had to achieve them.

These two landmark cases, *Cowan* and *Baxter*, offered contrasting views of sex and the purpose of marriage, and ignited fierce debate: at stake were the influence of Church and State over the regulation of marriage and the definition of 'normal' sex. Amidst an exchange of opinion on the letters' pages,[55] a *The Times* editorial in early 1948 argued that 'wilful refusal' was a 'curious clause' that allowed a marriage to be annulled because of an impediment *after* marriage, and the judgement in *Baxter* 'reveal[ed] a discrepancy between the legal and lay conceptions of the purpose of marriage'. The newspaper reminded lawmakers that procreation was 'the principle purpose of marriage' and the reason why it should be subject to 'regulation' by 'Church or State'.[56] The leader of the Catholic Church in England and Wales, the Archbishop of Westminster, agreed with *Baxter* but not its 'reasons' and restated the Canon Law stance against contraception.[57] Labour MP Marcus Lipton thought that *Baxter* was 'contrary to public policy' and suggested legislation as a solution.[58] The leader of the Anglican faith, the Archbishop of Canterbury, joined the debate on the meaning of 'consummation', which he defined as 'completion', and pointed out that contraception prevented 'complete' sex.[59] The judiciary however was undecided on whether *coitus interruptus* was 'complete' and gave contrasting decisions in two cases within three

[54] For example, 'Birth control marriage is declared void', *Daily Mirror*, 17 December 1947, 1.

[55] 'The purpose of marriage', *The Times*, 20 December 1947, 5; 'The purpose of marriage', *The Times*, 31 December 1947, 6; 'The purpose of marriage', *The Times*, 6 January 1948, 5.

[56] 'The purpose of marriage', *The Times*, 2 January 1948, 5.

[57] 'Primary purpose of marriage', *The Times*, 12 January 1948, 2.

[58] 'The Baxter case', *The Times*, 20 January 1948, 5.

[59] 'Primate on aim of marriage', *The Times*, 6 February 1948, 2; 'Primate welcomes nullity judgment', *Daily Express*, 6 February 1948, 3.

5 NON-CONSUMMATION 165

days.[60] The definition of 'complete' hinged on whether both *erectio* and *intermissio* were required.[61] The legal and theological definition of 'sex' was therefore entirely focused on the male body and the man's experience and pleasure.

By the mid-1950s, this debate about non-consummation of marriage became a potential divide between Church and State. In 1949, the Archbishop of Canterbury ordered a commission to tackle the subject of nullity of marriage in a direct challenge to judges who, in his opinion, 'don't know what constitutes consummation' and the 'medical profession [which] has brought it about that it is quite possible for a marriage to be both consummated and non-consummated at the same time'.[62] Four years later and in anticipation of the findings, some within the Church urged caution. A *Daily Express* front-page headline screamed 'Primate Rapped' and revealed that a leading clergyman warned of a 'disastrous clash between Church and State': one flashpoint being the remarriage of those who had wilfully refused to consummate a previous 'marriage'.[63] In June 1955, *The Times* editorial considered the issue of nullity of marriage to be 'what must now be regarded as the central problem in the relations of Church and State'.[64] In same year, the Church commission's report returned 'wilful refusal' to front-page news[65] and the widely reported findings specified exactly what the Church defined as 'complete' sex and therefore the 'normal' man. In a challenge to the 1937 'wilful refusal' clause, in which *concubitus* became more significant,[66] it ruled that marriage had the 'character of a sacrament'[67] and that consent was more important than consummation, since 'consent given in marriage involves consent to consummate the marriage and the capacity to do so'. Both

---

[60] *Grimes (otherwise Edwards) v Grimes* [1948] 2 All ER 147 and *White (otherwise Berry) vs White* [1948] 2 All ER 151 HC PDAD. 'Consummation of marriage', *The Times*, 13 May 1948, 2; 'This gives right to end marriage—Judge rules', *Daily Mirror*, 11 May 1948, 5.

[61] *R (otherwise F) v R* [1952] 1 All ER 1194.

[62] 'Primate leaves doctors out', *Daily Express*, 20 January 1950, 5.

[63] 'Divorce: Primate rapped', *Daily Express*, 10 June 1954, 1.

[64] 'Grounds for nullity', *The Times*, 20 June 1955, 11.

[65] 'Church told: End this divorce "loophole"', *Daily Mirror*, 20 May 1955, 1.

[66] Jackson, *Formation and annulment*, 329.

[67] 'Change in canon law on nullity proposed', *The Times*, 20 May 1955, 7.

husband and wife must be capable of *vera copula*—'true conjunction'— which 'involves penetration by the erect member of the man into the vagina of the woman so that ejaculation may there take place' such that 'in Nature... [it may] result in the procreation of Children'. Assuming the impossibility of proving the 'degree' of ejaculation the commission reluctantly accepted that although penetration is not equivalent to *vera copula* it was the only practical test of consummation and ruled that 'the ability to effect or permit penetration must be accepted as a practical test of capacity'.[68] Despite the Church's emphasis on procreation, this definition and test of consummation positions the 'normal' man as the active, penetrating (hetero)sexual partner regardless of his ability to ejaculate and to procreate children.

The Church commission embraced psychological theories of sexuality to draw the boundaries of the sexually 'normal' male. As part of its findings on nullity, the Church unveiled a 'Charter for Marriage' that restated that the 'principal purpose of marriage' was 'procreation of children' and further that marriage is 'the hallowing and directing aright of the natural instincts and affections'.[69] Demanding that 'wilful refusal' be repealed, the commission found that in 'very many cases where a partner refuses to consummate the marriage, refusal is due to some psychological incapacity and such cases can be effectively dealt with as cases of impotence'. Although the Church 'sympathise[d] with both partners to a marriage where one is homosexual and no cure has been effected [sic]',[70] it stipulated that 'inversion' should not be a ground for nullity. The report did not define 'homosexual *acts*' but did draw a distinction between the 'true invert [who] is really a sick man or woman, psychologically diseased' and the 'pervert [who] is a degenerate or vicious heterosexual who, for one reason or another, has taken to indulgence in homosexual acts'.[71] On unconsummated marriage, the Archbishop of Canterbury, Geoffrey Fisher by now, took the view that if 'there were psychological factors involved which medical or psychological treatment could put right' a marriage could be 'saved' and that non-consummation was more serious than a

[68] Church Commission, 33, 35, 47; 'The Church and divorce', *Daily Express*, 20 May 1955, 9.

[69] Church Commission, 47; 'The Church and divorce', *Daily Express*, 20 May 1955, 9.

[70] 'Change in canon law on nullity proposed', *The Times*, 20 May 1955, 7.

[71] Church Commission, 40.

'single act of adultery'.[72] Hence, from these confused pronouncements, the psychological 'normal' male is one who is capable of, and derives pleasure from, penetrating a vagina—ultimately any vagina.

In 1956, the year after the Church's commission on nullity, the Royal Commission on Marriage and Divorce delivered its findings. Although the Commission called witnesses from a range of Christian denominations, its 'duty' was to examine the subject 'from the point of view of the State, which has to legislate for all its citizens, whatever their religious beliefs'.[73] Unlike the 1912 Royal Commission, the 1956 one explicitly sought views on nullity for non-consummation. By 1952, when the Commissioners started hearing witnesses, many in the Church[74] and the legal profession[75] were calling for 'wilful refusal to consummate the marriage' to be a ground for divorce rather than nullity. This is despite the clause being re-enacted without parliamentary debate in the Matrimonial Causes Act 1950.[76] In addition to the evidence put forward by the Church of England commission on nullity, other Christian denominations gave their views on the purpose of marriage. The Methodist Church and the Free Church Federation Council stated, following its conference report of 1939,[77] that central to marriage were 'the two purposes of mutual fellowship and parenthood' and that 'Free Churches' accepted 'the conditions for a true and valid marriage [as] laid down in English law, namely—competence, consent, publicity and intention'.[78]

Most of the Royal Commission's witnesses wanted 'wilful refusal' to be a ground for *divorce* and their evidence defined the 'normal' married man. Those in the law, such as influential law professor L. C. B. Gower and Lord Merriman, President of the Probate, Divorce and Admiralty Division, thought that as a 'post-nuptial matrimonial offence' wilful refusal should be a ground for divorce. The General Council to the Bar

---

[72] 'Let the parents tell says Archbishop', *Daily Express*, 10 December 1954, 5.

[73] Royal Commission on Marriage and Divorce, *Royal Commission on Marriage and Divorce, report 1951–1955* (London, 1956), 7–8; this point is emphasised in 'What cannot be mended', *The Times*, 21 March 1956, 11.

[74] 'Social effects of divorce', *The Times*, 27 May 1952, 6.

[75] 'Lord Merriman on divorce', *The Times*, 20 June 1952, 3.

[76] Matrimonial Causes Act (1950) s. 8. 1. (a).

[77] 'Guidance before marriage', *The Times*, 25 July 1939, 9.

[78] Royal Commission on Marriage and Divorce, *Minutes of evidence taken before the Royal Commission on Marriage and Divorce, 1952–56* (London: HMSO, 1956), 63, 67.

contended that refusal could 'draw an inference of impotence or physical incapacity' and therefore an 'unfitness to marry' as set out by the 1912 Royal Commission's view on nullity. However, *wilful* refusal was a 'refusal of a marital duty' and as such should be a ground for divorce. This would also avoid a clash between civil and ecclesiastical law, reduce the possibly for collusion in cases where medical evidence is refused, and 'uphold the sanctity of the marriage tie'. Repealing the 'wilful refusal' nullity clause would also return English law to consistency with 'many foreign common law jurisdictions'.[79] Implicit in this definition of *wilful* is the creation of the 'normal' man who wants coitus and the abnormal one who does not. Whereas in *refusal* the 'normal' man is a one who is psychologically and physically capable of performing coitus.

Some argued for a return to the situation pre-1937. In her evidence to the Royal Commission, Marie Stopes, referring to herself as a 'biologist', stated that a 'recognition of biological facts should dominate legal niceties' and therefore called for the 'confusing' 1937 clause to be repealed. Stopes viewed marriage as 'complete' if it was both a 'legal marriage' and a 'natural marriage'. The former was the civil or religious ceremony and the latter, 'the voluntary biological action between the two sexes in which the erect male organ penetrates the feminine vagina'. For Stopes, the hymen was the key to determining whether a marriage was 'natural'. If the wife was '*virgo intacta*' then the marriage was unconsummated, but '[w]ilful refusal on the part of one or the other leaves the same biological condition but with a different moral atmosphere after the nullity suit is obtained'. She argued that '[l]egal terminology should be made to conform to biological facts'. In an attack on Roman Catholicism, Stopes argued that it was 'very deplorable that in 1937 we should have departed from the good old English idea that the *virgo intacta* got nullity and nobody else'. A similar recommendation was made by the Marriage Law Reform Society, but coming from the 'one flesh' theological angle set out by Anglo-Catholic Canon Lacey.[80] J. E. S. Simon, an influential Q.C., called for a repeal of the wilful refusal clause and considered that the

---

[79] Royal Commission on Marriage and Divorce, *Minutes of evidence taken before the Royal Commission on Marriage and Divorce, 1952–56* (London: HMSO, 1956), 16, 32, 419 and Appendix I, 1.

[80] Royal Commission on Marriage and Divorce, *Minutes of evidence taken before the Royal Commission on Marriage and Divorce, 1952–56* (London: HMSO, 1956), 223, 820–1; See also T. A. Lacey, *Marriage in Church and state* (London: SPCK, 1947), 200.

law before 1937 was adequate since in most cases of incapacity 'the refusal [had] in general a marked pathological element'. He further contended that 'wilful and unjustifiable refusal to procreate children is as destructive of matrimonial happiness, and as great a wrong to the other spouse, as, for example, adultery'. This latter proposal was also made by the Divorce Law Reform Union, which argued that refusal to have children should be allowed only with 'good cause'.[81]

The report of the Royal Commission recommended that 'wilful refusal to consummate the marriage' should be a ground for divorce, not nullity, and therefore repositioned the role of sex in marriage and restated the importance of sex to the individual within a companionate marriage. The report when published in March 1956 was widely covered in the newspapers.[82] *The Times* reported the Commission's view that there was a 'wider spread of knowledge in matters of sex' that was 'of great value' and there was 'in the popular mind an undue emphasis on the overriding importance of a satisfactory sex relationship without a similar emphasis on the other stable and enduring factors of a lasting marriage'.[83] A distinction was drawn between refusal as evidence of 'impotence in the psychological sense' or 'invincible aversion or repugnance', and *wilful* refusal, which connoted 'capacity' but 'unwillingness' to consummate.[84] This marked a triumph of psychological explanations of sexual desire and behaviour, central to which was the 'normal' man who was sexually active, and willing and capable of penetrating his wife's vagina. Anal penetration (between husband and wife, or anyone else) was deemed by the commission to be an 'unnatural practice' and should remain a ground for divorce.[85] Later that year, in the House of Lords debate on the Royal Commission report there was broad agreement on the change from nullity to divorce.[86] This shift from nullity to divorce was partly practical (to avoid the logical inconsistency of nullity being decreed for an event after the marriage)

---

[81] Royal Commission Minutes 1956, 194, 204–5.

[82] For example, 'Nine day YES, nine say NO to divorce by agreement', *Daily Express*, 21 March 1956, 9; 'The great marriage muddle', *Daily Mirror*, 21 March 1956, 1, 10–11.

[83] 'Three new grounds for divorce recommended', *The Times*, 21 March 1956, 5.

[84] Ibid.; 'What cannot be mended', *The Times*, 21 March 1956, 31.

[85] Royal Commission Report 1956, 63.

[86] 'Banns outdated', *The Times*, 25 October 1956, 4.

and partly political (to avoid further confrontation between Church and State). The suggested law change also symbolically drew a distinction between incapacity (whether deemed to be physical or psychological) and 'wilful refusal'. The former was to remain a ground for nullity and thus capacity to consummate would still be a requirement for marriage. The latter would now be a matrimonial offence on a par with adultery, cruelty and desertion. Penile-vaginal intercourse was an essential right for married people and by wilfully inflicting 'damage' to the spouse, and to the institution of marriage, the marriage should be dissolved.

Discourse about 'wilful refusal' was initially confined to the definition in the 1937 Act: that is, wilful refusal to *consummate* the marriage. This discussion centred on having coitus once and once only, but in 1946 the debate moved into new territory as 'wilful refusal' to *continue* to have penile-vaginal intercourse throughout marriage became the focus. This was to become an important feature of evidence and discussion of the Royal Commission and further defined sex and marriage and the relationship between the two. In *Weatherley v Weatherley* (1946),[87] the Court of Appeal found that 'refusal of marital relations' did not amount to desertion and that the 1937 'wilful refusal' clause did not explicitly cover 'wilful refusal to continue sexual intercourse'. The couple had 'lived a normal married life' but the wife later decided that she has '"finished with" marital intercourse': first, when her husband was home on leave from the Royal Air Force in 1941, and again when they resumed cohabitation in 1943. Though judging that the wife's actions were a 'cruel wrong' and 'a breach of one of the obligations of marriage', desertion did not apply. Lord Justice Scott gave a dissenting judgment that 'the wife had deliberately broken up the matrimonial home and brought an end to matrimonial life'. Although consummated, this marriage, argued Scott, went against all three of the central tenets of Christian marriage: 'procreation of children', 'remedy against sin', and for 'mutual society'.[88] On upholding the appeal, the Lord Chancellor stated if a 'marriage could be dissolved because further relations are refused after consummation, we might have to consider whether there was desertion if relations were only

---

[87] *Weatherley v Weatherley* [1946] 2 All ER 1 116.

[88] 'Law report', *The Times*, 17 April 1946, 8; '"Root of marriage" appeal fails', *Daily Mirror*, 17 April 1946, 5.

5 NON-CONSUMMATION   171

tolerated on rare and exceptional occasions'.[89] This was however precisely the discussion that took place during a call for a new ground for divorce.

The Royal Commission considered at length the creation of a new ground for divorce, 'wilful and persistent refusal of sexual intercourse'[90] and found that most of the witnesses thought that such a ground would be justified but impossible to prove in court. Renowned barrister Geoffrey H. Crispin, whose caseload was nearly 500 a year and who was involved in *Weatherley*, stated that 'wilful and unjustifiable refusal of sexual intercourse' should be a ground for divorce 'if continued without interruption for, say, three years, or possibly two years'. Crispin, arguing from a position in which sex is something the woman gives to the man, suggested that the 'present position is that a wife who submits to sexual intercourse on one occasion only may be comparatively secure for life'. In his experience, and applying a gendered view of sexual desire, 'a very great deal of matrimonial unhappiness and misery is the result of unbalanced sexual relations, and particularly the refusal of wives to have sexual intercourse'. He further argued that this often led men to commit adultery. The Bar Council took a similar view by claiming that it 'borders on the ludicrous that one act of sexual intercourse which may be followed by a refusal of all intercourse thereafter, should validate the marriage, leaving the subsequent refusal of intercourse without remedy'. The Council did however accept that the 'court has always recognised that it cannot enforce the marital duty of sexual intercourse'. Although they contended that 'wilful refusal of sexual intercourse... may offend seriously against the essential rights and basis of marriage', there was 'great difficulty in ascertaining whether such refusal is wilful'. The Council concluded that the law was sufficient as defined in the recent case, *Lawrance v Lawrance* (1950), in which refusal of sexual intercourse through the 'husband's sexual failings' was held to be desertion within in the context of insults and other behaviours.[91] He, a farm labourer, had refused his wife a 'vital aspect of married life' by refusing her 'invitations to sexual intercourse' after initially having 'intercourse perhaps once in three months'.[92]

---

[89] '"Dangerous" prayer book argument on marriage', *Daily Mirror*, 1 April 1947, 3.

[90] Royal Commission Report 1956, 28.

[91] Royal Commission Minutes 1956, 30, 32, 514.

[92] *Lawrance v Lawrance* [1950] 66 (1) TLR 9.

172   N. PENLINGTON

Pressure groups were less concerned with the burden of proof and revealed a range of social-class biased expectations of married masculinity. The Progressive League thought that divorce should be permitted, recommending divorce after three years for '[u]nreasonable refusal of sexual intercourse'. The Marriage Law Reform Society also sought a clause making three years of refusal a form of desertion. However, the desertion would be an aggregate of three years in the last five and not necessarily continuous. Marie Stopes was virtually alone in arguing against ongoing 'wilful refusal'. Stopes counselled against introducing such a ground because in her view 'apparently perfectly normal middle-class men' had a range of 'sexual capacity' from 'one union every two years' to 'sex union three times a day'.[93] Stopes first expounded the theory of the '"The Change" in men' in *Enduring Passion* (1928) in which she claimed that men can procreate at any age but have depressed sexual interests later in life Drawing on prevailing psychological discourses, Stopes argued that the 'most marked outward and obvious sign of the Change in Men' was 'a *mental* one'.[94] Ongoing refusal in middle-aged, middle-class men could therefore be 'normal' and should not be a ground for divorce. Stating his own view, the commissioner Mr Justice Pearce, argued that this kind of wilful refusal could be an 'annoyance' that most 'would put up with for the sake of family life and go on living together' rather than 'disruption to the home'.[95]

The Commission could not agree on almost all of the suggested new grounds for divorce. As the popular press pointed out, the Commissioners were resistant to change and did not want to make divorce 'easier'. In rejecting the suggested divorce ground 'wilful and persistent refusal of sexual intercourse', the Commission accepted that such a refusal was 'not infrequently an ingredient in cases of cruelty'. Without 'good cause', refusing sexual intercourse 'constitute[d] a serious breach of marital obligations' but the Commission decided that such a ground would open the door to 'false and collusive case[s]'. The evidence would be 'difficult to test' since there would be a 'variety of physiological and psychological factors' and the 'standards of frequency' in the 'intimate life of husband

[93] Royal Commission Minutes 1956, 226, 821, 906.

[94] Marie Stopes, *Enduring passion: Further new contributions to the solution of sex difficulties being the continuation of* Married Love (London: Hogarth, 1956. First published 1928), 135–45.

[95] Royal Commission Minutes 1956, 642.

and wife'. In contradiction, the Commission did not accept that refusal of sexual intercourse was the same as desertion as in 'separation of husband and wife'.[96] The *Daily Mirror* was dissatisfied with the 'Great Marriage Muddle'[97] created by a conservative Royal Commission, and reported that cruelty should be a ground for divorce when the 'normal husband and wife relationship were refused so as to inflict misery'.[98] Although the Royal Commission rejected ongoing refusal as a grounds for divorce, the discussion on the subject demonstrates the extent to which the relationship between sex and marriage had changed. A range of 'experts' now thought that continual sexual pleasure, narrowly defined as coitus in which the man was the active partner, was essential for a happy marriage.

Much of the foregoing debate about sex and the purpose of marriage started as a result of the 1940s contraception and non-consumption cases—*Cowan* and *Baxter*—but another strand of debate was opened up by cases involving artificial insemination: conception without coitus, the very opposite of contraception. In 1948, a wife successfully filed for nullity on the grounds of non-consummation although she had given birth to a child conceived by 'artificial insemination'.[99] As the *Daily Express* pointed out in its front-page coverage, 'although the husband is the father of the baby, he had not consummated the marriage in the *normal* sense'.[100] Citing this case,[101] in a Lords' debate the following year, the Marquis of Reading pointed out that the 1937 'wilful refusal' clause did not anticipate that a child could be born into an unconsummated marriage and this raised the possibility of the child being illegitimate if the marriage was annulled. He stated that '[p]ublic opinion' was asking for a lead on whether 'artificial insemination was going to be regarded as the consummation of marriage; an outcome he thought would have 'disastrous effects'.[102]

---

[96] Royal Commission Report 1956, 5.

[97] 'The great marriage muddle', *Daily Mirror*, 21 March 1956, 1.

[98] 'Refusal to have a child no ground for divorce', *Daily Mirror*, 21 March 1956, 10.

[99] 'Primary purpose of marriage', *The Times*, 1 December 1948, 2.

[100] With added emphasis, 'Is the test-tube baby legitimate?', *Daily Express*, 1 December 1948, 1; and front-page again: 'Test-tube babies to alter law', *Daily Express*, 10 December 1948, 1.

[101] *REL v REL (otherwise R)* [1948] P 211.

[102] 'Lords debate on artificial insemination', *The Times*, 17 March 1949, 4.

174   N. PENLINGTON

Although artificial insemination could allow a man to achieve an important attribute of contemporary manhood—paternity[103]—it did not mean that men who did not, or could not, penetrate could be 'normal'. In the logic of the Church, a husband's sperm (but not his penis) entering his wife's vagina was enough to consummate a marriage. The Archbishop of Canterbury drew the distinction between 'A. I. H. (artificial insemination by the husband)' and 'A. I. D. (artificial insemination by a donor)'. To cheering in the House of Lords, he claimed that the former satisfied 'one of the chief aims of... marriage, the procreation of children', but the latter was 'wrong in principle and contrary to all Christian standards'.[104] On its front page, the *Daily Mirror* quoted the Archbishop as saying, 'A.I.D. should be made a criminal offence'.[105] Preferring to defer to the forthcoming Royal Commission, the Church's commission on nullity recommended that 'when a married couple secure a child, either by adoption or by artificial insemination, their marriage should be protected from nullity proceedings, even though the legal test of sexual capacity has not been satisfied'.[106] This was taken up by the Royal Commission, which judged that the rights of the child(ren) should be more important than (lack of) sexual intercourse. In recommending that '[a]rtificial insemination by a donor without the husband's consent' should be a ground for divorce, the Commission stated that such an act would be 'deemed to be adultery'.[107] However, consensual artificial insemination 'whether by the seed of the husband or by the seed of a donor' amounted to 'acquiescence', which took precedence over impotence and therefore the Commissioners suggested it should be a bar to nullity for non-consummation.[108] It would appear that paternity was still regarded as an important element of being a 'normal' man. This echoed a much earlier nullity case from the 1920s in which Lord Birkenhead stated

[103] Sean Brady, *Masculinity and male homosexuality in Britain, 1861–1913* (Basingstoke: Palgrave, 2005), 35–6.

[104] 'Lords debate on artificial insemination', *The Times*, 17 March 1949, 4.

[105] '"Test tube" babies lead to perjury—Archbishop says "end this practice"', *Daily Mirror*, 17 March 1949, 1.

[106] 'Change in canon law on nullity proposed', *The Times*, 20 May 1955, 7; 'The Church and divorce', *Daily Express*, 20 May 1955, 9; Church Commission, 35–6, 39, 47.

[107] Royal Commission Report 1956, 28, 31.

[108] 'Nine say YES, nine say NO to divorce by agreement', *Daily Express*, 21 March 1956, 9; Royal Commission Report 1956, 84–91.

'the power of reproducing his species [is] a power which is commonly and rightly considered to be the most characteristic quality of manhood'.[109] However, in the era of the nascent 'test-tube baby'[110] an impotent father was marked as inflicting damage that 'few women can endure indefinitely without serious injury to health'.[111] To be truly 'normal' a man had to procreate *and* be the penetrative sexual partner.

The post-war 'wilful refusal' debates show that the definitions of 'normal' sex and marriage changed over time and further that the 'normal' man was increasingly defined by his ability and desire to penetrate a vagina continually for most of his adult life. As the Church lost influence over marriage and as contraception became more reliable and artificial insemination more established, the twin meanings and potential outcomes of coitus—pleasure and procreation—shifted. These changes were played out in the newspapers. The new secular definition of 'sex' was influenced by psychology and changing sexual mores, and posited the 'normal' man as married and continually (hetero)sexually active, as well as being a biological father.

RE-CONSUMMATION: 'SEX' AS CONDONATION

The 'wilful refusal' debate moved from a discussion about consummation of marriage to ongoing sex throughout the marriage. Another strand of marriage and divorce law also needs to be considered to show the changing meanings of 'sex' and 'marriage' and the continual (re)construction of the 'normal' man as (hetero)sexually active. 'Condonation', the 'complete forgiveness'[112] of a matrimonial offence such as adultery, had been law for centuries[113] but became increasingly defined in relation to 'sexual intercourse' in the first half of the twentieth

---

[109] *C v C* [1921] P 339, 400 quoted in Jackson, *Formation and annulment*, 314.

[110] For example, 'The Church and divorce', *Daily Express*, 20 May 1955, 9.

[111] *REL v REL* quoted in Collier, *Masculinity*, 163.

[112] This definition was clarified in the nineteenth century: 'complete' in *Ellis v Ellis and Smith* (1865) 164 ER 1475 and 'forgiveness' in *Hall v Hall and Kay* (1891) 64 LT 837. Cited in Leslie Brooks, *Matrimonial causes: Being an exposition of The Matrimonial Causes Act, 1937 and The Summary Procedure (Domestic Proceedings) Act, 1937* (London: Butterworth, 1937), 27; Fellows, *Popular divorce guide*, 5.

[113] For example, 'implied condonation' was defined in *Beeby v Beeby* (1799) 1 Hag Con 789, 162 ER 755.

century. The following discussion of test cases, the 1937 Act and the 1956 Royal Commission shows that penile-vaginal intercourse was a form of 're-consummation' and therefore the most important sexual act between men and woman—it was, and is, legally representative of '*all* sex*'. My term, 're-consummation', draws on feminist scholar Heather Brook's notion of penile-vaginal intercourse as a 'sexual performative' that '*re-performed* the marriage', since under the law 'corporeal unity repeatedly re-established *legal* unity'.[114] The law of condonation treated husband and wife unequally and (re)constructed the 'normal' man as (hetero)sexually active: a 'normal' man was married and continually penetrated his wife's vagina.

During the 1920s, coitus became the principle evidence of condonation. The 1912 Royal Commission did not consider the subject of sex as condonation but a series of test cases in the interwar period defined penile-vaginal intercourse as a form of 're-consummation'. Two test cases during and shortly after the First World War—*Roberts v Roberts and another* (1916–17)[115] and *Hare v Hare and Davidson* (1919–20)[116]—held that post-adultery sex between husband and wife was not necessarily condonation of the adultery. Then, in 1920, the judgement in *Cramp v Cramp and Freeman*[117] found that sexual intercourse between husband and wife 'necessarily infers condonation'. Although a contemporary judgment[118] held that sexual intercourse was not always necessary to demonstrate 'reinstatement' of a spouse, *Cramp* set the standard that 'the best evidence of reinstatement is resumption of intercourse between the parties'.[119] This was taken further five years later in *Turnbull v Turnbull and Coats* (1924–25).[120] The outcome of this case was that even though the husband did not forgive his wife's adultery, penetrating her vagina had the effect of forgiving her. This sexual act, and therefore every act of penile-vaginal intercourse, re-consummated the marriage and precluded divorce because of condonation.

[114] Brook, 'How to do things with sex', 140–1.

[115] *Roberts v Roberts and another* [1916–17] All ER 530.

[116] *Hare v Hare and Davidson* (1919–20) XXXVI TLR 331 HC PDAD.

[117] *Cramp v Cramp and Freeman* [1920] All ER 164.

[118] *Crocker v Crocker* [1921] All ER Rep 134.

[119] Brooks, *Matrimonial causes*, 28.

[120] *Turnbull v Turnbull and Coats* (1924–25) 69 SJ 574.

The interpretation of the law of condonation was gendered. The Matrimonial Causes Act (1937) reinforced the notion of 'sex' as condonation by adding a sexually defined condonation clause to the new grounds for nullity and by leaving the condonation of matrimonial offences (for divorce) undefined, and therefore subject to the prevailing interpretation of test cases. Three of the new nullity clauses—unsound mind at the time of marriage, venereal disease at the time of marriage, and pregnancy by another man at the time of marriage—were all subject to the requirement 'that marital intercourse with the consent of the petitioner has not taken place since the discovery by the petitioner of the existence of the grounds for decree'.[121] Such 'intercourse' would in effect re-consummate the marriage. The word 'consent' was to cover the 'rare cases [in which] it might be held that, though marital intercourse did take place after a woman petitioner had discovered the facts and before she filed the petition, yet such intercourse was practically forced upon her against her consent'.[122] The relevant section of the Act (Section 4) left condonation for divorce undefined. Following the relevant test cases, and nineteenth-century legislation, the Act was interpreted as being unequal for husband and wife. One act of sexual intercourse was enough for a husband to condone his wife's marital offence, but wives were sometimes given discretion by the judge, reflecting the economic dependency of most women on men and that the primary childcare role was a feminine one. As barrister Alfred Fellows put it in his *Popular Divorce Guide*, 'even intercourse with him [the husband] is not necessarily condonation, for, in his house, it may be virtually forced on her [the wife]'.[123] In general, for cruelty or desertion, 'implied condonation [was] usually the continuance or resumption of sexual intercourse'.[124] In England and Wales, the new divorce ground of desertion, enacted in 1938,[125] soon became subject to a sexual definition of condonation. Test cases in 1942 and 1951

---

[121] Section 7 of the Matrimonial Causes Act, 1937. See, for example, Fellows, *Popular divorce guide*, 45–6.

[122] Latey, *Matrimonial causes*, 39.

[123] Fellows, *Popular divorce guide*, 9–10, 43.

[124] Brookes, *Matrimonial causes*, 29.

[125] Matrimonial Causes Act, 1937, but a ground in Scotland since 1573, see Royal Commission Report 1956, 50.

178   N. PENLINGTON

held that sexual intercourse did not end desertion[126] especially if sex was followed by a refusal to cohabit.[127] The following year however, *Maslin v Maslin* (1952)[128] held that post-desertion penile-vaginal intercourse was condonation, regardless of whether reconciliation was intended.

When the Royal Commission hearing commenced in 1952, coitus and condonation were inextricably linked and many witnesses thought the gender bias of the law was unfair, but they instead reinforced a social-class bias. Influential legal scholar Prof. L. C. B. Gower advised the Commission that 'sexual intercourse' is 'conclusive evidence of condonation'.[129] The General Council to the Bar stated that 'most frequently... spouses signify their reconciliation by sexual intercourse' although it was sometimes the case that such intercourse could take place in 'circumstances where the parties thereafter allege condonation not to have been wholly effected'. Here, there was a reference to *Henderson v Henderson and Crellin* (1944),[130] in which one sex act was judged to have condoned the wife's adultery even though she promptly left home after the sex. The Bar Council felt this to be 'inequitable' to men since the Court often showed discretion to women by allowing other factors, and that this should be 'remedied by legislation'. The Council argued that the law was based on the nineteenth-century view that wives were '*inops consilii* and so oppressed by the duty of cohabitation that the dominant partner in the marriage might coax or coerce the wife to submit to sexual intercourse against her will and without her real consent'. They concluded, without considering that different 'women' may face different social and economic conditions and by assuming a middle-class norm, that in 'present-day experience... the wife more often than not is well aware of her rights and is an equal partner in the married state and often economically independent'. Leading barrister J. E. S. Simon agreed that the biased application of the law stemmed from 'the early years of the last century' but should be changed such that 'voluntary sexual intercourse by either party with knowledge of a matrimonial offence should amount to condonation of that offence'. Some witnesses were however calling for an end to a single

---

[126] *Mummery v Mummery* [1942] 1 All ER 553.

[127] *Whitney v Whitney* [1951] 1 All ER 301.

[128] *Maslin v Maslin* [1952] 1 All ER 477.

[129] Royal Commission Minutes 1956, 17.

[130] *Henderson v Henderson and Crellin* [1944] 1 All ER 44.

sexual act as condonation. The Marriage Law Reform Society stated that '[t]he breach of a condition imposed at the time of condoning an offence should in future put an end to the condonation, notwithstanding supervening acts of sexual intercourse'. Lord Merriman argued that 'the full extent of sleeping together as man and wife, is not to be regarded as the resumption of cohabitation or as condonation, as the case may be, I would be inclined to make it cut both ways, that is, in favour of both the husband and the wife'. The Law Society stated unequivocally that a 'single act of intercourse by a husband should not necessarily amount to condonation' and that 'the judge should have an unfettered discretion' as with the wife.[131]

The Report of the Royal Commission did not recommend a 'material change' to the law of condonation but its considerations and judgement reinforced the notion of 'sexual intercourse' as condonation. The Report suggested that the law of condonation should be equal between the sexes, and that 'sexual intercourse' should be taken as a 'presumption' of condonation, rather than an 'irrebuttable presumption'. The Commission considered that the law of condonation could prevent 'reconciliation' and suggested the introduction of a 'trial period of cohabitation of up to a month' that would be exempt from condonation. This proposal, like so many of the Commission's proposals, split the Commission fourteen to five. The majority suggested that '[a]cts of sexual intercourse between husband and wife which occur outside the trial period would give rise to a rebuttable presumption of condonation'. The minority stood against a trial period, which would be 'accompanied most probably by acts of sexual intercourse which may result in the birth of child'.[132] This strand of law, therefore, defined 'sex' as coitus and privileged it because it was potentially procreative.

Although the newspapers did not discuss the finer points of condonation, the law regarding condonation of matrimonial offences would have affected many couples seeking divorce. Between the First World War and the 1950s, 'sexual intercourse' became *the* evidence of condonation of a marital offence, and debates about its interpretation assumed middle-class power relations between husband and wife. Penile-vaginal intercourse was

[131] Royal Commission Minutes 1956, 33, 205, 225, 423, 742.

[132] Royal Commission Report 1956, 66, 70–3; 'The great marriage muddle', *Daily Mirror*, 21 March 1956, 1.

180   N. PENLINGTON

a 'sexual performative' that re-consummated marriage: in an era of near-universal marriage, *the* sexual act that defined the 'normal' male, and it was reinforced as the sexual act *par excellence* because of its potential for procreation.

PROOF OF (NON)CONSUMMATION

The foregoing debates placed penile-vaginal intercourse at the heart of married masculinity, but far from being a natural and timeless act, there was further disagreement on its precise definition as highlighted by the difficulty in proving whether the act had ever taken place at all. Medico-legal definitions of consummation defined the 'normal' man as sexually active and having a penis erect enough to penetrate his wife's vagina, as opposed to the unmanly, impotent man. In the absence of medical evidence, the bed was used to define 'normal' relations between men and women.

As has already been shown, medical explanations for incapacity gave way to the psychological; this coincided with a decreasing acceptance of the medical evidence in nullity cases. Roman Catholic Canon Law required a 'corporal inspection...[that] should be concerned exclusively with the female genitalia'[133] and some clinicians argued that the 'appearance of the vulva indicates elements of self-experience, the hymen exhibits the presence or absence of heterosexual experience, the vagina may record the history of mating'.[134] Although across the period, medical evidence secured a nullity decree in some cases,[135] the majority of medical and legal opinion gradually concluded that the 'the possible scope of the medical man in nullity suits was small' since 'impotence and virginity were [not]

---

[133] V. Harrington and J. B. Doyle, 'Indications and proof of non-consummation', *Linacre Quarterly: The Journal of the Catholic Medical Association* XIX (August 1952), 71.

[134] R. L. Dickinson and L. Beam, *A thousand marriages: A medical study of sex adjustment* (London: Williams and Norgate, 1932), 49.

[135] For example, 'Law report', *The Times*, 6 November 1925; 'Marriage is annulled after 23 years', *Daily Mirror*, 6 July 1951, 3.

absolute conditions'.[136] In *R. v R. (otherwise K)* (1907–8)[137] a nullity decree was granted although the putative wife was not *virgo intacta* and there were non-consummation cases widely reported in the newspapers of women who showed signs of virginity after giving birth.[138] In 1935, Seymour Edward Karminski, who in 1951 became a High Court Judge, 'remarked that physical defects were rare in nullity suits'.[139] The prevailing interpretation of the 1937 'wilful refusal' nullity clause was that parties could not be ordered to submit to a medical inspection.[140] Some medical inspectors felt that the *wilful* element of the new clause made medical evidence less relevant because it connoted choice.[141]

Unlike the centuries-old requirement of 'trial by congress', in which the man had to disprove the charge of impotence by engaging 'in sexual intercourse or masturbation before an audience',[142] the male body was not subject to scrutiny in non-consummation cases in the twentieth century. It was assumed that it was enough to determine the woman's virginity rather than the man's ability to gain an erection and penetrate a vagina. In the Roman Catholic Code of Canon Law, which required *erectio* and *emissio*, there was an assumption that 'once ['imperfect'] penetration has been established, minimum semination [sic] is presumed' since it was 'nigh on impossible to prove'.[143] The Church of England took a similarly practical stance in its nullity commission in the 1950s: 'After hearing the evidence of medical experts we are satisfied that the only test

[136] 'Reports of societies', *The British Medical Journal* 2, No. 3909 (December 7, 1935), 1127; See also 'Reports of societies', *The British Medical Journal* 1, No. 4035 (May 7, 1938), 1019–22.

[137] *R. v R. (otherwise K)* (1907–8) XXIV TLR 65 HC PDAD.

[138] For example, the widely reported 'Russell' case in 1922–3. See Adrian Bingham, *Family newspapers? Sex, private life, and the British popular press 1918–1978* (Oxford: Oxford University Press, 2009), 136.

[139] 'Reports of societies', *The British Medical Journal* 2, No. 3909 (December 7, 1935), 1127.

[140] Latey, *Matrimonial causes*, 36.

[141] William Latey, 'Consumption of marriage and the law', *The Medical-Legal and Criminological Review* XIV, No. 1–2 (January–June 1946), 59.

[142] Barbara Chuback, 'Male sexual dysfunction: Suing for sex in eighteenth-century England', *Urology* 71 (2008), 483.

[143] Harrington and Doyle, 'Indications and proof', 73.

which can be applied in law is that of penetration. Degrees of ejaculation may occur during intercourse which may be imperceptible to either party'.[144] This concurred with the commonly held medical view that *ejectio seminis* was a 'quite unprovable event'.[145]

In English Law by the 1950s, despite the lack of conclusive proof of penile-vaginal intercourse, 'true sex' legally required a 'real' erect penis to penetrate a vagina to a prescribed depth. The nullity case *B v B* (1955)[146] tested whether consummation could take place if the putative wife had an artificial (plastic) vagina. Following, the removal of 'certain male organs' at the age of seventeen,[147] the artificial vagina was fitted which subsequently collapsed to a length of two inches. This was deemed insufficient for *vera copula* and it was found that the artificial vagina should be replaced by one that was four to six inches long.[148] There are a number of outcomes to this case. First, the birth 'sex' of wife was not necessarily female at birth—this was not tested until *Corbett v Corbett* in 1970.[149] Secondly, the ruling in *B v B* stated that an artificial penis was not acceptable. This constructed the 'normal' man as one who could gain and sustain an erection in order to perform *vera copula*. Finally, this case demonstrates the variety of interpretations of 'complete' and 'true' 'sex'. The four inches of penetration required by English Civil Law was deeper than the Roman Catholic stipulation that

> there must be realised the apposition of an erect male organ against the hymeneal orifice with a definite pressure which will cause the membrane to be pushed aside and to be stretched, at least momentarily, so that part of the male organ can actually enter the vagina… coupled with a simultaneous semination [sic].

[144] Church Commission, 35.

[145] The Royal Society of Medicine, 'Discussion on birth control: Some medical and legal aspects', *Proceedings of the Royal Society of Medicine* 40, No. 2 (December 1946), 58.

[146] *B v B* [1955] P 42; This case is also discussed by Collier, but mainly as a starting point for later cases. Collier, *Masculinity*, 154–5.

[147] 'Medico-legal', *The British Medical Journal* 2, No. 4884 (14 August 1954), 418.

[148] Puxon and Dawkins, 'Non-consummation', 17–18.

[149] *Corbett v Corbett* [1970] 2 All ER 33.

5 NON-CONSUMMATION   183

The Catholic Church was aware that this legal definition differed from a commonly held assumption that 'consummation might be the perfect penetration of the vagina by the complete male organ'.[150]

In cases where medical evidence was inconclusive, sharing a bed was often evidence of penile-vaginal intercourse. The Roman Catholic Code of Canon Law worked on 'the principle that once the marriage ceremony ha[d] taken place and the spouses have cohabited, then it [was] *presumed* in law that proper and true consummation has taken place'.[151] This presumption that cohabitation equalled penile-vaginal intercourse could also be found in applications of English Civil Law: the important piece of evidence was *the bed*. In a case in 1920, *The Times* reported with incredulity that a women could still be a 'virgin' after 'sleeping in the same bed' with a man for four years.[152] In another case, it was found that '[n]ormal relations did not exist' since the 'parties occupied a bedroom with two beds in it'.[153] In some cases, separate bedrooms were taken as evidence of non-consummation.[154] In *Boynton v Boynton* (1952), the marriage was annulled because the husband and wife took turns sleeping in the double bed upstairs with the other on the 'couch and hearth rug downstairs'.[155] When a husband and wife shared a bed, the man was legally required to be the sexual initiator. From the mid-nineteenth century, the Court interpreted refusal to attempt sexual intercourse as incapacity, especially in the case of the husband. In *Lewis v Hayward* (1866)[156] 'it was held that when a husband abstains from or fails to attempt intercourse with his wife the inference of incapacity is stronger than the converse case'.[157] This inference of incapacity was tightened in *Kay v Kay (otherwise Gunson)* (1935)[158] in which the 'male' had never attempted intercourse after 'three years of occupying the same bed as

---

[150] Harrington and Doyle, 'Indications and proof', 65, 68.

[151] Harrington and Doyle, 'Indications and proof', 66.

[152] 'Gretna Green "marriage" revelations', *The Times*, 24 September 1920, 6.

[153] 'Law report', *The Times*, 7 May 1921, 4.

[154] 'Divorce suit wife accused of perjury', *Daily Express*, 22 November 1945, 3.

[155] '"Unusual case" of Mr. and Mrs. B.', *Daily Mirror*, 27 October 1952, 4.

[156] *Lewis v Hayward* [1866] 35 LJP.

[157] Latey, 'Consummation of marriage and the law', 51.

[158] *Kay v Kay (otherwise Gunson)* (1935) 152 LTR 264.

184   N. PENLINGTON

the female'.[159] This emphasis on the shared bed as evidence and with a legal bias between the sexes reinforced the notion that penile-vaginal intercourse is natural and irresistible for the 'normal' male subject. It also places 'normal' relations between men and women as (potentially) sexual; non-sexual male–female friendships were seen as unusual.

The medical evidence and presumptions in non-consummation cases, under both Canon Law and Civil Law, constructed the 'normal' male as heterosexual and physically and psychologically capable and willing to penetrate a vagina with his erect penis. Discussion focussed on the female body, but a *real* penis was required for *vera copula*. A 'normal' man was one who could not possibly share a bed with a woman without ever having penetrative sex with her.

CONCLUSION

The seemingly 'natural' act of consummation was subject to debates and redefinition during the period 1918–1960. Debates about non-consummation of marriage were debates about the purpose of sex and the purpose of marriage, and tested coitus with its possibilities for both pleasure and procreation. These gendered discourses defined normative married masculinity and male sexuality.

The legislative change in 1937 that introduced 'wilful refusal' and sex as condonation had long antecedents. The Royal Commission of 1912 and the nullity test cases leading up to it, found that sexual dysfunction could be psychological rather than physiological. During the 1920s, attempts to guide the entire package of divorce reforms through parliament failed, but the limited amount of discussion about 'wilful refusal' was gendered. Alongside eugenics concerns about the fitness of the 'race', married sex was presented as a right for husbands. Prominent test cases were brought by men whose wives had refused sex. A more mutual and companionate approach to sexual pleasure appeared in the debates in the 1930s, helped in part by a change in stance by the Church of England. The Established Church acknowledged sexual pleasure within marriage and decreed in 1930 that coitus could be about more than procreation. The 1937 Act brought monumental change to the laws of consummation, but there was no discussion of these changes during the passage

---

[159] Latey, 'Consummation of marriage and the law', 51–2.

of the Act through parliament. The inconsistencies, contradictions and lack of clarity in the new law stored up problems that were discovered, through practice, after the Second World War.

The debates about 'wilful refusal' and the purpose of sex and marriage, started in 1945 with a series of nullity test cases involving contraception. The discussion about the definition of 'natural' or 'complete' sex had repercussions for married masculinity. Newspapers reported these issues as a split between Church and State, but at the heart of these debates was the tension between procreation and pleasure in the required act of coitus between husband and wife. Initially, male sexual pleasure was held to be paramount, but this changed to a more mutual ideal of sex, narrowly defined as coitus. In 1955, the Church of England decreed, after much soul searching, that penetration was more important than procreation as long it was vaginal, not anal, penetration between husband and wife.

Most witnesses to the Royal Commission, which reported in 1956, wanted 'wilful refusal' to be a ground for divorce on a par with desertion and cruelty. In this vein, the discussion about 'wilful refusal' moved from a single act of coitus to consummate the marriage, to continual coitus throughout the marriage. Influenced by psychological theories, 'wilful refusal' defined the normal man as the willingly active, penetrative partner in a companionate marriage. Both partners had a right to sexual pleasure and it was 'cruel' to deny the other. In a separate strand of debate, the arrival of more reliable artificial insemination also caused a discussion about consummation of marriage. Although artificial insemination allowed a man to archive the masculine status of paternity, a normal man was still expected regularly to penetrate his wife's vagina.

Each act of coitus re-consummated a marriage and had the effect of legally reconciling a husband and wife even in the event of a marital offence such as adultery through the legal mechanism of condonation. The Royal Commission of 1912 did not consider sex as condonation, but an adultery test case in 1920 ensured that condonation appeared in the 1937 Matrimonial Causes Act. Condonation applied to the new nullity clauses, but was left undefined for divorce, for which earlier case law applied. The law was applied unequally. A man forgave his wife of a marital offence through one act of coitus, whereas a wife could receive discretion from the court because of her assumed less powerful economic and domestic status within the marriage. By the start of the 1950s Royal Commission, case law decreed that coitus was evidence of

186 N. PENLINGTON

reconciliation after desertion regardless of intention, and the Commissioners heard witnesses argue for gender equal law of condonation. The witnesses assumed a middle-class norm that women were now economically equal to men. The Majority report of the Commission recommended a trial period within which sex was allowed without assuming condonation; this was rejected by the Minority report which stated that every act of coitus was potentially procreative. The arrival of condonation and its application during this period reinforced the notion that coitus is *the* sexual act, and therefore vital to married masculinity.

The type of proof of consummation changed during this period to reflect the changing definitions of 'sex'. Roman Catholic Canon Law focused on female genitalia because ejaculation within the vagina was unprovable. It followed that penetration was taken as evidence of 'true sex'. Examination of the female body was not infallible, since there were cases under English Law of mothers who were *virgo intacta*. By the 1950s, case law required that true sex required a 'real' penis. A 'normal' man was therefore one who achieved and sustained an erection sufficient to penetrate a vagina. The shift to psychological definitions of impotence rendered physical examination less useful: *wilful* refusal implied 'choice'. In the absence of medical evidence, the bed was taken as proof, or otherwise, of consummation. By the end of the period, it was assumed under English Law that a normal man could not share a bed with a woman without achieving coitus. This sexual act, *the* sexual act, was increasingly expected to be achieved during the honeymoon holiday, which is the subject of the next chapter.

References

Abbott, Angus. 2001. *A history of celibacy*. Cambridge: Lutterworth

Anderson, Gary. 1989. Celibacy or consummation in the Garden? Reflections on early Jewish and Christian interpretations of the Garden of Eden. *The Harvard Theological Review* 82(2):121–48.

Anon. 1955. *The Church and the law of nullity of marriage: The report of a commission appointed by the Archbishops of Canterbury and York in 1949 at the request of the Convocations*. London: SPCK.

Barnes, H. Gorell and J. E. G. Montmorency. 1912. *The Divorce Commission: The Majority and Minority Reports summarised*. London: S. King and Son.

Barrett, Maxwell (ed.). 1998. *Blackstone's marriage breakdown law index: Case precedents, 1900–1997*. London: Blackstone.

Bingham, Adrian. 2009. *Family newspapers? Sex, private life, and the British popular press 1918–1978*. Oxford: Oxford University Press.

Brady, Sean. 2005. *Masculinity and male homosexuality in Britain, 1861–1913*. Basingstoke: Palgrave.

Brook, Heather. 2000. How to do things with sex. In *Sexuality in the legal arena* ed. Carl Stychin and Didi Herman, 132–50. London: Athlone.

Brooks, Leslie. 1937. *Matrimonial causes: Being an exposition of The Matrimonial Causes Act, 1937 and The Summary Procedure (Domestic Proceedings) Act, 1937*. London: Butterworth.

Church of England. 1935. *The Church and marriage: Being a report of the Joint Committees of the Convocations of Canterbury and York*. London: SPCK.

Civil Partnership Act (2004).

Collier, Richard. 1995. *Masculinity, law and the family*. London: Routledge.

Daily Express.

Daily Mirror.

Dickinson, R. L. and L. Beam. 1932. *A thousand marriages: A medical study of sex adjustment*. London: Williams and Norgate.

Fellows, Alfred. 1937. *The popular divorce guide: A guide to the Matrimonial Causes Act, 1937 (Mr A. Herbert's Marriage Bill)*. London: Watts.

Hall, Lesley. 1991. *Hidden anxieties: Male sexuality, 1900–1950*. Cambridge: Polity.

Harrington, V. and J. B. Doyle. 1952. Indications and proof of non-consummation. *Linacre Quarterly: The Journal of the Catholic Medical Association* XIX:61–76.

Herbert, A. 1937. *The ayes have it: The story of the Marriage Bill*. London: Methuen.

Jackson, Joseph. 1969. *The formation and annulment of marriage*. London: Butterworth.

Lacey, T. A. 1947. *Marriage in Church and state*. London: SPCK.

Latey, William. 1937. *The Matrimonial Causes Act 1937*. London: Sweet & Maxwell.

Latey, William. 1946. Consummation of marriage and the law. *The Medical-Legal and Criminological Review* XIV(1–2):51–9.

Matrimonial Causes Act (1950) s. 8. 1. (a)

McLaren, Angus. 2007. *Impotence: A cultural history*. London: University of Chicago Press.

Moyse, Cordelia. 1996. Reform of marriage and divorce law in England and Wales 1909–37. Unpublished PhD thesis: University of Cambridge.

Noonan, Jr., John T. 1972. *Power to dissolve: Lawyers and marriages in the courts of the Roman Curia*. Cambridge MA: Harvard University Press.

Proceedings of the Royal Society of Medicine.

188   N. PENLINGTON

Puxon, Margaret and Sylvia Dawkins. 1964. Non-consummation of marriage. *Medicine, Science and the Law* 4:15–21.

Royal Commission on Divorce and Matrimonial Causes. 1912. *Minutes of evidence taken before the Royal Commission on Divorce and Matrimonial Causes, Vol. 1.* London: HMSO.

Royal Commission on Divorce and Matrimonial Causes. 1912. *Minutes of evidence taken before the Royal Commission on Divorce and Matrimonial Causes, Vol. 3.* London: HMSO.

Royal Commission on Marriage and Divorce. 1956. *Minutes of evidence taken before the Royal Commission on Marriage and Divorce, 1952–56.* London: HMSO.

Royal Commission on Marriage and Divorce. 1956. *Royal Commission on Marriage and Divorce, report 1951–1955.* London: HMSO.

Seuffert, S. 1937. *The Matrimonial Causes Act, 1937.* London: Solicitors' Law Stationery Society.

Stone, Lawrence. 1990. *Road to divorce: England 1530–1987.* Oxford: Oxford University Press.

Stopes, Marie. 1956. First published 1928. *Enduring passion: Further new contributions to the solution of sex difficulties being the continuation of* Married Love. London: Hogarth.

The British Medical Journal.

The Marriage (Same Sex Couples) Act (2013).

The Times.

Urology.

Weeks, Jeffrey. 2012. First published 1989. *Sex, politics and society: The regulation of sexuality since 1800.* Harlow: Longman.

Wiegman, Robyn and Elizabeth A. Wilson. 2015. Introduction: Antinormativity's queer conventions. *differences* 26(1):1–25.

CHAPTER 6

Honeymoon

'There's something to be said, after all, for the sight-seeing kind of honeymoon—it does give one a programme'.—From Dorothy L. Sayers, *Busman's Honeymoon* (stage play 1936, novel 1937)[1]

By quoting her married friend, Harriet Vane encapsulates the feelings that many honeymoon couples would have had as they found themselves alone together, possibly for the first time. Harriet's quip, in Dorothy L Sayers' *Busman's Honeymoon*, demonstrates a social-class-specific response to the question of how to fill the time on a honeymoon, since Vane receives a house, Talboys, in Hertfordshire as a wedding present from her husband Lord Peter Wimsey. Many couples during this period could not afford a honeymoon, or a house, and, as will be seen, manual workers perhaps wanted a rest rather than a sightseeing programme. Sayers' observation is however both frank and typical of its time. Although historian Claire Langhamer shows that 'romance' increased during this period, there is here a pragmatic approach to love and marriage, and although couples embarked on their honeymoons with the desire, expectation and legal requirement to consummate their marriages, sex was not seen to be the dominant, or only, preoccupation of honeymooning men. How can the

---

[1] Dorothy L. Sayers, *Busman's Honeymoon* (London: Victor Gollancz, 1937), 372.

© The Author(s), under exclusive license to Springer Nature Switzerland AG 2023
N. Penlington, *Men Getting Married in England, 1918–60*, Genders and Sexualities in History, https://doi.org/10.1007/978-3-031-27405-3_6

honeymoon reveal codes of masculinity, and power relations between husband and wife during the early days of marriage?

The word 'honeymoon' has been part of the English language since the sixteenth century and originally described and defined a short period—typically a month—of conjugal happiness after getting married.[2] Here, the term 'honeymoon' will denote the holiday not the period after the wedding. Although, this is a modern usage it is more convenient as a tool to explore marrying masculinity. From the eighteenth century, upper-class couples could afford, in terms of both time and money, to go on a 'tour' visiting relatives and other associates.[3] By the mid-nineteenth century the honeymoon holiday was more widely available and 'it was becoming the fashion for middle-class couples to begin their honeymoon trips immediately after the wedding and to go unaccompanied'.[4] By the end of the nineteenth century, Thomas (and John) Cook had helped to make travel appear 'relatively risk-free', and honeymoons were available to some of the skilled working class.[5] Although increased availability of paid holidays[6] and the arrival of Butlin's holiday camps in the 1930s[7] made holidays more accessible to those on lower incomes, it was still the case in the 1940s that among the working class 'an extended honeymoon was largely confined to skilled workers' and did not become popular or possible until the 1960s.[8]

We are concerned here with the honeymoon as transformation, especially for men. English literature scholars have explored the meanings of the honeymoon and have contested its transformational nature. In

[2] Cele C. Otnes and Elizabeth H. Peck, *Cinderella dreams: The allure of the lavish wedding* (Berkeley: University of California Press, 2003), 134.

[3] Elizabeth Freeman, *The wedding complex: Forms of belonging in modern American culture*, (London: Duke University Press, 2002), 147.

[4] John Gillis, *For better, for worse: British marriages, 1600 to the present*, (Oxford: Oxford University Press, 1985), 138.

[5] John Urry, *Consuming places* (London: Routledge, 1994), 143.

[6] The Holidays with Pay Act (1938) recommended, but did not mandate, one week's paid holiday for full-time workers. Some employers were already agreeing paid holiday entitlements with trade unions in the 1920s. Sandra Dawson, 'Working-class Consumers and the Campaign for Holidays with Pay', *Twentieth Century British History* 18, No. 3 (2007), 277, 279.

[7] Steve Humphries, *A secret world of sex: Forbidden fruit: The British experience, 1900–1950* (London: Sidgwick & Jackson, 1988), 183.

[8] Gillis, *For better, for worse*, 296, 311.

her study of 'fictional and nonfictional' Victorian honeymoons, Helena Michie argues that for the upper-middle class the honeymoon was 'a transformation that was both highly visible and deeply private for both members of the newly married couple'. This transformation was asymmetrical because it was a change that was 'more acute for the bride' since for her there was change in legal and sexual status.[9] Elizabeth Freeman focuses on the man and argues that the American honeymoon 'transformed husband from suitor to tutor' since the 'couple-centred honeymoon put the husband in charge of both erotic knowledge and knowledge of life'. For Freeman, the honeymoon 'physically separates the couple from peers and natal family' and this retreat from the domestic sphere allowed the husband to start the marriage by demonstrating his 'cultural and sensual competence outside the home'. As an example of this, Freeman shows that in the American context before the 1960s the 'husband was in charge of paying for, picking the site of, and orchestrating the honeymoon'.[10] We shall explore the gendered transformation of English honeymooning couples in the period 1918 to 1960.

The honeymoon destination, if there was one, is an important area in which to unpack the gendered early days of marriage. An instructive way to interpret the honeymoon is by using the concept of the 'gaze'. Michie argues that the location of the honeymoon was important because the 'geographical displacements of the honeymoon often served as both backdrop and sign of the transformative cultural work of marriage'. By being in a strange place together, the newly formed married couple created 'the conjugal gaze with its attendant "we"', as they moved from 'a world essentially homosocial to a world defined around heterosexuality'.[11] Sociologist John Urry argues that travel is transformative since is it 'responsible for altering how people appear to experience the modern world'.[12] In 1990, Urry mapped out his conceptualisation of the 'tourist gaze'. Urry, builds on Michel Foucault's concept of 'the gaze', in which Foucault explains how the discipline of medicine changed such that 'the medical gaze ... was no longer of any observer, but that of a

---

[9] Helena Michie, 'Victorian Honeymoons: Sexual Reorientations and the "Sights" of Europe', *Victorian Studies* 43, No. 2 (Winter, 2001), 230, 233.

[10] Freeman, *Wedding complex*, 146–50.

[11] Michie, 'Victorian Honeymoons', 233–4, 240.

[12] Urry, *Consuming places*, 144.

192   N. PENLINGTON

doctor supported and justified by an institution'. Urry takes Foucault's gaze out of the institution and places it with the tourist to explore how the 'tourist gaze' is 'as socially organised and systematised as the gaze of the medic'. Although Urry gives many British examples of tourism, his only example of honeymoons is of Americans honeymooning at the Niagara Falls. The 'tourist gaze' allows the historian not just to focus on the honeymoon couple being alone but instead as part of a '"romantic" form of the tourist gaze' upon a holiday destination, and upon other people. This 'romantic gaze' places an 'emphasis' on 'solitude', but is nonetheless dependent upon others. Urry explains that 'Other people give atmosphere or a sense of carnival to a place' and 'indicate that this is *the* place to be and that one should not be elsewhere'.[13] By drawing on Urry's 'tourist gaze', a historian can therefore suggest the subjectivities of honeymooning couples within a wider context of place and people.

To uncover the honeymoon, and the experiences and expectations of newly married men, we shall examine first-person testimonies, etiquette manuals, railway posters and newspaper coverage of honeymoons. Oral history interviews are from the British Library Sound Archive. The sample of ninety-five interviews is not representative of the English population during the period but does contain a range of interviewees from fruit farmers to financiers. Since the social-class composition of those who talk about honeymoons is disproportionately middle and upper class, there are a further ten working-class autobiographies that have been added to the overall sample of first-person testimonies. First-person testimonies should however be read with caution; they are testimony, not truth. As Michie points out 'there would be cultural pressures to report that one's honeymoon was a success—and to convince oneself that this was the case'.[14] As literature scholar Allessandro Portelli explains, oral history 'tells us less about events as such than about their meaning'.[15] Etiquette manuals shed light on codes of behaviour expected of wealthier couples. A smaller number of manuals has been quoted here compared to previous chapters because the honeymoon featured in fewer manuals than the subjects of engagement and the wedding. This could be because the honeymoon

---

[13] John Urry, *The tourist gaze*, (London: Sage, 2002. First published 1990), 1, 11, 43; Urry cites Michel Foucault, *The birth of the clinic* (London: Tavistock, 1976), 89.

[14] Michie, 'Victorian Honeymoons', 250.

[15] Alessandro Portelli, 'The Peculiarities of Oral History', *History Workshop Journal* 12 (1981), 99.

holiday was evolving during this period and becoming a more culturally essential part of 'the wedding'. Railway posters are included as a way of unpacking the meanings associated with particular destinations.[16] These posters, typically displayed in railway stations, reached a large number of people during this period because the rail was the most popular mode of mid to long-distance transport. The newspaper sample of 921 articles is from over ten thousand articles in the *Daily Express* and *Daily Mirror* that contain the word 'honeymoon' in the period 1918 to 1960. The random ten per-cent sample, stratified by year,[17] excludes articles that were in fact advertisements for the well-known Dorothy L. Sayers' play, *Busman's Honeymoon*. Newspapers are not used to understand simply what the reports and editors wanted to say about honeymoons, but to suggest the ways in which the reader could narrativise her or his self through the daily reading of a newspaper.

Through interrogation of these sources, the subjectivities of married men are shown in relation to the notion of being a newlywed couple away from home within a wider social and cultural nexus. There are three sections in this chapter: planning, location and experience. The first section—'planning'—focuses on the planning and preparation of the honeymoon and the gendered knowledge and decision-making that led to the choice of holiday location and accommodation. The next section, 'location', looks at the particularity of honeymoon locations—especially Europe, countryside and the seaside—to explore the meanings of a newly married couple being in, and gazing upon, such places. Although potentially far from home, often for the first time, honeymooning couples travelled with the social and cultural expectations that they could not leave behind. The final section tackles the 'experience' of the honeymoon. Although the destination was supposedly romantic, the couple may not have had much privacy, and for some, consummating the marriage was less than straightforward. It has also been seen that many couples did not go on a honeymoon holiday but instead got on with daily life straight after the wedding. These different stages of the honeymoon highlight the social-class-inflected tensions and pressures of masculinity as men formed and performed the subject position of (newly) married man.

[16] The railway posters mentioned in this chapter are easily found online.

[17] For example, in 1928 there were 220 articles, therefore 22 appear in the sample. The proportion by each newspaper has been kept.

PLANNING

The honeymoon required planning—the choice of location, transport, accommodation and activities—and would have been greatly anticipated by the couple and to an extent by their families and friends. The idea of the honeymoon holiday was widely circulated in popular culture and the word 'honeymoon' came to mean a post-wedding holiday for the newlywed couple alone. Honeymoon planning reveals gendered power relations between husband and wife and that the man typically organised and orchestrated the honeymoon as it was an opportunity for him to show and rehearse masculine knowledge of places and processes outside the home.

Advertisers depicted the honeymoon period as one of intimacy, and the language was changing to equate 'honeymoon' with 'holiday'. Advertisers used romantic imagery to sell products in the interwar period and typified the honeymoon as a physical and intimate holiday. In the 1930s, Hinds Cream ran a series of advertisements with the strap-line 'Honeymoon Hands'. The hand cream in question promised 'to bring *honeymoon* enchantment' to the consumer's hands because '[h]oneymoon hands are more than beautiful... they are alluring, romantic, irresistible'. The accompanying picture shows an embracing couple admiring one pair of hands, the woman's. *Her* hands, complete with wedding and engagement rings, seem to remind the ecstatic-looking couple of their enchanted honeymoon.[18] Also in the 1930s, advertisements for 'Smarts' furniture featured an attractive couple walking along the beach (he manfully grips her around the waist, pulling her to him as he looks forward; she gazes *up* at him) as the man says 'I'm loving every minute of our honeymoon... our lovely new home... will be like a second honeymoon'. This makes a link between a (sexually) successful honeymoon and an equally successful marriage—that it will be one long honeymoon.[19] In this period, the usage of the word honeymoon changed from a period to a holiday.

---

[18] For example, 'Hinds Cream', *Daily Mirror*, 30 March 1932, 9; Also 'Men praise her honeymoon hands they could adore yours too' in 'Hinds Cream', *Daily Mirror*, 10 February 1932, 15.

[19] For example, 'Smarts', *Daily Express*, 6 July 1936, 7.

In 1951, The *Daily Express* (with a mostly middle-class readership)[20] ran a book review of the new *Webster's* dictionary of American English. Highlighting to historians the changing importance of marriage and the honeymoon, the reviewer honed in on the definition of 'honeymoon' as an example of how *Webster's* differed from the 'Oxford Dictionary'. The OED gave the definition as *'the first month after marriage'*, but *Webster's* as *'a holiday spent together by a newly married couple'*. The reviewer applauded this 'new approach to dictionary-making' because to 'most people a "honeymoon" means a "holiday"'.[21]

This changing definition of honeymoon appeared in popular culture,[22] especially when aimed at women; the honeymoon holiday became normal, or at least something to aspire to. In addition to Dorothy L Sayers' *Busman's Honeymoon*, discussed at the start of this chapter, other fictional accounts of honeymoons normalised the upper and middle-class honeymoon. Newspapers, especially in the interwar period, ran serialised fiction and these stories often involved a honeymoon.[23] In 1920, the *Daily Express* ran a lengthy serial entitled 'The Gates of Hope', which featured a honeymoon set in France in episode forty-six.[24] The *Daily Mirror* ran two-part stories, such as the 'The Muddled Marriage'[25] (1919) or one-off short stories, such as 'A Debt of Love'[26] (1921). Some stories contained disastrous honeymoons. The 1926 series 'Sandy: A Wonderful Love Story' featured a bride who ran away during her honeymoon because she found her new husband's 'presence to be absolutely repellent'.[27] Running in the *Daily Mirror* during the winter of 1932, 'Honeymoon Husband' contained the cautionary note that a good honeymoon is not necessarily

---

[20] Indeed, one definition of middle class was those 'who read the "popular" press, like the *Daily Mail* or *Daily Express*'. See Ross McKibbin, *Classes and cultures, England1918-1951* (Oxford: Oxford University Press, 1998), 44.

[21] With original emphasis, 'Read It', *Daily Express*, 5 March 1951, 4.

[22] Including British cinema films such as *Squibs' Honeymoon* (1923), *A Honeymoon Adventure* (1931), *Honeymoon for Three* (theatre 1932, film 1941) and *Is Your Honeymoon Really Necessary?* (theatre 1944, film 1953).

[23] Only a few examples are given here, but there are dozens of examples from every year in the interwar period.

[24] 'The gates of hope', *Daily Express*, 31 August 1920, 3.

[25] 'The Muddled Marriage', *Daily Mirror*, 2 October 1919, 10.

[26] 'A Debt of Love', *Daily Mirror*, 7 October 1921, 11.

[27] 'Sandy: A wonderful love story', *Daily Mirror*, 30 August 1926, 13.

196   N. PENLINGTON

a good omen since 'life is not a honeymoon and it was after the honeymoon was over that the real test of marriage began'.[28] A late example of the serialised story to involve a honeymoon is 'And Then I Grew Up' (1954). This was not fiction however, but the serialised biography of the actress Jean Simmons.[29] Newspaper book reviewers considered the romantic story to be unmanly, even if written by a man. Graham Greene's *Loser Takes All* (1955), involving a honeymoon in Monte Carlo, was dismissed by the reviewer a 'novel that reads as though it had been written for a woman's magazine'.[30]

If the romance of the honeymoon was supposedly feminine, the knowledge and organisation needed to plan a honeymoon were purportedly masculine. The newly married man was in effect taking over the father figure role in his wife's life. As shown in Chapter 3, he had received permission to marry from her father, the father had given her away in Chapter 4, and here the husband is becoming responsible for her. Etiquette manuals advised that men should plan and book the honeymoon. Mary Woodman in *Wedding Etiquette* (1929) advised that the couple could decide on the location, but 'it will be advisable for the man to secure the accommodation' and that 'every detail should be planned and booked-up before starting'.[31] Although M. and S. Bee stated in *Weddings without Worry* (1935) that the honeymoon location 'should be settled according to mutual taste' the accommodation and deposit, however, should be arranged by the 'best man'.[32] This reinforced men's dominant position in the public sphere. In 1950, Ann Page repeated this stance in *The Complete Guide to Wedding Etiquette* by asserting that the 'location and duration of the honeymoon depend upon the bridegroom's finances, his business responsibilities, and the personal preferences of his bride and himself'.[33] The man was therefore expected to be the breadwinner and provider, and to an extent to shield his new wife from the

---

[28] 'Honeymoon husband', *Daily Mirror*, 11 February 1932, 15.

[29] 'And Then I Grew Up', *Daily Express*, 2 November 1954, 4.

[30] 'Nancy Spain cheers on the gunrunner', *Daily Express*, 5 February 1955, 4.

[31] Mary Woodman, *Wedding etiquette* (London: W. Foulsham, 1929), 104.

[32] M. Bee and S. Bee, *Weddings without worry: A modern and practical guide to wedding conventions and ceremonies* (London: Methuen, 1935), 92, 94.

[33] Ann Page, *The complete guide to wedding etiquette* (London: Ward, Lock and Co., 1950), 124.

outside world by taking responsibility for financial transactions and other formal arrangements. Newspaper articles reflected the advice given in etiquette manuals. Some men allowed their fiancées to make the choice of honeymoon destination, and then paid for it themselves.[34] Even towards the end of the period, newspapers expected the man to pay for the honeymoon and could be contemptuous of a man who made his fiancée pay.[35]

Some working-class couples had honeymoons with the assistance of family or friends. For these couples, pragmatism was more important than convention: they wanted to have a honeymoon *somehow*. In the oral history sample, this help tended to be from the groom's side. This created an asymmetrical relationship between the newlyweds; the groom had more power and knowledge in these early days of marriage, but it also shows that men were often unable to stand on their own two feet and demonstrate their independence as head of household. In 1937, Middlesbrough steelworker Dickie Seymour and his wife stayed at his cousin's in Scarborough. The cousin stayed in Middlesbrough after the wedding to give the newlyweds some privacy.[36] In 1949, London market porter John Watts took his wife to Cornwall for a honeymoon. They stayed at a cottage owned by his mum's friends. They married on a Saturday and ran out of money by Wednesday, and his mum sent him money through the Post Office.[37] Some honeymooning couples did not necessarily have much privacy but still had a good honeymoon. Canning Town crane driver James Bushnell went on honeymoon to his mother's sister's in Watford because she invited them 'into her home'. James remembered that they 'had a good time' for a week before returning home.[38]

Instead of assistance from family, couples sometimes had help from friends to make a honeymoon possible. In the oral history sample, help came from the groom's friends and this reinforced the notion that the

---

[34] '£250 for a war heroine', *Daily Mirror*, 6 May 1921, 2.

[35] 'Honeymoon for two—but the bride paid', *Daily Express*, 12 February 1957, 9.

[36] C532/032 interview with Dickie Seymour, NLSC: Lives in Steel, BLSA.

[37] C821/190 interview with John Watts, NLSC: Food: From Source to Salespoint, BLSA.

[38] C707/302/1–7 interview with James Bushnell, Family Life and Work Experience before 1918, BLSA.

198   N. PENLINGTON

man was responsible for the honeymoon as it gave him the opportunity to demonstrate his connections outside the home. In the mid-1940s, Oxford-educated John Brown took his new wife to Switzerland for 'a delightful honeymoon'. As John explained in an interview, 'Lots of people helped ... you couldn't travel around unless you had influence'.[39] Relying on connections meant that a couple could not sever the link with home, even during their honeymoon. In 1942, shop worker Ron Stedman and his wife, Win, went on a honeymoon from South London to Brighton 'despite the war'. They were only able to do this because a friend's uncle and aunt kept a boarding house, or else they 'couldn't afford it'.[40] Staying with the husband's associates often came at the price of restricted privacy.[41] Humberside trawler man Jack Close was able to take his wife for a honeymoon on a Greek island as a 'guest' of his Greek captain.[42] When banker Anthony Akers married in the early 1950s, he arranged the honeymoon. He and his wife stayed with his friend, a 'famous restaurateur in London', in Switzerland.[43] Although there would have been different levels of spaciousness, the lack of privacy because of staying with friends applied to men in different social classes.

Some men, but no women, in the oral history sample were able to plan their honeymoons to coincide with work commitments or opportunities. Neville Conder and his wife Jean, a fellow architecture student, went on a honeymoon to Switzerland in the mid-1940s. Neville had a 'travel scholarship' and had to do a 'study' on chalets, but the 'school' authorities knew it was really a honeymoon.[44] In 1946, athlete Doug Wilson and his new wife Mavis went on a honeymoon to Ireland where he had to run in an invitation cross-country race.[45] In 1960, scientist John Glen

---

[39] C872/26/01–20 interview with John Brown, NLSC: Book Trade Lives, BLSA.

[40] C821/30/01–16 interview with Ronald Stedman, NLSC: Food: From Source to Salespoint, BLSA.

[41] For example, in 1946, colliery overseer George Pearson and his wife stayed with friends in County Durham for their honeymoon. C532/021/01–07 interview with George Pearson, NLSC: Lives in Steel, BLSA.

[42] C900/07067 interview with Jack Close, Millennium Memory Bank, BLSA.

[43] C1367/14 interview with Anthony Akers, An Oral History of Barings, BLSA.

[44] C467/42/01–08 interview with Neville Conder, NLSC: Architects' Lives, BLSA.

[45] C790/28/01–03 interview with Doug Wilson, Oral History of British Athletics, BLSA.

managed to plan his Scandinavian honeymoon to coincide with a conference in Helsinki.[46] These men were able to dominate the planning of the honeymoon and situate their new marriage in relation to their careers.

Not all husbands arranged the honeymoon and a few of the oral history interviews sampled show that a variety of other possibilities existed.[47] Towards the end of the period, a woman could plan the honeymoon and make all the arrangements, thus showing that financial and planning skills were not essentially or exclusively masculine.[48] Married in 1955, while on National Service, Scunthorpe man Harold Marshall had to get permission from his senior officer before he could go on honeymoon. As he was away in the army, his fiancée had to make the honeymoon arrangements. They went to London straight after the wedding reception and had 'a wonderful week's honeymoon' in Jersey.[49] A couple could embark on a mutual approach to decision-making.[50] Writer John Carey was clear in his interview that he and his wife 'both decided' on their honeymoon destinations in 1960. They travelled around Florence and Perugia by train, stayed in pensions and were determined to 'spend a lot of time in art galleries'.[51] A woman could demonstrate her wealth, knowledge and connections. Also married in 1960, Tessa Baring, member of the famous banking family, 'went off on honeymoon to Majorca where [her] aunt had a little house'.[52] These unusual examples show that the gendered positions of newlywed husband and wife were precarious, and negotiable according to context and wealth.

[46] C1379/26 interview with John Glen, An Oral History of British Science, BLSA.

[47] Bulcroft et al. found in their quantitative analysis of American honeymoons that the bride paid for ten per cent of honeymoons and that the men were typically responsible for 'planning and orchestrating' the honeymoon. Kris Bulcroft, Linda Smeins and Richard Bulcroft, *Romancing the honeymoon: Consummating the honeymoon in modern society* (London: Sage, 1999), 45, 50.

[48] For the 'symmetry between wives and secretaries' see Michael Roper, *Masculinity and the British organisational man* (Oxford: Oxford University Press, 1994), 181.

[49] C900/19547 C1 interview with Harold Marshall, Millennium Memory Bank, BLSA.

[50] While by no means universal, 'shared' decision-making could be found in a variety of marriages across the social spectrum. Marcus Collins, *Modern love: An Iitimate history of men and women in twentieth-century Britain* (London: Atlantic, 2003), 112–4.

[51] C1276/49 interview with John Carey, NLSC: Author's Lives, BLSA.

[52] C1367/18 interview with Tessa Baring, An Oral History of Barings, BLSA.

The honeymoon holiday became more prominent during the period 1918 to 1960, and it was typically the man's job to make the arrangements. Even when relying upon others for assistance, this allowed him to demonstrate his connections and knowledge outside the home and to replace the wife's father by taking responsibility for her. Some women did however arrange the honeymoon. Once the planning and preparations were complete, it was the location that mattered.

LOCATION

It is often impossible from the sources surveyed to discern how individual couples arrived at their choice of honeymoon destination, but the location can tell us something about the early days of marriage and the wider social and cultural nexus of expectations and norms. Although Kris Bulcroft, Linda Smeins and Richard Bulcroft have argued in their American interdisciplinary study of honeymoons that before the 1950s 'the emphasis on romantic fantasy was nominal',[53] it will be shown that couples gazed upon honeymoon destinations freighted with symbols and meanings, and they honeymooned in destinations that had romantic, and therefore gendered, associations.

Social class inflected the choice of location and the place in which newlyweds formed the 'we' of the 'conjugal gaze'. As Urry, drawing on Pierre Bourdieu, explains, different groups 'develop the social capital necessary for judging and discriminating between such different environments'.[54] Historian Barbara Penner argues that for wealthier Americans in the nineteenth century the honeymoon was not just 'an expression of this group's class privilege, but was integral to constructing them and making them visible in the first place'. The honeymoon was not just about the couple and was neither 'liberating' nor 'repressive' but 'suggested that certain beliefs were shared by its participants... and further enforced their feelings of allegiance'.[55] This social-class interpretation is applicable to twentieth-century English couples. Etiquette manuals suggested a range of places from which a couple could choose. Mary Woodman's *Wedding*

---

[53] Bulcroft et al., *Romancing the honeymoon*, 49.

[54] Urry, *Consuming Places*, 175.

[55] Barbara Penner, *Newlyweds on tour: Honeymooning in nineteenth-century America* (Durham NH: University of New Hampshire Press, 2009), 230.

Etiquette (1929) gave a list of possible honeymoon locations: Switzerland, the (French) Riviera, Paris, a tour from Belgium to the Rhine, the Dead Cities of Holland, a sea cruise to a Scandinavian city, Cornwall, Torquay for Devon, Aberystwyth for central Wales, the Lake District, Edinburgh, an 'English hydro' (for example, Harrogate, Malvern, Matlock), and the Yorkshire Moors.[56] M. and S. Bee's *Weddings without Worry* (1935) gave an almost identical list but additionally stated that '[c]ruises lasting from ten to thirty days to Norway or North Africa, around the British Isles, or through the Mediterranean Sea are becoming more popular with honeymoon couples'.[57] The oral history sample shows a range of honeymoon destinations that can highlight social class. As is shown below, Europe was beyond the reach of working-class and lower-middle class couples, while the countryside and seaside destinations were, on the face of it, more socially mixed. Choice of honeymoon destination reveals a wide range of options. The three most common—Europe, countryside and the seaside—are explored here to show some of the gender and class connotations of honeymoon location.

Wealthier couples were able to start their married life by gazing upon European places and people. A feature of the 'tourist gaze' as defined by Urry is that tourists construct it through 'the collection of signs'. Urry gives as examples Paris and the English village. When (potential) tourists 'see two people kissing in Paris', either directly or through photographs, postcards or films, they are 'gazing upon… timeless, romantic Paris'. The circulation of these signs 'enable[s] the gaze to be endlessly reproduced and recaptured'.[58] *Marriage Etiquette* (1936) by 'Best Man' suggested that.

[f]or a honeymoon in spring, a tour amongst the flowers fields of Holland, blazing with blossoming tulip and hyacinth bulbs, would be a pleasant variation from the orthodox visit to Paris, especially if the bridal couple are interested in picturesque architecture, quaintly dressed people and curious customs.[59]

---

[56] Woodman, *Wedding etiquette*,100–2.

[57] Bee and Bee, *Weddings without worry*, 92–3.

[58] Urry, *Consuming places*, 133.

[59] "Best Man", *Marriage etiquette: How to arrange a wedding* (London: W. Foulsham, 1936), 67 and "Best Man", *Marriage etiquette: How to arrange a wedding* (London: W. Foulsham, 1949), 68.

202   N. PENLINGTON

This places the newlywed couple within a setting in which they can form a conjugal gaze upon the 'quaintly dressed people and curious customs' of the European Other. Further, couples are immersed in the natural wonder of 'blossoming tulip and hyacinth bulbs', an instantly recognisable, romantic image of Holland, in what Michie calls, in her example of nineteenth-century Switzerland, the 'linking of romantic love with the tourist category of "scenery"'.[60] This combination of architecture, 'scenery' and romantic love is also present in later etiquette manuals. Ann Page in *The Complete Guide to Wedding Etiquette* (1950) gave a similar list of destinations but added some detail. Page described Switzerland as a 'tourist paradise' because of the 'beauty of its scenery', Paris as having 'the most famous art gallery in the world', and Norway and Sweden as famed for their mountains, forests and lakes.[61] When combined with the expectation that the man should plan and pay for the honeymoon, the husband was to start the marriage by providing his wife with transformative 'romance'.

A European honeymoon was not possible for most English newlyweds during this period. Even though the oral history sample is not representative of the English population, it is telling that only a narrow band of couples could achieve the aspiration of a honeymoon in continental Europe or Scandinavia. Those who went to such destinations were bankers, scientists, artists and architects. In 1935, stockbroker Peter Daniell demonstrated conspicuous consumption and took his wife on a 'whacking great honeymoon... all over Europe in a motorcar'[62] and, towards the end of the period, banker Anthony Akers took his new wife for a fortnight in Switzerland.[63] Less wealthy, but university educated, men took their new wives on European honeymoons. In the late 1950s, scientist James Crease had a 'conventional' honeymoon in Paris with 'not much money'[64] and engineer James McMahon, a Londoner of Australian origin, went on a holiday to Switzerland, Rome and Naples.[65] Artist couples also had the cultural capital to place their new marriage within a

---

[60] Michie, 'Victorian Honeymoons', 241.

[61] Page, *Complete guide*, 125–32.

[62] C409/031/01–05 interview with Sir Peter Daniell, NLSC: City Lives, BLSA.

[63] Interview with Anthony Akers.

[64] C1379/87 interview with James Crease, An Oral History of British Science, BLSA.

[65] C464/58 interview with James McMahon, NLSC: General, BLSA.

European setting. In 1934, artists Ursula Mommens and Julian Trevelyan honeymooned in Italy for six weeks.[66] In 1950, artist John Ward and his new wife Alison had a 'very' romantic time in Paris and then the Pyrenees.[67] This type of 'romantic gaze' upon the architecture, history and 'scenery' of Europe was perhaps only available to the wealthier and university educated.

A popular, and cross-class, choice for English honeymooners was the English countryside and the newlywed husband and wife started their first days of marriage by forming a conjugal 'we' and gazing upon their own country. As Urry explains, under the 'romantic tourist gaze' the English village becomes the 'real (merrie) England' and this allows the newlywed couple to place themselves within nature and Englishness since by consuming English holiday destinations they are, consciously or otherwise, 'worshipping their own society'.[68] In a deliberate contrast to exotic honeymoons, Anthony Thwaite and Ann, his wife and fellow writer wanted a 'very English honeymoon' before moving to Japan in 1955. They went from their 'rather grand' wedding in St Martin-in-the-Fields to a 'traditional country hotel' in Sussex. The six-week first-class boat journey to Japan was an 'extended honeymoon'.[69] Some couples stationed abroad honeymooned 'back home' in England. In the 1930s, English couples based in British India could have a honeymoon back in England.[70] In 1945, Chris Braithwaite married while still in the army. As his wife was in the Palestinian ATS,[71] the army arranged a honeymoon for them. They had a week in Rome, which was 'cut short' so that they could go to England to visit family while still on leave.[72] Of course, these couples used their honeymoons to visit family and friends, but inevitably, they would have made comparisons between England and their lives overseas, during the formative days of their marriage.

---

[66] C960/12/01–11 interview with Ursula Mommens, NLSC: Crafts Lives, BLSA.

[67] C466/203A interview with John Ward, NLSC: Artists' Lives, BLSA.

[68] Urry, Consuming Places, 133, 145.

[69] C1276/15 interview with Anthony Thwaite, NLSC: Authors' Lives, BLSA.

[70] For example, C63/139–141 interview with Mary Ffolliot Lambert, India Office Library: Oral History Recordings, BLSA.

[71] Auxiliary Territorial Service.

[72] C900/07166 C1 interview with Chris Braithwaite, Millennium Memory Bank, BLSA.

204 N. PENLINGTON

Countryside-bound honeymooners between 1918 and 1960 can be found from across the social-class spectrum. Urry gives as his chief countryside tourism example the Lake District. By this period, the Lake District had become synonymous with 'English Romanticism', a 'place-myth' that had developed since the eighteenth century.[73] Etiquette manuals were keen to promote the Lake District as an upmarket honeymoon destination,[74] but it was also accessible to working-class and lower-middle class couples in the oral history sample. In 1918, Londoner Frederick Allen made the long journey for a fortnight's honeymoon in Keswick.[75] Scunthorpe woman Barbara Jones went to Morecambe and the Lake District in 1950 with her steelworker husband.[76] A few years later, green grocer Douglas Kemp made the trip from Merseyside.[77] A wide range of men could provide a 'romantic' honeymoon destination across the period.

Another example of romantic English countryside during this period is Yorkshire, and one in which we can see the intertwining of romance, health and the outdoors. The Yorkshire Moors and the Yorkshire Dales, however defined, appeared in etiquette manuals[78] and oral history interviews.[79] As with the Lake District, the Yorkshire Moors had a literary connection. By this period, Emily Brontë's *Wuthering Heights* (1847), for example, had become very widely read, was an Academy Award-nominated film staring Laurence Olivier in 1939, and had helped to construct the rugged Yorkshire landscape, and unforgiving weather, as the epitome of English romance. Railway companies were keen to promote their stops as holiday destinations and angled romantic images at potential

[73] Urry, *Consuming places*, 194.

[74] For example, Woodman, *Wedding Etiquette*, 100–2 and Bee and Bee, *Weddings without worry*, 92–3.

[75] C707/107/1–2 C1 interview with Frederick Allen, Family Life and Work Experience before 1918, BLSA.

[76] C532/011 interview with Barbara Jones, NLSC: Lives in Steel, BLSA.

[77] C821/189 interview with Douglas Kemp, NLSC: Food: From Source to Salespoint, BLSA.

[78] For example, Woodman, *Wedding etiquette*, 100–2 and Bee and Bee, *Weddings without worry*, 92–3.

[79] In 1952, Leeds-born artist Ralph Brown and first wife Margaret honeymooned in the Yorkshire Dales before moving to London. C466/93/01-08 interview with Ralph Brown, NLSC: Artists' Lives, BLSA.

honeymooners. The number of holidaymakers travelling on the British rail network trebled in ten years from the late 1920s[80] and rail travel was of 'central importance... in structuring modern consciousness'.[81] The London and North Eastern Railway (LNER) promoted the Yorkshire Moors as a romantic getaway during a long-running poster campaign from 1923 to 1947.[82] The rugged landscape of the Brontës' Yorkshire is encapsulated in the remote, rocky setting with a couple, in romantic silhouette, standing together to admire a waterfall—a force of nature. As the woman leans on the man for masculine support, they become one (flesh), and form the conjugal gaze upon the English 'scenery'.[83] To borrow an observation from Urry, the 'historic association of waterfalls with passion, whether of love or death, further enhanced the salience of such a zone'.[84] Newlywed masculinity is in this example strong, supportive and romantic.

Two specific Yorkshire places mentioned by oral history interviewees and advertised by rail companies are Knaresborough and Ilkley. LNER advertised Knaresborough in a 1930s poster campaign[85] using the strapline 'Then-Now' and deliberately appealed to the notion of the real 'merrie' England. Englishness and coupledom are timeless: there is a direct link between the past and present, 'then' and 'now' as the poster puts it, but also the future since Mother Shipton was reputedly a seer who made accurate predictions. By venturing into the mystical Mother Shipton's Cave, the couple is heading into the unknown, or on an adventure. The woman in the foreground is by herself but it is unlikely that she is alone. She appears to be talking and gesturing to an unseen companion or is possibly posing for a photograph. and we are perhaps led to believe that this woman's unseen companion is a man. In another example, British

---

[80] John Walton, *The British seaside: Holidays and resorts in the twentieth century*, (Manchester: Manchester University Press, 2000), 82.

[81] Urry, *Consuming Places*, 119.

[82] Recently nationalised British Rail (BR) was keen to promote Yorkshire as a honeymoon destination. BR seized the opportunity of good publicity in 1954 by running a 'honeymoon special' for only two passengers to help a stranded couple reach their honeymoon destination in the dales. 'Honeymoon train for two', *Daily Express*, 17 December 1954, 5.

[83] See *Yorkshire Moors*, LNER poster, 1923–1947.

[84] Urry, *Tourist gaze*, 55.

[85] See *Knaresborough: Then and now*, LNER poster, c. 1930s.

Rail in the late 1950s advertised Ilkley, a spa town fashionable since the Victorian era, as the 'gateway to the Yorkshire Dales'. In a 1957 poster[86] the Dales, wild and romantic, are in the background. The 'gateway' is a path that leads the reader to people, mostly couples, frolicking in an outdoor lido. Our eye is drawn to a couple confidently walking together towards a future of social acceptance and romantic adventure. Both Knaresborough and Ilkley were therefore destinations with romantic associations, and they were accessible to the working class. The oral history sample throws up a number of honeymoons in these places[87] including wagonwright Thomas Harper in 1941[88] and steelworker Harry Taylor in 1946.[89]

The most popular destination for English honeymooners was the seaside, especially among middle- and working-class couples, but there were social distinctions between seaside towns. The seaside was appealing to couples, including newlyweds. Historian of the British seaside, John Walton explains that the coast held the promise, at least, of a transformative holiday experience because it was a '"place on the margin", where land and sea meet'. For holidaymakers of all classes, married or otherwise, there was 'the notion of a seaside holiday as liberating people from the leaden constraints of day-to-day identity'.[90] Oral historian Steve Humphries found that the seaside holiday and its saucy postcards 'came to acquire a mystique and became a byword for sexual licence'.[91] As Urry explains, by drawing on Pierre Bourdieu's *Distinction* (1984, in English), that as travel became 'democratised so extensive distinctions of taste were established between different *places*'. In Britain during the nineteenth century, there commenced the rise of a seaside 'resort hierarchy with considerable differences of "social tone" established between otherwise similar places'. For example, from the mid-nineteenth century Brighton and Southend had a 'lower social tone' than Bournemouth and

---

[86] See *Ilkley*, BR poster, 1957.

[87] For example, C900/12513 interview with Ruth Radley, Millennium Memory Bank, BLSA and C900/07043 C1 interview with Ella Thompson Millennium Memory Bank, BLSA.

[88] C532/022 interview with Thomas Harper, NLSC: Lives in Steel, BLSA.

[89] C532/008/01–07 interview with James Henry (Harry) Taylor, NLSC: Lives in Steel, BLSA.

[90] Walton, *British seaside*, 3–4.

[91] Humphries, *Secret world*, 166.

6 HONEYMOON   207

Torquay, partly because the former were within reach of day-trippers from London. Morecambe and Blackpool were generally more working class.[92] However, as Walton points out, seaside towns were not uniformly one social class or another in their appeal. For example, the North Shore of Blackpool was an 'enclave' of the 'better classes'.[93] Although unrepresentative, the oral history sample shows that honeymooning couples made seaside choices according to social class. Working-class and lower-middle class couples went to Southend-on-Sea, Blackpool, Bridlington and Brighton.[94] Lower-middle and middle-class honeymooners went to Sandgate-on-Sea, Eastbourne and Bournemouth,described by Malcolm Muggeridge in 1934 as 'more or less undiluted bourgeoisie'.[95]

The West Country is a good example of a seaside honeymoon destination because it appeared in newspapers,[96] etiquette manuals,[97] oral history interviews and railway advertisements. 'Glorious' Devon was advertised in newspapers as a 'honeymoon heaven'.[98] A 1928 article in the *Daily Mirror*, 'Ilfracombe's Honeymoonshine', reviewed the resort as a honeymoon destination. The article goes on to state that 'no wonder

[92] Urry, *Tourist gaze*, 21–2, 79; Urry, *Consuming places*, 130.

[93] Walton, *British Seaside*, 53.

[94] Grace Foakes, *My Life with Reuben*, (London: Shepheard-Walwyn, 1975), 26; C821/07/01–07 interview with Olive Wellings, NLSC: Food: from source to Salespoint, BLSA; Interview with Doug Grant; C821/166 interview with Samuel Kilburn, NLSC: Food: From Source to Salespoint, BLSA; Interview with Ronald Stedman.

[95] C900/11568 interview with Christine Peach, Millennium Memory Bank, BLSA; Marjorie Graham, *Love, dears!*, (London: Dobson, 1980), 35; Interview with Betty Judge; Interview with Derek Mate; C1154/01/01–09 interview with Desmond Moseley, An Oral History of the Wine Society, BLSA; Muggeridge uoted in Walton, *British seaside*, 21.

[96] For example: in 1922, the daughter of quintessential English composer Sir Edward Elgar honeymooned in Cornwall, 'A Diary of To-Day', *Daily Express*, 17 January 1922, 6; Two West County honeymoons, Ilfracombe and Torquay, were reported on the same front page of the *Daily Exspress* in 1922, 'Husband Crushed in a Lift' and 'Fish Bites a Bather', *Daily Express*, 28 August 1922, 1 and see also 'Tragic Honeymoon' and 'Bather Bitten by Fish', *Daily Mirror*, 28 August 1922, 2; In 1949, an eloped beauty queen made the front page with her honeymoon in on 'south Cornish coast', 'Ex-Beauty Queen Elopes at 2 a.m.', *Daily Express*, 6 January 1949, 1; Serialised short stories featured Cornish honeymoons, 'The Man Who Dared', *Daily Mirror*, 7 March 1922, 15 and 'Parents Are A Problem', *Daily Mirror*, 28 September 1932, 13.

[97] For example, Woodman, *Wedding etiquette*, 100–2; Bee and Bee, *Weddings without worry*, 92–3.

[98] For example, 'Glorious North Devon', *Daily Express*, 7 May 1938, 18.

Ilfracombe is famous for its loving honeymooners... They do get a little privacy here. Romantic privacy, too'. A cartoon shows a couple embracing and looking at each other 'in the sunshine of each other's smiles'.[99] In the oral history sample a range of couples honeymooned in the West Country.[100] Torquay, though promoted as an upmarket destination was accessible to the lower middle classes, even before the Second World War. In 1926, Geordie Labour Exchange counter clerk George Evers travelled almost the length of England to take his honeymoon in Torquay for a week.[101] Later in the period, working-class couples also honeymooned in the West Country, and some travelled long distances. After the Second World War, restaurant worker Janet Farrow and her husband went from Kent to Cornwall for their honeymoon.[102] In 1956, Frank Flear and his new wife honeymooned in the West Country and then toured their native Lincolnshire.[103]

Long, adventurous rail journeys were 'increasingly in vogue' during the interwar period'.[104] In the 1930s, the Great Western Railway (GWR) ran 'The Flower Harvest' poster for *Cornwall and the Isles of Scilly*[105] in which a woman joyfully carries a bouquet of flowers. The man in the background is the provider, he has harvested the flowers and the bouquet echoes the wedding day and the bride's bouquet,[106] possibly only a few days earlier if they are a honeymoon couple. The couple is placed within the tamed setting of production, consumption and perhaps

[99] 'Ilfracombe's Honeymoonshine', *Daily Mirror*, 1 September 1928, 27.

[100] For example, newly promoted steelworks' manager Les Peirson in the 1930s, banker's wife Margaret Lambert, and engineer John Duckworth both during the Second World War. C532/002 interview with Leslie (Les) Peirson, NLSC: Lives in Steel, BLSA; C1367/19 interview with Margaret Lambert, An Oral History of Barings, BLSA; C1495/02 interview with John Duckworth, An Oral History of the Electricity Supply Industry in the UK, BLSA.

[101] C707/223/1–2 C1 interview with George Henry Evers, Family Life and Work Experience before 1918, BLSA.

[102] C821/188 interview with Janet Farrow, NLSC: Food: From Source to Salespoint, BLSA.

[103] C821/113 interview with Frank Flear, NLSC: Food: From Source to Salespoint, BLSA.

[104] Walton, *British seaside*, 83.

[105] See *The flower harvest—Cornwall and Isles of Scilly*, GWR poster, c. 1930s.

[106] In Chapter 4, 'The Wedding', we saw that the woman chose her wedding flowers; here the man provides them.

domesticity, but the untamed, rugged Cornish coastline in the background suggests passion, romance and adventure. The 1956 British Rail *Torquay* poster[107] is a triptych of couples engaged in different romantic activities. A couple walking along cliffs stops to gaze upon a scenic, sandy cove, while another couple returns from or is about to play tennis. The third panel shows a man taking a photograph of a woman: he is in charge of the machinery (the camera); she, the object, strikes a pose in a scene reminiscent of the French Riviera and therefore links romantic coupledom with a modern cosmopolitan outlook that makes Torquay the 'International Resort', perhaps for those who cannot afford an international honeymoon. Torquay's famous palm trees evoke the exotic Other, but this is still firmly England. In the 1950s, British Rail also made short films to advertise its journeys and locations. The 1953 film *Devon Belle* featured the luxury train service from London's Waterloo to Exeter, Ilfracombe and Plymouth in Devon. A still from the film[108] shows a 'honeymooning couple' and conjures up the romance of the railway journey promoted during this period. The newly married couple travel, in comfort and civility, through rugged and hostile terrain seen through the train window. The couple are unmistakably newlyweds: the only hand in the frame is the left hand of the woman, and on her fourth finger is an overly large costume ring (perhaps bakelite or resin) drawing attention to their marital status. The man wears a conservative—by 1950s standards—wide-lapelled, double-breasted suit and is the epitome of masculine stoicism and responsibility.

Etiquette manuals, newspapers and advertising portrayed popular honeymoon destinations as romantic by circulating identifiable signs and symbols. These social-class-based destinations encapsulated sexuality as heterosexual and reinforced the position of husband as provider and protector. It is however important not to overstate the romantic choice of destination since couples may have had other, or a combination, of reasons for their choice.[109] For example, seaside holidaymakers

---

[107] See *Torquay*, BR poster, 1956.

[108] See *Honeymooners travelling to the West Country on the 'Devon Belle'*, May 1953.

[109] Bulcroft et al. found in their contemporary study of honeymooning couples in the mid-1990s that they tended to place 'Comfort/Relaxation' ahead of 'Romantic', Bulcroft et al., *Romancing the honeymoon*, 184.

210   N. PENLINGTON

liked 'sleep', 'sea air' and 'the sea' itself.[110] It is impossible to draw a direct connection between individual couples and their understanding of romantic advertising as each would have had subjective expectations and experiences.

EXPERIENCE

The romantic associations a honeymoon destination had did not necessarily mean that honeymooners were expecting or had a romantic experience. Although the actual experience of honeymoons is impossible to assess, historians can suggest the subjectivities of honeymooners through first-person testimonies, newspaper reporting and factors such as quality of accommodation. Many couples simply did not have a honeymoon. It is impossible to conclude from an oral history sample the true proportion of couples who did not have a honeymoon. The sample used in this chapter is mostly compiled by searching for the word 'honeymoon' in the British Library Sound Archive. It is therefore a biased sample of those who mention honeymoons. Unsurprisingly, most interviewees mention honeymoons because they went on one, and only a few mention honeymoons because they did not. The interviews used in the rest of this book do not necessarily shed light on whether a couple went on a honeymoon.[111] Towards the end of the period, newspapers increasingly reported ordinary people going on extraordinary honeymoons. For example, bank clerk twins going on honeymoon together.[112] It is not therefore possible to calculate from newspaper reports the proportion of couples who honeymooned.

In the oral history sample, the commonest reason given for not having a honeymoon was lack of money. In the 1930s, those working in the Lancashire cotton industry had the problem of 'budgeting for unpaid holidays'. This improved with the growth of 'holidays with pay' during and after the Second World War,[113] following the Holidays with Pay

---

[110] Gary Cross (ed.), *The worktowners at blackpool: Mass-observation and popular leisure in the 1930s* (Abingdon: Routledge, 1990), 190.

[111] If an interviewee mentions an engagement or a wedding it does not simply follow that she or he will talk about honeymoons, and silence on the subject of the honeymoon is not an indication of whether it took place or not.

[112] 'Twins Marry', *Daily Express*, 26 March 1956, 9.

[113] Walton, *British seaside*, 60, 62.

Act (1938).[114] As social historian John Gillis shows, lower paid couples could not afford honeymoons until the 1940s, or even the 1960s,[115] after 'working class living standards were undeniably improved by full employment and comprehensive welfare provision'.[116] Gillis also argues that many working-class couples 'had already worked out the heterosexuality that would be the pattern for their married lives. No honeymoon was needed, and most were back to work the next day'.[117] Sociologists Kanin and Howard found in the 1950s that American couples were more likely to go on a honeymoon if they had not had pre-marital sex.[118] After her wedding in 1925, 'Yorkshire girl' Alice Bond returned to her 'daily life' in Goole.[119] Although honeymoons were becoming increasingly common, some oral history interviewees narrated their situation as normal. In the early 1930s, Shropshire woman Nellie Rowson married at the age of nineteen. She did not have a honeymoon because they were 'scarce in those days' because people 'couldn't afford it'.[120] It is unlikely that these working-class husbands would have felt less manly for not being able to provide a honeymoon during the interwar period, since it appears 'normal' not to have had a honeymoon. Indeed the memory of working-class people not having honeymoons was so strong for some, that even when they had time off work after the wedding they did not class it as a 'honeymoon'. In 1939, David Lewis had two nights and one day off from work after his wedding. He and his wife were married in Leeds synagogue on a Sunday and he went back to work on Tuesday, but she was off for the rest of the week. They spent the first night of married life at her sister's and did not see this as a honeymoon.[121] In 1948, Richard Perks had to go back to the Navy after a period of leave. He and his new

[114] Dawson, 'Working-class consumers', 277, 279.

[115] Gillis, *For better, for worse*, 189.

[116] Stephen Brooke, 'Gender and Working Class Identity in Britain during the 1950s', *Journal of Social History* 34, No. 4 (Summer, 2001), 773.

[117] Gillis, *For better, For worse*, 189.

[118] 47% of those who had pre-martial sex, 87% who had not, went on a honeymoon. E. Kanin and D. Howard, 'Postmarital consequences of premarital sex', *American Sociological Review* 23 (1958), 556–562 cited in Bulcroft et al., *Romancing the honeymoon*, 12.

[119] Alice Bond, *Life of a Yorkshire Girl* (Hull: Bradley, 1981), 70.

[120] C900/15073 interview with Nellie Rowson, Millennium Memory Bank, BLSA.

[121] C900/08557 interview with David Lewis, Millennium Memory Bank, BLSA.

wife Margaret managed a week in a 'little cottage' in their native Shropshire. Richard did not however class this as a honeymoon because they 'didn't have them in those days'.[122] These working-class couples were clearly not the intended readership for etiquette manuals. In 1929, Mary Woodman's *Wedding Etiquette* suggested that readers should be aiming to spend £20 on a fortnight's honeymoon,[123] the same figure was quoted by 'Best Man' in 1936.[124] This was well beyond the reach of almost all working-class and lower-middle-class couples. The pressure to have an expensive honeymoon would have been more keenly felt by men from the middle and upper-middle classes.

Other couples had very specific reasons for not having a honeymoon and this also shows that the honeymoon was not an essential element of married masculinity. During a period of limited access to effective contraception, the 'shotgun wedding' was 'quite a common occurrence in the first half of the twentieth century'.[125] For a man in this situation it was more important to seen to be taking responsibility for his pregnant wife than to provide a honeymoon. In the late 1930s, Workington steelworker Stan Hullock had to marry at twenty-four because he and his partner 'made a slip' and she became pregnant. They did not have a honeymoon.[126] Some couples had more radical reasons for not going on a honeymoon. In 1935, London-based actress Muriel Box did not have a honeymoon, but the decision was not financial. They had got married after many years of living together as an attempt to ward off a 'blasphemy' case involving one of his plays.[127] For this man, marriage was not important for demonstrating masculinity, but he was nonetheless in a visible, indeed high-profile, long-term, marriage-like relationship with a woman.

Social class was likely to determine the length of (any) honeymoon.[128] Etiquette manuals advised against a long honeymoon and gave

---

[122] C900/15089 interview with Richard Gordon Perks, Millennium Memory Bank, BLSA.

[123] Woodman, *Wedding etiquette*, 100.

[124] "Best Man", *Marriage etiquette* [1936], 67. The expected cost of a honeymoon is not mentioned in the 1949 edition.

[125] Humphries, *Secret world*, 114.

[126] C532/042 interview with Stan Hullock, NLSC: Lives in Steel, BLSA.

[127] Muriel Box, *Odd woman out* (London: Leslie Frewin, 1974), 141–2.

[128] During the Second World War, couples of different social classes had similar experiences when one or both spouses had to squeeze a wedding and a honeymoon into a

a gendered explanation. Mary Woodman's *Wedding Etiquette* (1929) cautioned against a honeymoon that was longer than a fortnight because it 'may begin to drag'. The boredom and anxiety caused by a long honeymoon was gendered since 'the wife, especially, may begin to wish herself installed in her new home'.[129] This shows that marriage was expected to change the lives of the man and the woman in different ways—that they would travel along together but in different directions. The woman now had a home to run; the man continued his paid employment, but now had a wife and home to support. The woman did however have the power to cancel a honeymoon, especially in relation to her role as homemaker. In 1950, Ann Page advised that it would be '[f]ar better for the bride to cancel or at least postpone her honeymoon than to spoil or delay the setting up of their new home'.[130] Contrary to this advice, upper-class couples could go away on honeymoon for months.[131] In 1921, the Queen's Maid of Honour had an 'unfashionably long honeymoon' of over three months.[132] Long honeymoons still took place in the 1930s. American golfer Charles Sweeney, a friend of the Prince of Wales, and his English wife went on a two-month honeymoon.[133] At the other extreme, some working-class couples could only manage a honeymoon of a weekend, typically so that the man could return to work. In 1929, East Ender Grace Foakes managed a weekend in Southend-on-Sea before her husband returned to work on the Thames tub boats.[134] Gordon Medlock left school at fifteen and married Dorothy at nineteen in 1956. They had their 'honeymoon in Clapham Junction for three days' before he returned to work at the Hawker Aircraft factory in Kingston. Despite the short honeymoon being in less than exotic surroundings, Gordon was keen to

short period of leave. Interview with FlorenceWadlow; Interview with John Duckworth; Interview with Ruth Radley.

[129] Woodman, *Wedding etiquette*, 104.

[130] Page, *Complete guide*, 125.

[131] For example, 'A Diary of To-Day', *Daily Express*, 22 February 1922, 6.

[132] 'To-Day's Gossip', *Daily Mirror*, 13 April 1921, 4.

[133] 'Party to See a Trousseau', *Daily Mirror*, 17 February 1933, 7.

[134] Foakes, *My life*, 26.

214   N. PENLINGTON

stress that they were still married after fifty-one years at the time of writing his autobiography.[135]

Expectations of privacy and honeymoon activities were also inflected by class-based masculinity. Etiquette manuals initially advised couples to lower their expectations of honeymoons, but there was a hint later in the period that couples might actually want to be alone. As Bulcroft, Smeins and Bulcroft found in the American context, 'signs of the activity-centred script were evident' in the 1930s.[136] Mary Woodman explained in 1929 that during the honeymoon 'husband and wife really see each other, for the first time, in their true colours'. Woodman, in a similar vain to Dorothy L. Sayers at the start of this chapter, warned that engaged couples might 'think that gazing into each other's eyes will prove a sufficiently exciting pastime' but it would be 'sensible to put a few things in one's trunks that will help pass a pleasant hour'. She suggested novels, cameras, golf clubs and tennis racquets.[137] Films involving characters from this social class could draw on the same idea, that the honeymoon should be full of the same improving activities. The 1920 comedy film *The Indestructible Wife* was advertised with a blurb explaining that the protagonist Charlotte 'exhausted' her 'young husband' with a honeymoon that 'was a ceaseless round of golfing, walking, riding, boating, swimming, polo-playing, mountain-climbing'. The joke here seems to be that the wife is the one who leads the way, with her husband trailing 'behind her', and further that these exhausting activities detracted from sex. Tapping into the myth of the sexually exhausting honeymoon, gender normality is restored as the husband 'eventually tamed this tireless young wife'.[138] Later in the period, etiquette manuals changed their tone slightly. In 1949, "Best Man", in a change from the 1936 edition of *Marriage Etiquette*, acknowledged that 'all newly married couples have one desire in common: to be as far as possible, on their own'. This expectation of being 'alone' was tempered by a warning that couples were unlikely 'to find their own company... sufficient' and that 'a wise pair' would 'decide

---

[135] Gordon Richard Medlock, *My working life, 1952 –1994* (Frimley: Medlock, 2009), 6–7.

[136] Bulcroft et al., *Romancing the honeymoon*, 44.

[137] Woodman, *Wedding etiquette*, 104–108.

[138] 'Walturdaw Pictures', *Daily Express*, 27 March 1920, 10.

to pack one or two diversions for odd half-hours or a rainy afternoon'.[139] Not all agreed, even in 1950 Ann Page advised her readers to 'avoid solitude at all costs' and 'make sure that every moment is occupied'.[140]

Honeymooners did not always desire privacy and some newly married men performed their new status in the company of others. As we have seen, many working-class and lower-middle-class couples stayed with family or friends and may not have had much privacy. Some working-class couples chose to spend time with company on part of their honeymoon and for these couples, the gendered early days of marriage were set within a wider nexus of familial and social relationships.[141] This was not perhaps unusual since working-class people from 'the Midlands and the industrial north… would troop off to a favourite resort together' for summer holiday in large groups including 'family, relatives, neighbours, friends and workmates'.[142] During the interwar period, working-class newly-weds could go on honeymoon on mass. For example, in 1923 the *Daily Express* reported that 300 'honeymoon couples' from Oldham went for a weekend in London because it was 'Wakes Week'.[143] Middle-class sensibilities and expectations were possibly different. In 1950, artist John Ward and his wife had a 'very' romantic time in Paris before 'end[ing] in the Pyrenees along with another English honeymoon couple'. At this point in the interview, John laughed at the notion that neither couple was alone on honeymoon.[144] John's nervous laughter highlights two things. When interviewed later in life, the interviewee is perhaps comparing his own honeymoon experience with the romantic, sexualised expectations of the late twentieth century. Secondly, John is perhaps expressing a middle-class attitude towards privacy that did not necessarily resonate with working-class men of his generation.

Couples who honeymooned alone may not have had much privacy. In the 1920s, newspaper reports show that many upper-class couples

---

[139] "Best Man", *Marriage etiquette* [1936], 69–70 and [1949], 67, 70.

[140] Page, *Complete guide*, 124.

[141] For example, C532/025 interview with Harold Leech, NLSC: Lives in Steel, BLSA and interview with Barbara Jones.

[142] Humphries, *Secret world*, 171.

[143] 'All The Way Fra' Oldham', *Daily Express*, 27 August 1923, 5.

[144] Interview with John Ward.

took their honeymoons in other people's houses.[145] To our twenty-first-century eyes, these couples would not have had a lot of privacy. There would have been servants nearby and if staying as houseguests they may have had to spend time being sociable. At the other end of the economic spectrum, working-class and lower-middle-class couples who were not staying with family or friends were likely to honeymoon at a boarding house. Many of these places would have had strict rules and hours, perhaps enforced by the 'landlady'—stereotypically the 'matriarch, the time clock, and the booking clerk'[146]—and couples staying at such establishments would have had to spend many hours a day without access to their accommodation.[147] As well as being prey to the weather, these couples would have had little privacy since they would have to spend so much time in the early days of marriage in public places.

Those who could afford to honeymoon in a mid-market or upmarket hotel may not have had much solitude either. In London, the price difference between a 'simple Bed Room' and a 'Private Sitting Room' was such that many guests had to spend most of their time in the public rooms.[148] In Blackpool, the famous Metropole hotel had cold bedrooms that 'were less comfortable than today'.[149] Based in the North Shore 'enclave' of the 'better classes'[150] and known locally as 'the Honeymoon Hotel', there was an emphasis on 'country house living' and spending time in the drawing room and billiard room. Although 'life at the Metropole changed very little' between the 1890s and the Second World War, one thing that did change was the style of dancing in its famous ballroom. Before the Great War, dancing in 'sets' was popular, but 'dancing in

---

[145] 'A Diary of To-Day', *Daily Express*, 5 October 1922, 6; 'Diary of To-Day', *Daily Express*, 7 May 1923, 6.

[146] Cross, *Worktowners*, 190.

[147] Steve Humphries points out that many landladies were of a more 'sympathetic character', but nonetheless strict about time-keeping. Humphries, *Secret world*, 172.

[148] Mary Cathcart Borer, *The British hotel through the ages* (London: Lutterworth, 1972), 192–3.

[149] Bryan Perrett, *Honeymoon hotel: A brief history of the metropole hotel, Blackpool* (Ormskirk: Bryan Perrett, 1992), pages unnumbered.

[150] Walton, *British seaside*, 53.

couples became the norm during the inter-war years'.[151] This public display of coupling coincided with etiquette manuals across the period strongly advising couples to pack well, because 'the newly married couple will wish to appear at their best'.[152] Hotels at the 'luxury' end of the market 'would insist on guests wearing full evening dress'.[153] Even at Blackpool, which 'was never as formal as some resorts, guests at the best hotels dressed for dinner as a matter of course'.[154] As Walton shows in his research on seaside tourism, 'people brought their own internal controls and assumptions about proper behaviour with them'.[155] Honeymooners would have mixed with people of their own social class, and the wealthier were concerned with keeping up appearances. As Bulcroft, Smeins and Bulcroft have argued in their American study, perhaps honeymooning couples needed 'others' 'in order that their experience be defined and reinforced'.[156] Across the social spectrum, the newly married man spent his honeymoon—if he had one—surrounded by the people and norms of his own social class as he was carving out his own role as husband.

Whichever way the couple spent their honeymoon, there was the expectation to consummate the marriage. Etiquette manuals and newspapers were not sexually explicit during this period, and only a few first-person testimonies shed any light on honeymoon sex. East Ender Dorothy (Dolly) Scannell took advantage of both her writing abilities and the medium of the 1970s autobiography, to construct a humorous narrative of how a couple can struggle to consummate their marriage during their honeymoon. Dolly devotes the final chapter, 'Holy Honeymoon', of the first volume of her 1974 autobiography to her 1930s honeymoon on which she and her husband grew 'a little more bored each day'. Dolly framed the calamitous attempt at consummation within a hotel on the Isle of Wight that 'catered for religious conventions'. As the hotel was full, she and her husband found themselves in the 'annexe' and 'warned' that it

---

[151] Perrett, *Honeymoon hotel*, pages unnumbered; also for the Metropole's ballroom see, Elaine Denby, *Grand hotels: Reality and illusion, An architectural and social history* (London: Reaktion, 1998), 78.

[152] For example, Bee and Bee, *Weddings without worry*, 94; Page, *Complete guide*, 124.

[153] Derek Taylor, *British hotels, 1837–1987* (London: Milman, 2003), 211.

[154] Perrett, *Honeymoon hotel*, pages unnumbered.

[155] Walton, *British seaside*, 5.

[156] Bulcroft et al., *Romancing the honeymoon*, 48.

'had only thin asbestos walls and … that everything, just everything could be heard through these walls'. The hotel staff, therefore, knew exactly what the purpose of a honeymoon was, and Dolly sets this in opposition to the supposed prudery of those attending a 'religious convention', emphasising this by stressing that at dinner the couple was 'the object of many staring eyes'. In anticipation that the expected purpose of the honeymoon was to 'commence [their] nuptials',Dolly and her husband bought a 'sheath', nicknamed the 'tyre'. Dolly draws on a stock scene in which the woman waits in bed for the man: she got dressed in her 'beautiful wedding nightie' while he went to put the 'tyre' on in the bathroom. Since the man in the shop had sold them a 'small' size, her husband struggled to get it on and managed to spring it across the bathroom. It 'took an effort to retrieve it' from behind the bath. Her husband returned to the bedroom 'with a look of pain on his weary face' and all he wanted was a good night's sleep because he worked in a restaurant. In among the comedy, pathos and brilliant storytelling, Scannell perhaps hits on an important point about working-class masculinity in the 1930s. As she 'lay awake and wondered how many bridegrooms had looked forward to these two weeks just to be able to get some good nights' sleep', she was making a point that can be found in other first-person narratives covering the 1930s. As historian Joanna Bourke has shown, working-class men sometimes stated that their demanding physical labour made them too tired for sex. Dolly reinforces this point by drawing it down through previous generations of working-class couples. When she arrived home and told her mother about the honeymoon, her mother simply replied, 'I could have told you it was overrated'.[157]

Other first-person testimonies gave a range of narratives about the consummation of marriage on honeymoon. Some, like Dolly Scannell, had a difficult start to married sex. The previous chapter showed that there was a small, but steady stream, of unconsummated marriages that appeared before the courts. In the oral history sample, two couples clearly stated that they did not consummate their marriage during their honeymoon. Humberside woman Ella Thompson remembered that her 1941 honeymoon in Ilkley did not go as planned. She and her husband had not had sex before marriage and were prevented from having a 'first night' because of her period. Their next opportunity did not come until after

---

[157] Dorothy Scannell, *Mother knows best: An east end childhood*, (London: MacMillan, 1974), 177, 179–81; Joanna Bourke, *Working-class cultures*, 42.

the war.[158] Married in 1946, Preston shopkeepers' son Samuel Kilburn was looking forward to a week's seaside honeymoon in a boarding house in Bridlington. The newlyweds had a not a 'very exotic or exhilarating honeymoon... in fact, a bit of a disaster' because his wife caught a 'terrible cold'. Samuel then had to get a 'doctor's note' so that he could apply for extended leave from the army to look after his new wife.[159] There was a nervousness about sex, and who should be doing it and when. In 1942, Betty Judge went from Dulwich straight after the wedding reception to Bournemouth for her honeymoon. As her ration book still showed her maiden name they needed to show the hotel staff their marriage certificate to 'explain that [they] were on [their] honeymoon, because, otherwise it would have been a, you know, terrible sin to be there'. The hotel staff could see that they 'were in love'.[160] Here there was an assumption that the hotel staff would not allow unmarried sex, which is presented in the Christian language of sin. Also in 1942, twenty-five-year-old South London shop worker Ron Stedman had his wedding night but 'it wasn't a good night'. From a Baptist background, Ron assumed it was 'not unusual' that 'both sexes were virgins' before marriage. He and his wife, Win, went on a honeymoon to Brighton but the sex was 'disappointing at first'.[161] Ron seems to link sexual inexperience with religion, but hints that their sex life improved over time. Other couples were more matter of fact about consummating their marriage on honeymoon. Humberside farm-worker Doug Grant married in 1938 aged twenty-seven. It was on their honeymoon to Bridlington that he and his wife 'shared a bed for the first time'.[162] On the other hand, Cadbury's chocolate 'enrober' Olive Wellings went on her honeymoon to Blackpool in 1953. As it was Boxing Day it was 'not very exciting' and also the couple 'knew each other very well', a euphemism that alludes to their pre-marital sex life.[163] Only one first-person testimony in the material surveyed gave a fully positive account of honeymoon sex. In 1930, former chorus girl Marjorie Graham went on her honeymoon to a hotel in Eastbourne. In an unusual,

[158] C900/07043 C1 interview with Ella Thompson, Millennium Memory Bank, BLSA.

[159] Interview with Samuel Kilburn.

[160] Interview with Betty Judge.

[161] Interview with Ronald Stedman.

[162] Interview with Doug Grant.

[163] Interview with Olive Wellings.

frank autobiography, the well-known actress reminisced that '[s]exually' she and her husband 'got on well' and were 'two in one'. During the honeymoon, she 'couldn't care less if it happened every half an hour' because she was 'healthy and strong'.[164]

Couples did not necessarily have much privacy on honeymoon and for many working-class men it was normal not to have a honeymoon. Men who had honeymoons started their marriages learning and performing married masculinity within the context of their own social class. Although consummating the marriage was important to newlyweds, it was not the only thing that mattered. Many couples seem to have had a pragmatic attitude to sex and wanted to spend time together, perhaps in the company of others.

Conclusion

The honeymoon holiday became more visible in popular culture between 1918 and 1960 and is, therefore, an important site for gender historians to examine masculinity and power relations between husband and wife, especially in relation to social class. Novels, plays and films normalised the honeymoon holiday. Newspaper reports of honeymoon holidays shifted from those about the upper classes to more accessible celebrities and ordinary people. The popular meaning of 'honeymoon' became more firmly a 'holiday', rather than a 'period of time'.

Although the honeymoon was not part of the marriage process for many working-class men, a close reading of the sources has revealed class-inflected masculinities and newlywed power relations. Working-class men often did not go on a honeymoon, and instead returned to work straight after the wedding. In many working-class communities, this would have been normal, especially in the interwar period. The husband's status as a man depended on paid employment and the fact of being married, rather than going on a romantic honeymoon.

The planning of the honeymoon allowed the man to demonstrate his abilities and connections outside the home and position himself in the public sphere, in relation to his wife, from the onset of the marriage. The planning and booking of transport and accommodation was not essentially masculine because towards the end of the period, some women

[164] Graham, *Love, dears!*, 35.

did it. In most cases, however, the husband took ownership of orchestrating the honeymoon arrangements from start to finish, although as seen in Chapter 4 'The Wedding', the man was not typically involved in the wedding preparations. In all social classes, the man was acting as father figure to his wife in the public realm and taking over the position of her father, from whom he had received permission to marry shortly before. But my evidence questions this because arranging the honeymoon in some cases was largely symbolic as the man was often dependent on others to make a class-appropriate honeymoon happen and to provide 'romance' for his new wife to consume.

Using the concept of 'the gaze' revealed that the most popular destinations—seaside, countryside and Europe—each had romantic associations. Men across the social spectrum could provide a honeymoon in a romantic location. Couples were not necessarily expecting a romantic honeymoon and some, especially the working class, simply wanted a rest. The honeymoon often involved spending time with other people. Couples tended to choose locations, activities and (incidental) companions based on social class. Working-class couples were more likely to go away with other couples, although upper-class couples also stayed with family and friends albeit in very different circumstances. Middle-class and upper-middle-class couples stayed in hotels that would have encouraged residents to spend time in the public areas. There would not have been much privacy by today's standards. Men started their married lives immersed in the people and norms of their own social class. It is within this context that a man forged the subject position of husband, and negotiated power relations with his new wife.

It is difficult to assess men's honeymoon experience, since the relevant historical sources are opaque. By considering a range of sources, a complex tissue of masculinities has shown that men were able to transform and position themselves as husband and prospective father, sometimes without being independent of their own parents or in-laws. Honeymoons in the period 1918 to 1960 were not necessarily riddled with 'anxiety' as suggested by academics from other disciplines.[165] First-person testimonies tended to be matter of fact about honeymoons, with a few following the example of the literary 'bad' honeymoon. Many honeymooners however had a 'nice time'. The romantic, sexually charged

---

[165] Bulcroft et al., *Romancing the Honeymoon*, 188.

honeymoon is perhaps more in the mind of twenty-first-century observers than the reality at the time. The marrying men surveyed here were interested in sex, but not obsessed with it: they were also interested in spending time with their wives and keeping in contact with their families and friends, and with becoming the breadwinner and starting a family.

REFERENCES

An Oral History of Barings, British Library Sound Archive

An Oral History of British Science, British Library Sound Archive

An Oral History of the Electricity Supply Industry in the UK, British Library Sound Archive

An Oral History of the Wine Society, British Library Sound Archive

Artists' Lives, British Library Sound Archive

Bee, M., and S. Bee. 1935. *Weddings without worry: A modern and practical guide to wedding conventions and ceremonies*. London: Methuen.

"Best Man". 1936. *Marriage etiquette: How to arrange a wedding*. London: W. Foulsham.

"Best Man". 1949. *Marriage etiquette: How to arrange a wedding*. London: W. Foulsham.

Bond, Alice. 1981. *Life of a Yorkshire girl*. Hull: Bradley.

Bourke, Joanna. 1994. *Working-class cultures: Gender, class and ethnicity*. London: Routledge.

Box, Muriel. 1974. *Odd woman out*. London: Leslie Frewin.

Brooke, Stephen. 2001. Gender and working class identity in Britain during the 1950s. *Journal of Social History* 34 (4): 773–795.

Bulcroft, Kris, Linda Smeins, and Richard Bulcroft. 1999. *Romancing the honeymoon: Consummating the honeymoon in modern society*. London: Sage.

Collins, Marcus. 2003. *Modern love: An intimate history of men and women in twentieth-century Britain*. London: Atlantic.

Cross, Gary, ed. 1990. *The Worktowners at blackpool: Mass-Observation and popular leisure in the 1930s*. Abingdon: Routledge.

Daily Express

Daily Mirror

Dawson, Sandra. 2007. Working-class consumers and the campaign for holidays with pay. *Twentieth Century British History* 18 (3): 277–305.

Denby, Elaine. 1998. *Grand hotels: Reality and illusion, an architectural and social history*. London: Reaktion.

Family Life and Work Experience before 1918, British Library Sound Archive

Foakes, Grace. 1975. *My life with Reuben*. London: Shepheard-Walwyn.

Foucault, Michel. 1976. *The birth of the clinic*. London: Tavistock.

Freeman, Elizabeth. 2002. *The wedding complex: Forms of belonging in modern American culture.* London: Duke University Press.

Gillis, John. 1985. *For better, for worse: British marriages, 1600 to the present.* Oxford: Oxford University Press.

Graham, Marjorie. 1980. *Love, dears!* London: Dobson.

Humphries, Steve. 1988. *A secret world of sex: Forbidden fruit: The British experience, 1900–1950.* London: Sidgwick & Jackson.

India Office Library: Oral History Recordings, British Library Sound Archive

Kanin, E., and D. Howard. 1958. Postmarital consequences of premarital sex. *American Sociological Review* 23: 556–562.

McKibbin, Ross. 1998. *Classes and cultures, England 1918–1951.* Oxford: Oxford University Press.

Medlock, Gordon Richard. 2009. *My working life, 1952 – 1994.* Frimley: Medlock.

Michie, Helena. 2001. Victorian honeymoons: Sexual reorientations and the "sights" of Europe. *Victorian Studies* 43 (2): 229–251.

Millennium Memory Bank, British Library Sound Archive

National Life Stories Collection: Architects' Lives, British Library Sound Archive

National Life Stories Collection: Author's Lives, British Library Sound Archive

National Life Stories Collection: Book Trade Lives, British Library Sound Archive

National Life Stories Collection: City Lives, British Library Sound Archive

National Life Stories Collection: Crafts Lives, British Library Sound Archive

National Life Stories Collection: Food: From Source to Salespoint, British Library Sound Archive

National Life Stories Collection: General, British Library Sound Archive

National Life Stories Collection: Lives in Steel, British Library Sound Archive

Oral History of British Athletics, British Library Sound Archive

Otnes, Cele, and Elizabeth H. Peck. 2003. *Cinderella dreams: The allure of the lavish wedding.* Berkeley: University of California Press.

Page, Ann. 1950. *The complete guide to wedding etiquette.* London: Ward, Lock and Co.

Penner, Barbara. 2009. *Newlyweds on tour: Honeymooning in nineteenth-century America.* Durham NH: University of New Hampshire Press.

Perrett, Bryan. 1992. *Honeymoon hotel: A brief history of the Metropole Hotel, Blackpool.* Ormskirk: Bryan Perrett.

Portelli, Alessandro. 1981. The peculiarities of oral history. *History Workshop Journal* 12: 96–107.

Roper, Michael. 1994. *Masculinity and the British organisational man.* Oxford: Oxford University Press.

Sayers, Dorothy L. 1937. *Busman's honeymoon.* London: Victor Gollancz.

Scannell, Dorothy. 1974. *Mother knows best: An East End childhood.* London: MacMillan.

Taylor, Derek. 2003. *British hotels, 1837–1987*. London: Milman.
Urry, John. 1994. *Consuming places*. London: Routledge.
Urry, John. 2002. First published 1990. *The tourist gaze*. London: Sage.
Walton, John. 2000. *The British seaside: Holidays and resorts in the twentieth century*. Manchester: Manchester University Press.
Woodman, Mary. 1929. *Wedding etiquette*. London: W. Foulsham.

CHAPTER 7

Conclusion

Although not an exhaustive study of marriage and masculinity, or even of the marriage process, this book makes an unusual contribution to gender and cultural history. There are many ways of tackling the subject of men and marriage in mid-twentieth-century England, but looking narrowly at consent, celebration and consummation has shown elements of masculinity such as domesticity, breadwinning, romance and sexuality in relation to social class, race, religion, locality and generation. This book has unravelled the process of getting married, and by drawing on a variety of sources has highlighted some of the changes, continuities and contradictions of masculinity.

Different archival sources have shown the nuances of masculinity by suggesting the ways in which men could narrativise their gendered selves through available discourses. Taking a narrow approach to marriage and masculinity—by looking only at the process of marriage—has yielded complex results. Newspapers show the cultural reach of marriage discourses and also change over time as the white wedding and romantic honeymoon were normalised. Oral histories are less good for detecting change over time, partly because the interviewees were trying to remember events that had taken place decades earlier. They were prone to using linguistic tropes of the later period rather than of the time of the wedding, and were consciously, or otherwise, making comparisons with the present day. Although relying on an oral history archive rather than

© The Author(s), under exclusive license to Springer Nature Switzerland AG 2023
N. Penlington, *Men Getting Married in England, 1918–60*, Genders and Sexualities in History, https://doi.org/10.1007/978-3-031-27405-3_7

225

conducting live interviews is limiting, the archived interviews are however a rich source for suggesting the vast array of subjectivities. 'Official' sources show the politically contested nature of masculinity and further how masculinity was yoked to Englishness, class and Christianity. Even within a source base—for example legal discourse—we have seen differences between individual sources when historicising masculinity. Legislative debates highlight some of the long-term concerns about marriage and masculinity, whereas case law reveals how the judicial process minutely tested and defined boundaries of legally acceptable marriage, and therefore married masculinity. Omitting sources or looking more broadly at 'marriage' would have led to wildly different outcomes. This approach— a wide source base, and narrow scope—adds granularity and nuance to the history of masculinity in mid-twentieth-century England.

The process of getting married was in many ways a rehearsal for married life itself: the relative subject positions of femininity and masculinity have been seen by looking at who did what during the engagement, and wedding and honeymoon preparations. During the engagement, the man gave the woman gifts (especially an engagement ring), prefiguring his future role as provider, but he was not to overstate this role until they were married. The bride and her mother, and sometimes the groom's mother, made most of the wedding preparations. The bride's father typically paid, but in an era of increasing female access to paid employment, the bride sometimes made a financial contribution to the wedding costs, especially in the 1950s, and this would have meant a challenge to the status of her father. Although posited as the bride's day, the man often staked his interest by helping to choose the venue, and therefore the type of wedding. On the day, the woman was the centre of attention but passive as she was passed from father to groom. The gender roles were crystallised at the reception, at which the women provided the catering and the men the speeches. There was a difference between pre-marital and married gender roles as the man made most of the arrangements for the honeymoon holiday to take place as soon as possible after the wedding. This allowed him to be the provider husband and to demonstrate his knowledge of the world outside the home, but it was largely symbolic since most men were dependent upon friends and family in order to provide a social-class appropriate honeymoon.

Throughout the process of getting married, and also in parliamentary debates and case law judgements, men were providers and protectors, and women the homemakers and child carers. This is in keeping with the 'family' model of the Welfare State. With the rise of the companionate ideal of marriage came an increase in the theatrical white wedding and romantic honeymoon holiday, both of which were normalised in the popular press from the 1930s, at a time of increased consumerism, especially for the middle classes. Men were largely invisible in the newspaper presentation of the white wedding, but they were increasingly expected, and wanted, to provide romance for their new wives to consume. Although some middle-class men wanted to be 'unconventional', working-class men often strove to achieve elements of the idealised, romantic, white wedding and have the biggest wedding they could.

Tropes of romantic masculinity became increasingly visible, but within constraints. The rise of the romantic white wedding came at a time of further decline in, but not eradication of, breach of promise. Men were to follow codes of honour towards women, but were less likely to branded as 'fickle' in the newspapers from the 1930s and could change their minds and marry for love. Men's words could be duplicitous in order to secure sex, but men were to an extent legally protected from mendacious young women who might seduce them into marriage. Romantic letters were a feature of engagements across the period, and some men wrote hundreds of them. The wedding ceremony became more romantically choreographed. The increased romance and mutuality of weddings was however underpinned by the static gendered positions of breadwinning husband, and child-rearing housewife, which were presented as natural and therefore unquestionable. Men typically narrated the wedding as a site of class-based homosociality: they remembered the work colleagues in attendance, and the best man in particular, and this demonstrated the masculine privilege of passing freely over the boundaries of home, work and all-male association. The honeymoon, often in a romantic location, was also set within a social context. Men performed their new position of husband surrounded by their own social class. Despite the rise of the romantic wedding and honeymoon, debates about affinity showed that marriage for many men was pragmatic and perhaps primarily about finding someone to do the housework and look after the children. The idealised, formal, romantic proposal was often matter of fact. The romantic honeymoon was also beyond reach of most lower-paid working-class people across the period. In some working-class communities, it was normal for men to go back to work the day after the wedding.

Sex marked the boundary between different stages of a relationship. Coitus was a legal requirement to complete the marriage, and was evidence of commitment to marry, something that appeared in newspaper reports of a breach of promise cases from the 1930s. The theatricality of the wedding made the sexes of male and female appear timeless and unquestionable, and coitus as the only natural form of 'sex'. Sex, narrowly defined as coitus and assuming middle-class norms of agency, was legal condonation of a marital offence and every act of penile-vaginal intercourse effectively re-consummated the marriage.

Debates about 'wilful refusal' to consummate a marriage, were debates about the purpose of sex, the purpose of marriage, and the sexual 'normal' man. Across the period, class-inflected eugenics discourses influenced marriage law by stressing the fitness of the race and the need to encourage the right people to marry, and therefore consent and capacity laws denied those deemed unfit access to the institution of marriage. Paternity was a vital requirement of masculinity and the purpose of marriage was procreation, but there was from the 1930s increasing emphasis on continued mutual sexual pleasure throughout a marriage. After the Second World War, debates reported in newspapers, stemming from 'wilful refusal' cases, tested the tension between procreation and pleasure in relation to contraception and artificial insemination. The 'wilful refusal' debates in the 1950s moved from discussion about one act of coitus to continual penetrative sex throughout the marriage and impotence was increasingly defined psychologically rather than medically. 'Mutual' sexual pleasure was asymmetrical in favour of the husband, and in the era of the Wolfenden Committee, concerns about homosexuality and the solidifying of the hetero/homo binary, the 'normal' man was defined as being continually able and willing to penetrate a vagina. First-person testimonies gave a range of consummation narratives, from the sexually charged honeymoon to the new husband who desperately wanted a rest from manual work. Legally, a 'reasonable' man was to 'bring his wife to bear' and consummate the marriage, and although the sexual agency was complicated, sexual consent was something that was required by the man and given by the women once for the duration of the marriage. Mental capacity case law however demonstrated that although the psychologically 'normal' man found women desirable and was the pursuer and capturer, a woman could negotiate, in advance, a sex-free marriage.

During the marriage process there was a potential conflict between generations as a man sought to achieve the status of married head of an

7 CONCLUSION **229**

independent household, but found himself dependent on others. Politicians passed age of marriage laws with class and gender assumptions about age and responsibility. There was not the same perception of a 'generation gap' as there was just after the period 1918 to 1960, and few couples resorted to eloping to Gretna Green. Across the period and in all social classes, men sought permission to marry from the woman's father. Exercising patriarchal authority or at least taking the opportunity to set a standard to a younger man, some fathers immediately agreed, while others refused permission. A father had no legal right to refuse if his daughter was of age but generally had more influence if he had economic power. The man's father could also influence a son's marriage choice, especially if there was a role in the family business at stake. Some men had to seek permission from an employer or senior officer, especially in the 1950s era of National Service. Men therefore often had to confront an older more powerful man, or perhaps men, and prove themselves before being allowed to marry. The marrying man also had to strike a balance between being respectful of his own mother but not be unduly under her influence, and similarly he had to stand up respectfully to his prospective mother-in-law. The wedding itself was increasingly, and literally, a procession of different generations and potential couples. The bride's mother was invisible on the day but the father gave the woman away to the man, before an entourage that included a replica couple comprising the best man and chief bridesmaid. The gradual normalisation of 'child attendants'—girl bridesmaids and pageboys—across the period created a sense of marriage, and its concomitant gender roles and sexuality, as naturally iterative.

English marriage and masculinity were to an extent defined against the non-White, non-Christian Other. At a time of rising individualism and a perceived move away from 'traditional authority', the decline of the Church of England influence over legal definitions of marriage was seen in the 'wilful refusal' debates. The Church still had, and has, a say in the House of Lords and the Church's views on sex and marriage were, and are, extensively reported in the popular press, often on the front page. Most weddings took place in a church, and most men in the oral history sample wanted it to be 'proper', by which they meant a church wedding. The archaic language and tropes of *The Book of Common Prayer* created a timeless sense of Englishness. Englishness was bolstered by honeymoons in the English seaside and countryside locations.

Case law—through judgements in nullity test cases—asserted Anglican definitions of marriage and masculinity in cases involving Hindu, Muslim, or Roman Catholic marriage. Nullity test cases brought English Law into the judgement of Indian and Egyptian marriage at a time of imperial anxiety when those countries were pushing for independence. While polygamy was judged to be acceptable among non-White people in India, it was not in England, and judgements were framed within a narrative of Englishmen protecting women from a less civilised masculinity and male sexuality. Parliamentarians, and lobbyists, had expressed similar concerns when arguing in favour of a higher marriage age in the 1920s. English masculinity was to be protective of vulnerable women, set an example to the colonies and compare favourably with other 'civilised' nations. At home in the 1950s, Black married, masculinity was invisible to the White majority, even when in the form of large extravagant weddings and at a time of highly visible racial tensions, especially in London. The West Indian community in Brixton held large weddings on a par with, or possibly outdoing, White 'white weddings' of a similar social class, but these locally important weddings went largely unnoticed, and seem to have left few historical traces.

It is hoped that the approach of this book will prove useful to other scholars. The multivalent approach to a narrow (marriage) process has produced findings and a methodology of relevance to historians of family and historians of religion, as well as historians of gender and sexuality. More generally, cultural historians may be interested in the interaction between official discourses, popular culture and personal testimony demonstrated here. Beyond academic history, the close reading of a variety of sources brought to bear upon a single, dense point of analysis may be useful to literary scholars, sociologists and those beyond the academy seeking to show the sexed and gendered 'reality' of the everyday.

The issues discussed throughout are resonant today. There is clearly a need for a brave, open-minded, national conversation about sex, love, kinship and procreation. This book makes a modest contribution to that debate by asking people, especially men, to question *how* they marry and *why* they marry, or perhaps even *should* they marry. The findings here are of changes and continuities of masculinities, but not biologically determined permanency: men and boys can do their genders differently.

Index

A
Active (Active-Passive), 116–118
Activities, 194, 209, 214, 221
Advertisements, 193, 194, 207
Affinity, 29–34, 36–40, 64, 65
Age, 29–33, 45–55, 59, 60, 64, 65
Age of Marriage Act (1929), 29, 45, 47, 48, 54
Althusser, Louis, 7
Anglican, 229
Archbishop of Canterbury, 37, 53, 60, 164–166, 174
Archbishop of Westminster, 164
Army, 77, 84, 94, 99, 100
Arnold, John, 10
Artificial insemination, 149, 173–175, 185
Austin, J.L., 16, 17, 155
Autobiographies, 19, 20, 128, 131, 145

B
Baindail (otherwise Lawson) vs Baindail, 41, 42

Balliol College, 138
Bates, Denise, 70–72, 79
Baxter v Baxter, 163, 164, 173
BBC Millennium Memories, 20
Bed, 180, 183, 184, 186
Bee, M., 196, 201, 204, 207, 217
Bee, S., 196, 201, 204, 207, 217
Bell, Catherine, 18, 19
Benn, Sir Arthur Shirley, 35
"Best Man", 75, 85, 90, 91, 96, 108, 111–120, 125, 135, 141–144, 196, 201, 212, 214, 215
Beveridge, Lord, 36, 37
Bingham, Adrian, 18
Birkbeck College, 10
Birkenhead, 79, 84
Birmingham, 137
Black, 230
Blackpool, 207, 216, 217, 219
Blackstone's Index, 31
Bodkin, Sir Archibald, 51, 52
Book of Common Prayer, 29
Bourdieu, Pierre, 200, 206
Bourke, Joanna, 5, 13, 15, 20, 76

© The Editor(s) (if applicable) and The Author(s), under exclusive license to Springer Nature Switzerland AG 2023
N. Penlington, *Men Getting Married in England, 1918–60*, Genders and Sexualities in History, https://doi.org/10.1007/978-3-031-27405-3

232 INDEX

Bournemouth, 131, 139, 206, 207, 219
Bower v Ebsworth, 71
Boynton v Boynton, 183
Brady, Sean, 10, 13
Breach of promise, 69–73, 76, 79–84, 86, 87, 89, 90, 94–101, 103
Breadwinner, 13
Bride, 107, 108, 111–130, 132, 134–141, 143, 145, 226, 229
Bridesmaids, 108, 113, 115–119, 122–126, 131, 132, 134, 135, 141, 144
Bridlington, 207, 219
Brighton, 198, 206, 207, 219
Bristol, 138
British Empire, 33, 39, 65
British Library Sound Archive (BLSA), 20, 192, 210
British Medical Association, 158
British Medical Journal, 56, 63
British Nationality and Status of Aliens Act (1914), 55
British rail (BR), 205, 206, 209
Brontë, Emily, 204, 205
Brooke, Stephen, 9
Brook, Heather, 155, 176
Buckmaster, Lord, 48–50, 52, 53, 158, 159
Bulcroft, Kris, 199, 200, 214, 217
Bulcroft, Richard, 199, 200, 214, 217
Busfield, Joan, 57
Butler, Judith, 17, 155
Butlin's, 190
B v B, 182

C
Cake, 108, 118, 131, 134, 135
Cannadine, David, 15
Canon Law, 164, 184
Capacity, 2, 17, 21, 23, 161, 165, 166, 169, 170, 174

Caribbean, 140, 141, 144, 230
Carr (otherwise Fowler) vs Carr, 45, 46
Case law, 226, 228, 229
Cathedral, Westminster, 122, 159
Cheshire, 97
Child attendant, 125, 126, 128, 142
Childhood, 46, 47, 55, 60
Chivalry, 100, 113, 117, 125, 137
Choreography (of wedding), 109, 110, 115, 144
Christian, 2, 3, 110, 137, 138, 150, 159, 167, 170, 174, 219
Christianity, 226
Church, 2, 8, 22, 108, 110, 112–120, 122, 123, 125–128, 130, 132–140, 144, 229
Church of England, 3, 4, 110–112, 118, 119, 132, 137, 138, 141, 150, 160–162, 165–167, 174, 175, 181, 184, 185
Civil Law, 182–184
Class, 1–3, 7, 11–16, 21–23, 32–34, 46, 47, 55–57, 60, 63–65, 73, 75, 80, 85, 89, 90, 92, 94, 96, 99, 102, 104, 107, 108, 110, 111, 114, 117, 120, 122, 129, 131–136, 138, 139, 143–145, 190–192, 195, 197, 200, 201, 203, 204, 206–209, 211–218, 220, 221, 225–230
Coitus, 149, 150, 157, 159, 160, 162, 163, 168, 170–186
Collier, Richard, 152
Collins, Marcus, 5, 141
Company, 214, 215, 220
Condonation, 157, 175–179, 184–186
Connell, R.W., 12, 13
Consent, 2, 3, 12, 17, 21, 23
Consummate, 217

INDEX 233

Consummation, 2, 3, 17, 21–23,
149–151, 154, 155, 157, 159,
160, 162–166, 170, 173, 175,
180, 182–186, 189, 217, 218,
225, 228
Contraception, 5, 6, 149, 162–164,
173, 175, 185
Convocations of Canterbury and
York, 159
Cook, Hera, 6
Cook, Matt, 8
Cornwall, 130, 142, 197, 201, 207,
208
Countryside, 193, 201, 203, 204, 221
Cowan v Cowan, 162, 164, 173
Cramp v Cramp and Freeman, 176
Criminal Law Amendment Act
(1885), 46, 47, 49
Cruelty, 170, 172, 173, 177, 185
Cumbria, 88

D

Daily Express, 17, 35, 45, 48, 50, 54,
56, 71, 81–83, 86, 87, 97,
120–123, 125–127, 165, 173,
193, 195, 215
Daily Mirror, 17, 33, 51, 69, 71, 76,
79, 80, 87, 100, 120–127, 163,
173, 174, 193, 195, 207
Deceased Wife's Sister's Marriage Act
(1907), 35
Deceased Wife's Sister's Marriage Act
(1907) Amendment (1921), 35
Dein, Alan, 20
Derrida, Jacques, 17
Desertion, 170–173, 177, 178, 185,
186
Devereux, G.R.M., 84, 85, 90, 92,
96, 97
*Dickenson v Dickenson otherwise
Philips*, 160

Divorce, 5, 18, 149, 151, 152, 154,
158, 161, 167–169, 171–177,
179, 184, 185
Divorce Law Reform Union, 161,
169
Domesticity, 127, 128, 143
Dorothy (Dolly) Scannell, 217
Double burden, 5
Double standard, 12
Dress, 107, 108, 111, 113–116,
118–121, 124, 126, 130, 131,
135, 139, 140, 143, 145
Dr Lushington, 163
Durham v Durham (1885), 58
Dyer, Richard, 110

E

Edgar and Diana Woods, 86, 91
Egypt, 40, 44, 45, 52, 65, 230
Ejaculation, 166, 182, 186
Elopement, 127, 128, 144
Enfield, 133
Engagement, 8, 20, 22, 69, 70,
72–74, 77–81, 83–92, 96, 98,
100–104, 226, 227
Engagement ring(s), 73, 84–88, 90,
94, 98
England, 1, 2, 11, 13, 14, 21, 22
English, 29, 32–34, 39–45, 52–55,
57, 62, 64, 65, 107, 109–111,
119, 123, 143, 144
English Law, 150, 167, 168, 182,
186
Englishness, 226, 229
Etiquette manual(s), 2, 19, 22, 23,
70, 73, 74, 76, 84, 86–88,
90–93, 96, 97, 101–103, 107,
110–121, 123, 125, 128, 129,
134, 135, 137, 139, 141,
143–145, 192, 196, 197, 200,
202, 204, 207, 209, 212, 214,
217

234 INDEX

Eugenics, 32, 56, 57, 59, 63, 65
European, 193, 201–203, 221
Expectations, 189, 192, 193, 200, 202, 210, 214, 215, 217
Experience, 9, 11, 15, 16, 20, 191–193, 206, 210, 212, 215, 217, 221
Exton, Rev, 88, 96
Exton, Rev. D., 112

F

Family, 2, 8, 9, 190, 191, 197–199, 203, 215, 216, 221, 222
Father, 78, 91–94, 96–99, 101, 102, 104, 108, 115–117, 120, 122, 128, 129, 135, 136, 139, 144, 196, 200, 221, 226, 229
Fellows, Alfred, 161, 177
Female, 226, 228
Femininity, 5, 6, 108, 114, 116, 119, 128, 143
Feminist historians, 5
Fiancée/Fiancé, 69, 78, 81–84, 86–90, 92, 95–101, 103
First-person testimonies, 2, 23
First World War, 109, 131
Fisher, Kate, 6, 20
Flowers, 113, 119
Forster (otherwise Street) v Forster (1923), 58
Foucauldian, 16
Foucault, Michel, 191, 192
Free Church Federation Council, 167
Freeman, Elizabeth, 8, 108, 190, 191
Friends, 194, 197, 198, 203, 215, 216, 221
Frost, Ginger, 70–72

G

Gable, Clark, 115

Gaze, 191, 192, 194, 200, 201, 203, 205, 209, 221
Gender, 2, 3, 5, 7–9, 12, 13, 16, 17, 19, 21–23, 30–37, 39, 41, 42, 44–46, 48, 50, 53, 55, 57, 59, 60, 63, 64, 69, 70, 72, 73, 75, 81, 82, 84–86, 89, 91, 93–95, 97, 102–104, 108–111, 113, 115, 117, 118, 125, 127, 129, 132, 140, 142, 144, 191, 193, 194, 199–201, 213–215, 220, 225–227, 229, 230
Generation(s), 115, 122, 142, 225, 228, 229
Gift(s), 85, 88–91, 101, 103
Gillis, John, 7, 15, 108, 190, 211
Gilman, Sander, 62, 63
Giving away, 117, 118, 144
Gladstone, William, 38
Goffman, Erving, 107
Gower, L.C.B., 167, 178
Gramsci, Antonio, 12
Grant, Cary, 115
Great Western Railway (GWR), 208
Greek island, 198
Green, Gretna, 127, 229
Groom, 107, 112–118, 120, 122, 124, 126, 128, 130, 133, 135, 136, 139, 141–145, 226
Guests, 109, 112, 131–134, 141, 143, 144

H

Hall, Lesley, 153, 154
Hanson, Clare, 56, 57
Hardwick Act (1753), 46
Hardwicke Marriage Act (1753), 70
Hare v Hare and Davidson, 176
Harvey, Karen, 10, 11
Hasson, Ezra, 57, 58, 62
Hegemonic masculinity, 12, 13, 18
Helsinki, 199

INDEX 235

Henderson v Henderson and Crellin,
    178
Herbert, A.P., 160, 161
Herefordshire, 77
Heterosexual, 109, 110, 115, 116,
    132, 142
Hindu, 32, 33, 39–43, 45, 64, 65,
    229
Historians, 230
Hobsbawm, Eric, 18
Holden, Katherine, 8
Holiday, 190, 192–195, 200,
    202–204, 206, 210, 215, 220
Homosocial, 109, 143, 145, 191, 227
Honeymoon, 1, 8, 10, 16, 19, 20,
    23, 189–204, 206–222, 225–229
Hotel, 198, 216–219, 221
Houlbrook, Matt, 6, 7, 31, 47, 48
Humberside, 129, 131, 132, 198,
    218, 219
Hume-Williams, Sir Ellis, 160
Humphries, Steve, 6
Husband, 189–191, 194–196, 198,
    199, 202–204, 208, 209, 211,
    213, 214, 217, 218, 220, 221

I
Impotence, 153, 154, 157, 158,
    160–162, 166, 168, 169, 174,
    180, 181, 186
India, 32–34, 39–41, 43, 44, 52, 53,
    65, 230
Ingraham, Chrys, 1, 2, 7, 8, 109,
    110, 112, 120, 128, 132
In the estate of Park; Park v Park
    (1953), 60, 61
Invented tradition, 3, 18
Isle of Wight, 217

J
Jewish, 119

Jobling, Paul, 115
Joynson-Hicks, Sir William, 52, 53

K
Karminski, Seymour Edward, 181
Kay v Kay (otherwise Gunson), 183

L
Lacan, Jacques, 7
Lacey, T.A., 159, 168
Lake District, 201, 202, 204
Langhamer, Claire, 1, 5, 9, 70–72,
    79, 80, 82, 100, 102, 189
Law, 226, 228, 229
Lawrance v Lawrance, 171
League of Nations Advisory
    Commission for the Protection
    and Welfare of Children and
    Young People, 53
Leech, Kenneth, 110
Leonard, Diana, 109
Letchworth, 138
Lettmaier, Saskia, 71, 72
Lewis v Hayward, 183
Liverpool, 78, 84, 98, 129, 130, 136
Locality, 225
Location, 191–194, 196, 197,
    199–210, 221
London, 79, 87, 89, 97, 114, 124,
    130–132, 135, 139–141,
    197–199, 205, 207, 209, 212,
    213, 215, 216, 219
London and North Eastern Railway
    (LNER), 205
Lord Lyndhurst's Act (1836), 54
Love, 69, 72, 75, 78–80, 82, 84, 86,
    97, 98, 100, 101, 103
Love letter(s), 69, 73, 74, 79, 80, 84,
    90, 103

M

Male, 228, 230
Mancroft, Lord, 36, 38
Manhood, 174, 175, 180
Manly, 74, 85, 92, 97, 100, 101
Marriage, 1–10, 13–19, 21–23, 225–230
Marriage Act (1949), 35
Marriage (Enabling) Act (1960), 29, 35, 36
Marriage Law Reform Society, 168, 172, 179
Marriage (Prohibited Degrees of Relationship) Act (1931), 29, 35
Masculinity, 1–3, 5–7, 10–13, 15–18, 20–23, 30–33, 37, 40, 41, 44, 45, 48, 55, 64–66, 69, 70, 73–75, 82, 83, 85, 91, 92, 95, 97, 98, 101–103, 107–111, 113–116, 119, 121, 124, 125, 128, 133, 141, 143–145, 149, 150, 154, 158, 159, 162, 164, 172, 180, 184–186, 190, 193, 205, 212, 214, 218, 220, 225–230
Maslin v Maslin, 178
Matrimonial Causes Act (1937), 29, 56, 58, 60, 156, 160, 161, 167, 177, 185
McKibbin, Ross, 14, 15
McLaren, Angus, 153, 154
Medical inspection, 151, 181
Mehta (otherwise Kohn) vs Mehta, 42, 43
Men, 1–6, 8–13, 15, 16, 19–23
Mental deficiency, 56–59, 63, 65
Mental Deficiency Acts (1913 to 1928), 56, 59
Merriman, Lord, 167, 179
Merseyside, 204
Methodist, 130, 133, 137, 138, 167
Michie, Helena, 191, 192, 202

Middlesbrough, 197
Mistress, 81, 83, 103
Mort, Frank, 6, 16, 115, 140
Mother, 69, 73, 87, 93, 95–98, 101, 102, 104, 226, 229
Moyse, Cordelia, 151, 152, 161
Muslim, 32, 33, 40, 44, 45, 64, 65, 229
Mutuality, 227, 228

N

Napier v Napier, 160
National Council of the Evangelical Free Churches, 159
National Union of Societies for Equal Citizenship (NUSEC), 52
Natural sex, 162
Newlyweds, 193, 194, 197, 199, 200, 202, 203, 205, 206, 209, 215, 219, 220
News of the World, 71
Newspaper(s), 1, 17, 18, 22, 23, 69–72, 79–81, 83, 87, 95, 97, 99–101, 103, 107, 110, 112, 120–125, 127–129, 131, 134, 137, 139, 141, 143–145, 153, 154, 158, 160, 162–164, 169, 175, 179, 181, 185, 192, 193, 195–197, 207, 209, 210, 215, 217, 220, 225, 227, 228
Niagara Falls, 192
Nonconformist, 118
Non-consummation, 149, 151, 152, 154, 156–158, 161, 165–167, 173, 174, 181, 183, 184
Non-sexual marriage, 61
Norfolk, 129, 130, 134
Normal, 2, 7–9, 17, 23, 151, 154, 157, 164–170, 172–176, 180, 182, 184–186, 227, 228
Northampton, 97
Northumberland, 129, 135

INDEX 237

Nullity, 30, 31, 33, 39, 41–45, 54, 57–59, 62–64, 66, 149, 151, 152, 154, 156–158, 160–170, 173, 174, 177, 180–182, 184, 185, 229, 230

O

Occupation, 13–15
Oldham, 215
One flesh, 159, 168
Oral history, 6, 8, 20, 70, 73, 74, 78, 79, 84, 87, 91, 93, 95, 96, 98, 99, 101–103, 107, 128, 130, 134, 137, 138, 141, 143, 145, 192, 197–199, 201, 202, 204–208, 210, 211, 218, 225, 229
Oratory, Brompton, 122
Oxford, 198

P

Page, Ann, 75, 76, 86, 88, 92, 93, 196, 202, 213, 215
Parents, 72, 76, 89, 91–94, 96, 97, 99, 102, 104, 112, 113, 117, 127, 128, 135–137
Paris, 201–203, 215
Parker, Andrew, 108, 109, 118
Parliament, 157–161, 184, 185
Passive, 109, 116–118
Paternity, 164, 174, 185, 228
Peal v Peal, 33, 34
Penetration, 166, 169, 181–183, 185, 186
Penis, 155, 157, 174, 180, 182, 184, 186
Penner, Barbara, 200
Performativity, 3, 8, 16, 17
Permission, 229
Personal testimonies, 6, 19, 130, 136, 144, 145

Planning, 193, 194, 197, 199, 200, 212, 220, 221
Polygamy, 30–33, 39–45, 64, 65, 230
Portelli, Allessandro, 192
Portsmouth, 124
Power relations, 2, 3, 5, 9, 12, 16, 21, 22, 190, 220, 221
Pragmatic, 227
Pragmatism, 197, 200
Preparations, 110, 117, 130, 131, 134, 135, 139, 143, 144
Presbyterian, 137
Preston, 133
Privacy, 193, 197, 198, 208, 214–216, 220, 221
Procession, 108, 116, 117, 126, 143, 144
Procreation, 150, 156, 158–160, 162, 164, 166, 170, 174, 175, 180, 184, 185, 228, 230
Proposal, 73–79, 81, 84, 85, 87, 91, 93, 101–103
Pugh v Pugh, 54, 55
Purley, 98

Q

Quaker, 119, 138

R

Race, 107, 109–111, 129, 140, 141, 143, 225, 228
Railway posters, 192, 193
Rathbone, Eleanor, 52
Reception, 107, 108, 117, 118, 131–136, 141, 143, 144
Refused permission (to marry), 93, 94, 99
Register office, 124, 129, 131, 138, 139
Ritual, 3, 8, 18, 19, 108
Roberts v Roberts and another, 176

238 INDEX

Roman Catholic, 34, 54, 119, 122, 133, 137, 138, 142, 150, 164, 180–183, 186, 230
Romance, 2, 3, 7–10, 22, 23, 69, 76, 78, 80, 81, 86, 87, 89, 100, 189, 192–194, 196, 200–206, 208–210, 215, 220, 221
Romantic, 111, 120, 124, 125, 127, 128, 143–145, 225, 227
Roper, Michael, 133, 143
Royal Commission, 149, 153, 156–158, 160–162, 167–171, 173, 174, 176, 178, 179, 184, 185
Royal Commission on Divorce and Matrimonial Causes, 59
Russian, 123
R. v R. (otherwise K), 181

S
Salisbury, Lord, 48, 50
Sandhurst, 136
Sayers, Dorothy L., 189, 193, 195, 214
Scandinavia, 199, 201, 202
Scarborough, 142
Scott, Joan, 20
Scunthorpe, 199, 204
Seaside, 193, 201, 206, 207, 209, 217, 219, 221
Second World War, 3, 75, 77, 79, 88, 90, 93, 100, 149, 156, 162, 185, 208, 210, 212, 216
Sedgwick, Eve, 108, 109, 118
Seduction, 72
Serialised fiction, 195
Sex, 30, 32, 46, 61, 62, 69, 70, 73, 81–83, 91, 101, 103, 149–151, 153–160, 162–165, 169–173, 175–179, 182, 184–186, 189, 211, 214, 217–220, 222, 227–230

Sexual dysfunction, 160, 184
Sexuality, 2, 6–9, 15–18, 22, 108–111, 115, 125, 133, 140, 144, 149, 150, 155, 157, 160, 162, 166, 184, 209, 225, 229, 230
Sexual performative, 176, 180
Sexual pleasure, 149, 156, 157, 159, 161, 164, 173, 184, 185
Sexual revolution, 6
Shepard, Alexandra, 10, 11
Shropshire, 87, 93, 129, 211, 212
Simon, J.E.S., 168, 178
Single, 4, 8, 22
Slesser, Sir H., 35
Smeins, Linda, 199, 200, 214, 217
Smith v Smith (otherwise Hand), 30, 62
Society weddings, 111, 122, 125, 126, 144
Somerset, 132
Southend-on-Sea, 206, 207, 213
St James', Spanish Place, 122
Stone, Lawrence, 151, 152, 158
Stopes, Marie, 153, 168, 172
Subjectivities, 226
Suit, 114, 115, 120, 131, 139, 140, 144
Summerfield, Penny, 5, 20
Surbiton, 142
Surprise, 77, 81, 103
S v S (otherwise M), 158
Switzerland, 198, 201, 202
Szreter, Simon, 6

T
Teesside, 133–135
Terry, Eileen, 85, 88–92
Testimonies, 192, 210, 217–219, 221
The Progressive League, 172
The Times, 17, 158, 159, 162, 164, 165, 169, 183

INDEX

Thomas (and John) Cook, 190
Thompson, E.P., 7
Thompson, Peter, 115
Tosh, John, 10–13, 15–18
Tradition, 108, 110, 111, 118–120,
   127, 131, 143, 144
Traditional, 19, 22
Transformation, 190, 191
Troubridge, Lady, 74, 86
Trousseau(s), 73, 84, 89, 91, 103
Turnbull v Turnbull and Coats, 176

U
Urry, John, 190–192, 200, 201,
   203–207

V
Vagina, 155, 157, 166–169, 174–176,
   180–186
Venue, 112, 136–139, 143, 145
vera copula, 166, 182, 184
Victoria, Queen, 120, 121
Vigier v Smith, 71
Virgin, 168, 180, 181, 183, 186, 219
Vulva, 180

W
Walton, John, 205–208, 210, 216,
   217
Watford, 197

Weatherley v Weatherley, 170, 171
Wedding, 1–3, 7, 8, 16–20, 22, 189,
   190, 192–194, 197, 199, 203,
   208, 211, 218–221, 225–230
Wedding March, 117, 130
Weeks, Jeffrey, 6, 150, 162
Week, Wakes, 215
Welfare State, 36
Welshman, John, 56
West Country, 197, 201, 207–209
Weymouth, 138
White, 230
Whiteness, 109–111
White wedding, 1, 7, 8, 10, 22,
   107–112, 119–132, 134–136,
   139–145, 225, 227, 230
Wiegman, Robyn, 7
Wife, 190, 194, 196–200, 202–204,
   208, 211–215, 219–221
Wilful refusal, 149, 151, 156–173,
   175, 181, 184–186, 228, 229
Wilson, Elizabeth A., 7
Wirral, 137
Woodman, Mary, 75, 85, 91, 196,
   200, 201, 204, 207, 212–214
Work colleagues, 132
Wouters, Cas, 19
W v W, 158

Y
Yorkshire, 78, 94, 96, 201, 204–206,
   211, 218

Printed in the United States
by Baker & Taylor Publisher Services